2015

D1111526

MODEL RULES
OF
PROFESSIONAL
CONDUCT

CENTER FOR
PROFESSIONAL
RESPONSIBILITY

Defending Liberty
Pursuing Justice

AMERICAN BAR ASSOCIATION

ABA STANDING COMMITTEE ON ETHICS AND PROFESSIONAL RESPONSIBILITY
2014–2015

Dedicated to the memory of
Jeanne P. Gray
Director, ABA Center for Professional Responsibility,
1982–2013

CONTENTS

COUNSELOR

ADVOCATE

TRANSACTIONS WITH PERSONS OTHER THAN CLIENTS

LAW FIRMS AND ASSOCIATIONS

APPENDICES

PREFACE

For more than one hundred years, the American Bar Association has provided leadership in legal ethics and professional responsibility through the adoption of professional standards that serve as models of the regulatory law governing the legal profession.

On August 27, 1908, the Association adopted the original Canons of Professional Ethics. These were based principally on the Code of Ethics adopted by the Alabama Bar Association in 1887, which in turn had been borrowed largely from the lectures of Judge George Sharswood, published in 1854 as Professional Ethics, and from the fifty resolutions included in David Hoffman's A Course of Legal Study (2d ed. 1836). Piecemeal amendments to the Canons occasionally followed.

In 1913, the Standing Committee on Professional Ethics of the American Bar Association was established to keep the Association informed about state and local bar activities concerning professional ethics. In 1919 the name of the Committee was changed to the Committee on Professional Ethics and Grievances; its role was expanded in 1922 to include issuing opinions "concerning professional conduct, and particularly concerning the application of the tenets of ethics thereto." In 1958 the Committee on Professional Ethics and Grievances was separated into two committees: a Committee on Professional Grievances, with authority to review issues of professional misconduct, and a Committee on Professional Ethics with responsibility to express its opinion concerning proper professional and judicial conduct. The Committee on Professional Grievances was discontinued in 1971. The name of the Committee on Professional Ethics was changed to the Committee on Ethics and Professional Responsibility in 1971 and remains so.

In 1964, at the request of President Lewis F. Powell Jr., the House of Delegates of the American Bar Association created a Special Committee on Evaluation of Ethical Standards (the "Wright Committee") to assess whether changes should be made in the then-current Canons of Professional Ethics. In response, the Committee produced the Model Code of Professional Responsibility. The Model Code was adopted by the House of Delegates on August 12, 1969, and subsequently by the vast majority of state and federal jurisdictions.

In 1977, the American Bar Association created the Commission on Evaluation of Professional Standards to undertake a comprehensive rethinking of the ethical premises and problems of the legal profession. Upon evaluating the Model Code and determining that amendment of the Code would not achieve a comprehensive statement of the law governing the legal profession, the Commission commenced a six-year study and drafting process that produced the Model Rules of Professional Conduct. The Model Rules were adopted by the House of Delegates of the American Bar Association on August 2, 1983.

Between 1983 and 2002, the House amended the Rules and Comments on fourteen different occasions. In 1997, the American Bar Association created the Commission on Evaluation of the Rules of Professional Conduct ("Ethics 2000 Commission") to comprehensively review the Model Rules and propose amendments as deemed appropriate. On February 5, 2002 the House of Delegates adopted a series of amendments that arose from this process.

In 2000, the American Bar Association created the Commission on Multijurisdictional Practice to research, study and report on the application of current ethics and bar admission rules to the multijurisdictional practice of law. On August 12, 2002 the House of Delegates adopted amendments to Rules 5.5 and 8.5 as a result of the Commission's work and recommendations.

In 2002, the American Bar Association created the Task Force on Corporate Responsibility to examine systemic issues relating to corporate responsibility arising out of the unexpected and traumatic bankruptcy of Enron and other Enron-like situations that had shaken confidence in the effectiveness of the governance and disclosure systems applicable to public companies in the United States. In August 11-12, 2003, the House of Delegates adopted amendments to Rules 1.6 and 1.13 as a result of the Task Force's work and recommendations.

In 2009, the American Bar Association created the Commission on Ethics 20/20 to perform a thorough review of the ABA Model Rules of Professional Conduct and the U.S. system of lawyer regulation in the context of advances in technology and global legal practice developments. On August 6, 2012 and February 11, 2013 the House of Delegates adopted a series of amendments to the Rules and Comments as a result of the Commission's work and recommendations.

The American Bar Association continues to pursue its goal of assuring the highest standards of professional competence and ethical conduct. The Standing Committee on Ethics and Professional Responsibility, charged with interpreting the professional standards of the Association and recommending appropriate amendments and clarifications, issues opinions interpreting the Model Rules of Professional Conduct and the Model Code of Judicial Conduct. The opinions of the Committee are published by the American Bar Association in a series of bound volumes containing opinions from 1924 through 2013 and as individual PDFs starting with the 1984 opinions.

Requests that the Committee issue opinions on particular questions of professional and judicial conduct should be directed to the American Bar Association, Center for Professional Responsibility, 321 N. Clark Street, Chicago, Illinois 60654.

ABA COMMISSION ON
EVALUATION OF PROFESSIONAL STANDARDS
(1977–1983)

ROBERT W. MESERVE, *Chair*
Boston, Massachusetts

MARVIN E. FRANKEL
New York, New York

RICHARD H. SINKFIELD
Atlanta, Georgia

ALAN BARTH
Washington, D.C.

LOIS C. HARRISON
Lakeland, Florida

WILLIAM B. SPANN, JR.
Atlanta, Georgia

ARNO H. DENECKE
Salem, Oregon

ROBERT O. HETLAGE
St. Louis, Missouri

SAMUEL D. THURMAN
Salt Lake City, Utah

THOMAS EHRLICH
Washington, D.C.

ROBERT B. McKAY
New York, New York

ROBERT J. KUTAK
Omaha, Nebraska
Former Chair

JANE FRANK-HARMAN
Washington, D.C.

L. CLAIR NELSON
Washington, D.C.

LIAISONS

MICHAEL FRANCK
Lansing, Michigan
*Standing Committee on
Professional Discipline*

JOHN C. DEACON
Jonesboro, Arkansas
Board of Governors

H. WILLIAM ALLEN
Little Rock, Arkansas
*Standing Committee on
Ethics and Professional
Responsibility*

THOMAS Z. HAYWARD, JR.
Chicago, Illinois

CONSULTANTS

BETTY B. FLETCHER
Seattle, Washington

L. RAY PATTERSON
Atlanta, Georgia

JOHN F. SUTTON, JR.
Austin, Texas

REPORTER

GEOFFREY C. HAZARD, JR.
New Haven, Connecticut

ASSISTANT REPORTERS

THOMAS J. McCORMICK
Washington, D.C.

DANIEL S. REYNOLDS
DeKalb, Illinois

COMMISSION ON EVALUATION OF PROFESSIONAL STANDARDS
CHAIR'S INTRODUCTION

The Commission on Evaluation of Professional Standards was appointed in the summer of 1977 by former ABA President William B. Spann, Jr. Chaired by Robert J. Kutak until his death in early 1983, the Commission was charged with evaluating whether existing standards of professional conduct provided comprehensive and consistent guidance for resolving the increasingly complex ethical problems in the practice of law. For the most part, the Commission looked to the former ABA Model Code of Professional Responsibility, which served as a model for the majority of state ethics codes. The Commission also referred to opinions of the ABA Standing Committee on Ethics and Professional Responsibility, as well as to decisions of the United States Supreme Court and of state supreme courts. After thoughtful study, the Commission concluded that piecemeal amendment of the Model Code would not sufficiently clarify the profession's ethical responsibilities in light of changed conditions. The Commission therefore commenced a drafting process that produced numerous drafts, elicited voluminous comment, and launched an unprecedented debate on the ethics of the legal profession.

On January 30, 1980, the Commission presented its initial suggestions to the bar in the form of a Discussion Draft of the proposed Model Rules of Professional Conduct. The Discussion Draft was subject to the widest possible dissemination and interested parties were urged to offer comments and suggestions. Public hearings were held around the country to provide forums for expression of views on the draft.

In the year following the last of these public hearings, the Commission conducted a painstaking analysis of the submitted comments and attempted to integrate into the draft those which seemed consistent with its underlying philosophy. The product of this analysis and integration was presented on May 31, 1981, as the proposed Final Draft of the Model Rules of Professional Conduct. This proposed Final Draft was submitted in two formats. The first format, consisting of blackletter Rules and accompanying Comments in the so-called restatement format, was submitted with the Commission's recommendation that it be adopted. The alternative format was patterned after the Model Code and consisted of Canons, Ethical Considerations, and Disciplinary Rules. In February 1982, the House of Delegates by substantial majority approved the restatement format of the Model Rules.

The proposed Final Draft was submitted to the House of Delegates for debate and approval at the 1982 Annual Meeting of the Association in San Francisco. Many organizations and interested parties offered their comments in the form of proposed amendments to the Final Draft. In the time allotted on its agenda, however, the House debated only proposed amendments to Rule 1.5. Consideration of the remainder of the document was deferred until the 1983 Midyear Meeting in New Orleans. The proposed Final Draft, as amended by the House in San Francisco, was reprinted in the November 1982 issue of the *ABA Journal*.

At the 1983 Midyear Meeting the House resumed consideration of the Final Draft. After two days of often vigorous debate, the House completed its review of the proposed amendments to the blackletter Rules. Many amendments, particularly in the area of confidentiality, were adopted. Debate on a Preamble, Scope, Terminology, and Comments, rewritten to reflect the New Orleans amendments, was deferred until the 1983 Annual Meeting in Atlanta, Georgia.

On March 11, 1983, the text of the blackletter Rules as approved by the House in February, together with the proposed Preamble, Scope, Terminology, and Comments, was circulated to members of the House, Section and Committee chairs, and all other interested parties. The text of the Rules reflected the joint efforts of the Commission and the House Drafting Committee to incorporate the changes approved by the House and to ensure stylistic continuity and uniformity. Recipients of the draft were again urged to submit comments in the form of proposed amendments. The House Committees on Drafting and Rules and Calendar met on May 23, 1983, to consider all of the proposed amendments that had been submitted in response to this draft. In addition, discussions were held among concerned parties in an effort to reach accommodation of the various positions. On July 11, 1983, the final version of the Model Rules was again circulated.

The House of Delegates commenced debate on the proposed Preamble, Scope, Terminology, and Comments on August 2, 1983. After four hours of debate, the House completed its consideration of all the proposed amendments and, upon motion of the Commission, the House voted to adopt the Model Rules of Professional Conduct, together with the ancillary material as amended. The task of the Commission had ended and it was discharged with thanks.

Throughout the drafting process, active participants included not only the members of the Commission but also the Sections and Committees of the American Bar Association and national, state, and local bar organizations. The work of the Commission was subject to virtually continuous scrutiny by academicians, practicing lawyers, members of the press, and the judiciary. Consequently, every provision of the Model Rules reflects the thoughtful consideration and hard work of many dedicated professionals. Because of their input, the Model Rules are truly national in derivation. The Association can take immense pride in its continued demonstration of leadership in the area of professional responsibility.

The Model Rules of Professional Conduct are intended to serve as a national framework for implementation of standards of professional conduct. Although the Commission endeavored to harmonize and accommodate the views of all the participants, no set of national standards that speaks to such a diverse constituency as the legal profession can resolve each issue to the complete satisfaction of every affected party. Undoubtedly there will be those who take issue with one or another of the Rules' provisions. Indeed, such dissent from individual provisions is expected. And the Model Rules, like all model legislation, will be subject to modification at the level of local implementation. Viewed as a whole, however, the Model Rules represent a responsible approach to the ethical practice of law and are consistent with professional obligations imposed by other law, such as constitutional, corporate, tort, fiduciary, and agency law.

I should not end this report without speaking of the Commission's debt to many people who have aided us in our deliberations, and have devoted time, energy, and goodwill to the advancement of our work over the last six years. It would probably be impossible to name each of the particular persons whose help was significant to us, and it surely would be unfortunate if the name of anyone were omitted from the list. We are, and shall remain, deeply grateful to the literally hundreds of people who aided us with welcome and productive suggestions. We think the bar should be grateful to each of them, and to our deceased members, Alan Barth of the District of Columbia, who we hardly had time to know, Bill Spann, who became a member after the conclusion of his presidential term, and our original chair, Bob Kutak.

The long work of the Commission and its resulting new codification of the ethical rules of practice demonstrate, it is submitted, the commitment of the American lawyer to his or her profession and to achievement of the highest standards.

Robert W. Meserve
September 1983

ABA COMMISSION ON EVALUATION
OF THE RULES OF PROFESSIONAL CONDUCT
(1997–2002)

HON. E. NORMAN VEASEY, *Chair*
Wilmington, Delaware

MARGARET C. LOVE
Washington, D.C.

LAWRENCE J. FOX
Philadelphia, Pennsylvania

SUSAN R. MARTYN
Toledo, Ohio

ALBERT C. HARVEY
Memphis, Tennessee

DAVID T. MCLAUGHLIN
New London, New Hampshire

GEOFFREY C. HAZARD, JR.
Swarthmore, Pennsylvania

RICHARD E. MULROY
Ridgewood, New Jersey

HON. PATRICK E. HIGGINBOTHAM
Dallas, Texas

LUCIAN T. PERA
Memphis, Tennessee

W. LOEBER LANDAU
New York, New York

HON. HENRY RAMSEY, JR. (Ret.)
Berkeley, California

HON. LAURIE D. ZELON
Los Angeles, California

LIAISONS

JAMES B. LEE
Salt Lake City, Utah
Board of Governors

SETH ROSNER
Greenfield Center, New York
Board of Governors

REPORTERS

NANCY J. MOORE
Boston, Massachusetts
Chief Reporter

THOMAS D. MORGAN (1998–1999)
Washington, D.C.

CARL A. PIERCE
Knoxville, Tennessee

CENTER FOR PROFESSIONAL RESPONSIBILITY

JEANNE P. GRAY
Chicago, Illinois
Director

CHARLOTTE K. STRETCH, *Counsel*
Chicago, Illinois

SUSAN M. CAMPBELL, *Paralegal*
Chicago, Illinois

COMMISSION ON EVALUATION OF THE
RULES OF PROFESSIONAL CONDUCT ("ETHICS 2000")
CHAIR'S INTRODUCTION

In mid-1997, ABA President Jerome J. Shestack, his immediate predecessor, N. Lee Cooper, and his successor, Philip S. Anderson had the vision to establish the "Ethics 2000" Commission. These three leaders persuaded the ABA Board of Governors that the Model Rules adopted by the ABA House of Delegates in 1983 needed comprehensive review and some revision, and this project was launched. Though some might have thought it premature to reopen the Model Rules to such a rigorous general reassessment after only fourteen years, the evaluation process has proven that the ABA leadership was correct.

One of the primary reasons behind the decision to revisit the Model Rules was the growing disparity in state ethics codes. While a large majority of states and the District of Columbia had adopted some version of the Model Rules (then thirty-nine, now forty-two), there were many significant differences among the state versions that resulted in an undesirable lack of uniformity—a problem that had been exacerbated by the approximately thirty amendments to the Model Rules between 1983 and 1997. A few states had elected to retain some version of the 1969 Model Code of Professional Responsibility, and California remained committed to an entirely separate system of lawyer regulation.

But it was not only the patchwork pattern of state regulation that motivated the ABA leaders of 1997 to take this action. There were also new issues and questions raised by the influence that technological developments were having on the delivery of legal services. The explosive dynamics of modern law practice and the anticipated developments in the future of the legal profession lent a sense of urgency as well as a substantive dimension to the project. These developments were underscored by the work then underway on the American Law Institute's *Restatement of the Law Governing Lawyers*.

There was also a strong countervailing sense that there was much to be valued in the existing concepts and articulation of the Model Rules. The Commission concluded early on that these valuable aspects of the Rules should not be lost or put at risk in our revision effort. As a result, the Commission set about to be comprehensive, but at the same time conservative, and to recommend change only where necessary. In balancing the need to preserve the good with the need for improvement, we were mindful of Thomas Jefferson's words of nearly 185 years ago, in a letter concerning the Virginia Constitution, that "moderate imperfections had better be borne with; because, when once known, we accommodate ourselves to them, and find practical means of correcting their ill effects."

Thus, we retained the basic architecture of the Model Rules. We also retained the primary disciplinary function of the Rules, resisting the temptation to preach aspirationally about "best practices" or professionalism concepts. Valuable as the profession might find such guidance, it would not have—and should not be misperceived as having—a regulatory dimension. We were, however, always conscious of the educational role of the Model Rules. Finally, we tried to keep our changes to a minimum: when a particular provision was found not to be "broken" we did not try to "fix" it. Even so, as the reader will note, the Commission ended up making a large number of changes: some are relatively innocuous and nonsubstantive, in the nature of editorial or stylistic changes; others are substantive but not particularly controversial; and a few are both substantive and controversial.

The deliberations of the Commission did not take place in a vacuum and our determinations are not being pronounced *ex cathedra*. Rather, they are products of thorough research, scholarly analysis, and thoughtful consideration. Of equal importance, they have been influenced by the views of practitioners, scholars, other members of the legal profession, and the public. All these constituencies have had continual access to and considerable—and proper—influence upon the deliberations of the Commission throughout this process.

I must pause to underscore the openness of our process. We held over fifty days of meetings, all of which were open, and ten public hearings at regular intervals over a four-and-a-half-year period. There were a large number of interested observers at our meetings, many of whom were members of our Advisory Council of 250-plus persons, to offer comments and suggestions. Those observations were very helpful and influential in shaping the Report. Our public discussion drafts, minutes, and Report were available on our website for the world to see and comment upon. As a consequence, we received an enormous number of excellent comments and suggestions, many of which were adopted in the formulation of our Report.

Moreover, we encouraged state and local bar associations, ABA sections and divisions, other professional organizations, and the judiciary to appoint specially designated committees to work with and counsel the Commission. This effort was successful, and the Commission benefitted significantly from the considered views of these groups.

In heeding the counsel of these advisors, we were constantly mindful of substantial and high-velocity changes in the legal profession, particularly over the past decade. These changes have been highlighted by increased public scrutiny of lawyers and an awareness of their influential role in the formation and implementation of public policy; persistent concerns about lawyer honesty, candor, and civility; external competitive and technological pressures on the legal profession; internal pressures on law firm organization and management raised by sheer size, as well as specialization and lawyer mobility; jurisdictional and governance issues, such as multidisciplinary and multijurisdictional practice; special concerns of lawyers in nontraditional practice settings, such as government lawyers and in-house counsel; and the need to enhance public trust and confidence in the legal profession.

At the end of the day, our goal was to develop Rules that are comprehensible to the public and provide clear guidance to the practitioner. Our desire was to preserve all that is valuable and enduring about the existing Model Rules, while at the same time adapting them to the realities of modern law practice and the limits of professional discipline. We believe our product is a balanced blend of traditional precepts and forward-looking provisions that are responsive to modern developments. Our process has been thorough, painstaking, open, scholarly, objective, and collegial.

It is impossible here to go into detail about the changes proposed by the Commission. The changes recommended by the Commission clarified and strengthened a lawyer's duty to communicate with the client; clarified and strengthened a lawyer's duty to clients in certain specific problem areas; responded to the changing organization and structure of modern law practice; responded to new issues and questions raised by the influence that technological developments are having on the delivery of legal services; clarified existing Rules to provide better guidance and explanation to lawyers; clarified and strengthened a lawyer's obligations to the tribunal and to the justice system; responded to the need for changes in the delivery of legal services to low- and middle-income persons; and increased protection of third parties.

The ABA House of Delegates began consideration of the Commission's Report at the August 2001 Annual Meeting in Chicago and completed its review at the February 2002 Midyear Meeting in Philadelphia.

At the August 2002 Annual Meeting in Washington, D.C., the ABA House of Delegates considered and adopted additional amendments to the Model Rules sponsored by the ABA Commission on Multijurisdictional Practice and the ABA Standing Committee on Ethics and Professional Responsibility. As state supreme courts consider implementation of these newly revised Rules, it is our fervent hope that the goal of uniformity will be the guiding beacon.

In closing, the Commission expresses its gratitude to the law firm of Drinker Biddle & Reath, whose generous contribution helped make possible the continued, invaluable support of the Commission's Chief Reporter. I also want to express personally my gratitude to and admiration for my colleagues. The chemistry, goodwill, good humor, serious purpose, collegiality, and hard work of the Commission members, Reporters, and ABA staff have been extraordinary. The profession and the public have been enriched beyond measure by their efforts. It has been a pleasure and a privilege for me to work with all of them.

Hon. E. Norman Veasey
August 2002

PREAMBLE AND SCOPE

PREAMBLE:
A LAWYER'S RESPONSIBILITIES

[1] A lawyer, as a member of the legal profession, is a representative of clients, an officer of the legal system and a public citizen having special responsibility for the quality of justice.

[2] As a representative of clients, a lawyer performs various functions. As advisor, a lawyer provides a client with an informed understanding of the client's legal rights and obligations and explains their practical implications. As advocate, a lawyer zealously asserts the client's position under the rules of the adversary system. As negotiator, a lawyer seeks a result advantageous to the client but consistent with requirements of honest dealings with others. As an evaluator, a lawyer acts by examining a client's legal affairs and reporting about them to the client or to others.

[3] In addition to these representational functions, a lawyer may serve as a third-party neutral, a nonrepresentational role helping the parties to resolve a dispute or other matter. Some of these Rules apply directly to lawyers who are or have served as third-party neutrals. See, e.g., Rules 1.12 and 2.4. In addition, there are Rules that apply to lawyers who are not active in the practice of law or to practicing lawyers even when they are acting in a nonprofessional capacity. For example, a lawyer who commits fraud in the conduct of a business is subject to discipline for engaging in conduct involving dishonesty, fraud, deceit or misrepresentation. See Rule 8.4.

[4] In all professional functions a lawyer should be competent, prompt and diligent. A lawyer should maintain communication with a client concerning the representation. A lawyer should keep in confidence information relating to representation of a client except so far as disclosure is required or permitted by the Rules of Professional Conduct or other law.

[5] A lawyer's conduct should conform to the requirements of the law, both in professional service to clients and in the lawyer's business and personal affairs. A lawyer should use the law's procedures only for legitimate purposes and not to harass or intimidate others. A lawyer should demonstrate respect for the legal system and for those who serve it, including judges, other lawyers and public officials. While it is a law-

yer's duty, when necessary, to challenge the rectitude of official action, it is also a lawyer's duty to uphold legal process.

[6] As a public citizen, a lawyer should seek improvement of the law, access to the legal system, the administration of justice and the quality of service rendered by the legal profession. As a member of a learned profession, a lawyer should cultivate knowledge of the law beyond its use for clients, employ that knowledge in reform of the law and work to strengthen legal education. In addition, a lawyer should further the public's understanding of and confidence in the rule of law and the justice system because legal institutions in a constitutional democracy depend on popular participation and support to maintain their authority. A lawyer should be mindful of deficiencies in the administration of justice and of the fact that the poor, and sometimes persons who are not poor, cannot afford adequate legal assistance. Therefore, all lawyers should devote professional time and resources and use civic influence to ensure equal access to our system of justice for all those who because of economic or social barriers cannot afford or secure adequate legal counsel. A lawyer should aid the legal profession in pursuing these objectives and should help the bar regulate itself in the public interest.

[7] Many of a lawyer's professional responsibilities are prescribed in the Rules of Professional Conduct, as well as substantive and procedural law. However, a lawyer is also guided by personal conscience and the approbation of professional peers. A lawyer should strive to attain the highest level of skill, to improve the law and the legal profession and to exemplify the legal profession's ideals of public service.

[8] A lawyer's responsibilities as a representative of clients, an officer of the legal system and a public citizen are usually harmonious. Thus, when an opposing party is well represented, a lawyer can be a zealous advocate on behalf of a client and at the same time assume that justice is being done. So also, a lawyer can be sure that preserving client confidences ordinarily serves the public interest because people are more likely to seek legal advice, and thereby heed their legal obligations, when they know their communications will be private.

[9] In the nature of law practice, however, conflicting responsibilities are encountered. Virtually all difficult ethical problems arise from conflict between a lawyer's responsibilities to clients, to the legal system and to the lawyer's own interest in remaining an ethical person while earning a satisfactory living. The Rules of Professional Conduct often prescribe terms for resolving such conflicts. Within the framework of these Rules,

however, many difficult issues of professional discretion can arise. Such issues must be resolved through the exercise of sensitive professional and moral judgment guided by the basic principles underlying the Rules. These principles include the lawyer's obligation zealously to protect and pursue a client's legitimate interests, within the bounds of the law, while maintaining a professional, courteous and civil attitude toward all persons involved in the legal system.

[10] The legal profession is largely self-governing. Although other professions also have been granted powers of self-government, the legal profession is unique in this respect because of the close relationship between the profession and the processes of government and law enforcement. This connection is manifested in the fact that ultimate authority over the legal profession is vested largely in the courts.

[11] To the extent that lawyers meet the obligations of their professional calling, the occasion for government regulation is obviated. Self-regulation also helps maintain the legal profession's independence from government domination. An independent legal profession is an important force in preserving government under law, for abuse of legal authority is more readily challenged by a profession whose members are not dependent on government for the right to practice.

[12] The legal profession's relative autonomy carries with it special responsibilities of self-government. The profession has a responsibility to assure that its regulations are conceived in the public interest and not in furtherance of parochial or self-interested concerns of the bar. Every lawyer is responsible for observance of the Rules of Professional Conduct. A lawyer should also aid in securing their observance by other lawyers. Neglect of these responsibilities compromises the independence of the profession and the public interest which it serves.

[13] Lawyers play a vital role in the preservation of society. The fulfillment of this role requires an understanding by lawyers of their relationship to our legal system. The Rules of Professional Conduct, when properly applied, serve to define that relationship.

SCOPE

[14] The Rules of Professional Conduct are rules of reason. They should be interpreted with reference to the purposes of legal representation and of the law itself. Some of the Rules are imperatives, cast in the terms "shall" or "shall not." These define proper conduct for purposes of professional discipline. Others, generally cast in the term "may," are

permissive and define areas under the Rules in which the lawyer has discretion to exercise professional judgment. No disciplinary action should be taken when the lawyer chooses not to act or acts within the bounds of such discretion. Other Rules define the nature of relationships between the lawyer and others. The Rules are thus partly obligatory and disciplinary and partly constitutive and descriptive in that they define a lawyer's professional role. Many of the Comments use the term "should." Comments do not add obligations to the Rules but provide guidance for practicing in compliance with the Rules.

[15] The Rules presuppose a larger legal context shaping the lawyer's role. That context includes court rules and statutes relating to matters of licensure, laws defining specific obligations of lawyers and substantive and procedural law in general. The Comments are sometimes used to alert lawyers to their responsibilities under such other law.

[16] Compliance with the Rules, as with all law in an open society, depends primarily upon understanding and voluntary compliance, secondarily upon reinforcement by peer and public opinion and finally, when necessary, upon enforcement through disciplinary proceedings. The Rules do not, however, exhaust the moral and ethical considerations that should inform a lawyer, for no worthwhile human activity can be completely defined by legal rules. The Rules simply provide a framework for the ethical practice of law.

[17] Furthermore, for purposes of determining the lawyer's authority and responsibility, principles of substantive law external to these Rules determine whether a client-lawyer relationship exists. Most of the duties flowing from the client-lawyer relationship attach only after the client has requested the lawyer to render legal services and the lawyer has agreed to do so. But there are some duties, such as that of confidentiality under Rule 1.6, that attach when the lawyer agrees to consider whether a client-lawyer relationship shall be established. See Rule 1.18. Whether a client-lawyer relationship exists for any specific purpose can depend on the circumstances and may be a question of fact.

[18] Under various legal provisions, including constitutional, statutory and common law, the responsibilities of government lawyers may include authority concerning legal matters that ordinarily reposes in the client in private client-lawyer relationships. For example, a lawyer for a government agency may have authority on behalf of the government to decide upon settlement or whether to appeal from an adverse judgment. Such authority in various respects is generally vested in the attorney

general and the state's attorney in state government, and their federal counterparts, and the same may be true of other government law officers. Also, lawyers under the supervision of these officers may be authorized to represent several government agencies in intragovernmental legal controversies in circumstances where a private lawyer could not represent multiple private clients. These Rules do not abrogate any such authority.

[19] Failure to comply with an obligation or prohibition imposed by a Rule is a basis for invoking the disciplinary process. The Rules presuppose that disciplinary assessment of a lawyer's conduct will be made on the basis of the facts and circumstances as they existed at the time of the conduct in question and in recognition of the fact that a lawyer often has to act upon uncertain or incomplete evidence of the situation. Moreover, the Rules presuppose that whether or not discipline should be imposed for a violation, and the severity of a sanction, depend on all the circumstances, such as the willfulness and seriousness of the violation, extenuating factors and whether there have been previous violations.

[20] Violation of a Rule should not itself give rise to a cause of action against a lawyer nor should it create any presumption in such a case that a legal duty has been breached. In addition, violation of a Rule does not necessarily warrant any other nondisciplinary remedy, such as disqualification of a lawyer in pending litigation. The Rules are designed to provide guidance to lawyers and to provide a structure for regulating conduct through disciplinary agencies. They are not designed to be a basis for civil liability. Furthermore, the purpose of the Rules can be subverted when they are invoked by opposing parties as procedural weapons. The fact that a Rule is a just basis for a lawyer's self-assessment, or for sanctioning a lawyer under the administration of a disciplinary authority, does not imply that an antagonist in a collateral proceeding or transaction has standing to seek enforcement of the Rule. Nevertheless, since the Rules do establish standards of conduct by lawyers, a lawyer's violation of a Rule may be evidence of breach of the applicable standard of conduct.

[21] The Comment accompanying each Rule explains and illustrates the meaning and purpose of the Rule. The Preamble and this note on Scope provide general orientation. The Comments are intended as guides to interpretation, but the text of each Rule is authoritative.

RULE 1.0: TERMINOLOGY

(a) "Belief" or "believes" denotes that the person involved actually supposed the fact in question to be true. A person's belief may be inferred from circumstances.

(b) "Confirmed in writing," when used in reference to the informed consent of a person, denotes informed consent that is given in writing by the person or a writing that a lawyer promptly transmits to the person confirming an oral informed consent. See paragraph (e) for the definition of "informed consent." If it is not feasible to obtain or transmit the writing at the time the person gives informed consent, then the lawyer must obtain or transmit it within a reasonable time thereafter.

(c) "Firm" or "law firm" denotes a lawyer or lawyers in a law partnership, professional corporation, sole proprietorship or other association authorized to practice law; or lawyers employed in a legal services organization or the legal department of a corporation or other organization.

(d) "Fraud" or "fraudulent" denotes conduct that is fraudulent under the substantive or procedural law of the applicable jurisdiction and has a purpose to deceive.

(e) "Informed consent" denotes the agreement by a person to a proposed course of conduct after the lawyer has communicated adequate information and explanation about the material risks of and reasonably available alternatives to the proposed course of conduct.

(f) "Knowingly," "known," or "knows" denotes actual knowledge of the fact in question. A person's knowledge may be inferred from circumstances.

(g) "Partner" denotes a member of a partnership, a shareholder in a law firm organized as a professional corporation, or a member of an association authorized to practice law.

(h) "Reasonable" or "reasonably" when used in relation to conduct by a lawyer denotes the conduct of a reasonably prudent and competent lawyer.

(i) "Reasonable belief" or "reasonably believes" when used in reference to a lawyer denotes that the lawyer believes the matter in question and that the circumstances are such that the belief is reasonable.

(j) "Reasonably should know" when used in reference to a lawyer denotes that a lawyer of reasonable prudence and competence would ascertain the matter in question.

(k) "Screened" denotes the isolation of a lawyer from any participation in a matter through the timely imposition of procedures within a firm that are reasonably adequate under the circumstances to protect information that the isolated lawyer is obligated to protect under these Rules or other law.

(l) "Substantial" when used in reference to degree or extent denotes a material matter of clear and weighty importance.

(m) "Tribunal" denotes a court, an arbitrator in a binding arbitration proceeding or a legislative body, administrative agency or other body acting in an adjudicative capacity. A legislative body, administrative agency or other body acts in an adjudicative capacity when a neutral official, after the presentation of evidence or legal argument by a party or parties, will render a binding legal judgment directly affecting a party's interests in a particular matter.

(n) "Writing" or "written" denotes a tangible or electronic record of a communication or representation, including handwriting, typewriting, printing, photostating, photography, audio or videorecording, and electronic communications. A "signed" writing includes an electronic sound, symbol or process attached to or logically associated with a writing and executed or adopted by a person with the intent to sign the writing.

Comment
Confirmed in Writing

[1] If it is not feasible to obtain or transmit a written confirmation at the time the client gives informed consent, then the lawyer must obtain or transmit it within a reasonable time thereafter. If a lawyer has obtained a client's informed consent, the lawyer may act in reliance on that consent so long as it is confirmed in writing within a reasonable time thereafter.

Firm

[2] Whether two or more lawyers constitute a firm within paragraph (c) can depend on the specific facts. For example, two practitioners who share office space and occasionally consult or assist each other ordinarily would not be regarded as constituting a firm. However, if they present themselves to the public in a way that suggests that they are a firm or conduct themselves as a firm, they should be regarded as a firm for purposes of the Rules. The terms of any formal agreement between associated lawyers are relevant in determining whether they are a firm, as

is the fact that they have mutual access to information concerning the clients they serve. Furthermore, it is relevant in doubtful cases to consider the underlying purpose of the Rule that is involved. A group of lawyers could be regarded as a firm for purposes of the Rule that the same lawyer should not represent opposing parties in litigation, while it might not be so regarded for purposes of the Rule that information acquired by one lawyer is attributed to another.

[3] With respect to the law department of an organization, including the government, there is ordinarily no question that the members of the department constitute a firm within the meaning of the Rules of Professional Conduct. There can be uncertainty, however, as to the identity of the client. For example, it may not be clear whether the law department of a corporation represents a subsidiary or an affiliated corporation, as well as the corporation by which the members of the department are directly employed. A similar question can arise concerning an unincorporated association and its local affiliates.

[4] Similar questions can also arise with respect to lawyers in legal aid and legal services organizations. Depending upon the structure of the organization, the entire organization or different components of it may constitute a firm or firms for purposes of these Rules.

Fraud

[5] When used in these Rules, the terms "fraud" or "fraudulent" refer to conduct that is characterized as such under the substantive or procedural law of the applicable jurisdiction and has a purpose to deceive. This does not include merely negligent misrepresentation or negligent failure to apprise another of relevant information. For purposes of these Rules, it is not necessary that anyone has suffered damages or relied on the misrepresentation or failure to inform.

Informed Consent

[6] Many of the Rules of Professional Conduct require the lawyer to obtain the informed consent of a client or other person (e.g., a former client or, under certain circumstances, a prospective client) before accepting or continuing representation or pursuing a course of conduct. See, e.g., Rules 1.2(c), 1.6(a) and 1.7(b). The communication necessary to obtain such consent will vary according to the Rule involved and the circumstances giving rise to the need to obtain informed consent. The lawyer must make reasonable efforts to ensure that the client or other person

9

possesses information reasonably adequate to make an informed decision. Ordinarily, this will require communication that includes a disclosure of the facts and circumstances giving rise to the situation, any explanation reasonably necessary to inform the client or other person of the
material advantages and disadvantages of the proposed course of conduct and a discussion of the client's or other person's options and alternatives. In some circumstances it may be appropriate for a lawyer to advise
a client or other person to seek the advice of other counsel. A lawyer need
not inform a client or other person of facts or implications already known
to the client or other person; nevertheless, a lawyer who does not personally inform the client or other person assumes the risk that the client
or other person is inadequately informed and the consent is invalid. In
determining whether the information and explanation provided are reasonably adequate, relevant factors include whether the client or other
person is experienced in legal matters generally and in making decisions
of the type involved, and whether the client or other person is independently represented by other counsel in giving the consent. Normally,
such persons need less information and explanation than others, and
generally a client or other person who is independently represented by
other counsel in giving the consent should be assumed to have given informed consent.

[7] Obtaining informed consent will usually require an affirmative
response by the client or other person. In general, a lawyer may not assume consent from a client's or other person's silence. Consent may be
inferred, however, from the conduct of a client or other person who has
reasonably adequate information about the matter. A number of Rules require that a person's consent be confirmed in writing. See Rules 1.7(b)
and 1.9(a). For a definition of "writing" and "confirmed in writing," see
paragraphs (n) and (b). Other Rules require that a client's consent be obtained in a writing signed by the client. See, e.g., Rules 1.8(a) and (g). For
a definition of "signed," see paragraph (n).

Screened

[8] This definition applies to situations where screening of a personally disqualified lawyer is permitted to remove imputation of a conflict of
interest under Rules 1.10, 1.11, 1.12 or 1.18.

[9] The purpose of screening is to assure the affected parties that confidential information known by the personally disqualified lawyer remains protected. The personally disqualified lawyer should acknowledge

the obligation not to communicate with any of the other lawyers in the firm with respect to the matter. Similarly, other lawyers in the firm who are working on the matter should be informed that the screening is in place and that they may not communicate with the personally disqualified lawyer with respect to the matter. Additional screening measures that are appropriate for the particular matter will depend on the circumstances. To implement, reinforce and remind all affected lawyers of the presence of the screening, it may be appropriate for the firm to undertake such procedures as a written undertaking by the screened lawyer to avoid any communication with other firm personnel and any contact with any firm files or other information, including information in electronic form, relating to the matter, written notice and instructions to all other firm personnel forbidding any communication with the screened lawyer relating to the matter, denial of access by the screened lawyer to firm files or other information, including information in electronic form, relating to the matter and periodic reminders of the screen to the screened lawyer and all other firm personnel.

[10] In order to be effective, screening measures must be implemented as soon as practical after a lawyer or law firm knows or reasonably should know that there is a need for screening.

CLIENT-LAWYER RELATIONSHIP

RULE 1.1: COMPETENCE

A lawyer shall provide competent representation to a client. Competent representation requires the legal knowledge, skill, thoroughness and preparation reasonably necessary for the representation.

Comment
Legal Knowledge and Skill

[1] In determining whether a lawyer employs the requisite knowledge and skill in a particular matter, relevant factors include the relative complexity and specialized nature of the matter, the lawyer's general experience, the lawyer's training and experience in the field in question, the preparation and study the lawyer is able to give the matter and whether it is feasible to refer the matter to, or associate or consult with, a lawyer of established competence in the field in question. In many instances, the

required proficiency is that of a general practitioner. Expertise in a particular field of law may be required in some circumstances.

[2] A lawyer need not necessarily have special training or prior experience to handle legal problems of a type with which the lawyer is unfamiliar. A newly admitted lawyer can be as competent as a practitioner with long experience. Some important legal skills, such as the analysis of precedent, the evaluation of evidence and legal drafting, are required in all legal problems. Perhaps the most fundamental legal skill consists of determining what kind of legal problems a situation may involve, a skill that necessarily transcends any particular specialized knowledge. A lawyer can provide adequate representation in a wholly novel field through necessary study. Competent representation can also be provided through the association of a lawyer of established competence in the field in question.

[3] In an emergency a lawyer may give advice or assistance in a matter in which the lawyer does not have the skill ordinarily required where referral to or consultation or association with another lawyer would be impractical. Even in an emergency, however, assistance should be limited to that reasonably necessary in the circumstances, for ill-considered action under emergency conditions can jeopardize the client's interest.

[4] A lawyer may accept representation where the requisite level of competence can be achieved by reasonable preparation. This applies as well to a lawyer who is appointed as counsel for an unrepresented person. See also Rule 6.2.

Thoroughness and Preparation

[5] Competent handling of a particular matter includes inquiry into and analysis of the factual and legal elements of the problem, and use of methods and procedures meeting the standards of competent practitioners. It also includes adequate preparation. The required attention and preparation are determined in part by what is at stake; major litigation and complex transactions ordinarily require more extensive treatment than matters of lesser complexity and consequence. An agreement between the lawyer and the client regarding the scope of the representation may limit the matters for which the lawyer is responsible. See Rule 1.2(c).

Retaining or Contracting With Other Lawyers

[6] Before a lawyer retains or contracts with other lawyers outside the lawyer's own firm to provide or assist in the provision of legal services to a client, the lawyer should ordinarily obtain informed consent

from the client and must reasonably believe that the other lawyers' services will contribute to the competent and ethical representation of the client. See also Rules 1.2 (allocation of authority), 1.4 (communication with client), 1.5(e) (fee sharing), 1.6 (confidentiality), and 5.5(a) (unauthorized practice of law). The reasonableness of the decision to retain or contract with other lawyers outside the lawyer's own firm will depend upon the circumstances, including the education, experience and reputation of the nonfirm lawyers; the nature of the services assigned to the nonfirm lawyers; and the legal protections, professional conduct rules, and ethical environments of the jurisdictions in which the services will be performed, particularly relating to confidential information.

[7] When lawyers from more than one law firm are providing legal services to the client on a particular matter, the lawyers ordinarily should consult with each other and the client about the scope of their respective representations and the allocation of responsibility among them. See Rule 1.2. When making allocations of responsibility in a matter pending before a tribunal, lawyers and parties may have additional obligations that are a matter of law beyond the scope of these Rules.

Maintaining Competence

[8] To maintain the requisite knowledge and skill, a lawyer should keep abreast of changes in the law and its practice, including the benefits and risks associated with relevant technology, engage in continuing study and education and comply with all continuing legal education requirements to which the lawyer is subject.

Definitional Cross-References

"Reasonably" *See* Rule 1.0(h)

RULE 1.2: SCOPE OF REPRESENTATION AND ALLOCATION OF AUTHORITY BETWEEN CLIENT AND LAWYER

(a) Subject to paragraphs (c) and (d), a lawyer shall abide by a client's decisions concerning the objectives of representation and, as required by Rule 1.4, shall consult with the client as to the means by which they are to be pursued. A lawyer may take such action on behalf of the client as is impliedly authorized to carry out the representation. A lawyer shall abide by a client's decision

whether to settle a matter. In a criminal case, the lawyer shall abide by the client's decision, after consultation with the lawyer, as to a plea to be entered, whether to waive jury trial and whether the client will testify.

(b) A lawyer's representation of a client, including representation by appointment, does not constitute an endorsement of the client's political, economic, social or moral views or activities.

(c) A lawyer may limit the scope of the representation if the limitation is reasonable under the circumstances and the client gives informed consent.

(d) A lawyer shall not counsel a client to engage, or assist a client, in conduct that the lawyer knows is criminal or fraudulent, but a lawyer may discuss the legal consequences of any proposed course of conduct with a client and may counsel or assist a client to make a good faith effort to determine the validity, scope, meaning or application of the law.

Comment
Allocation of Authority between Client and Lawyer

[1] Paragraph (a) confers upon the client the ultimate authority to determine the purposes to be served by legal representation, within the limits imposed by law and the lawyer's professional obligations. The decisions specified in paragraph (a), such as whether to settle a civil matter, must also be made by the client. See Rule 1.4(a)(1) for the lawyer's duty to communicate with the client about such decisions. With respect to the means by which the client's objectives are to be pursued, the lawyer shall consult with the client as required by Rule 1.4(a)(2) and may take such action as is impliedly authorized to carry out the representation.

[2] On occasion, however, a lawyer and a client may disagree about the means to be used to accomplish the client's objectives. Clients normally defer to the special knowledge and skill of their lawyer with respect to the means to be used to accomplish their objectives, particularly with respect to technical, legal and tactical matters. Conversely, lawyers usually defer to the client regarding such questions as the expense to be incurred and concern for third persons who might be adversely affected. Because of the varied nature of the matters about which a lawyer and client might disagree and because the actions in question may implicate the interests of a tribunal or other persons, this Rule does not prescribe how

such disagreements are to be resolved. Other law, however, may be applicable and should be consulted by the lawyer. The lawyer should also consult with the client and seek a mutually acceptable resolution of the disagreement. If such efforts are unavailing and the lawyer has a fundamental disagreement with the client, the lawyer may withdraw from the representation. See Rule 1.16(b)(4). Conversely, the client may resolve the disagreement by discharging the lawyer. See Rule 1.16(a)(3).

[3] At the outset of a representation, the client may authorize the lawyer to take specific action on the client's behalf without further consultation. Absent a material change in circumstances and subject to Rule 1.4, a lawyer may rely on such an advance authorization. The client may, however, revoke such authority at any time.

[4] In a case in which the client appears to be suffering diminished capacity, the lawyer's duty to abide by the client's decisions is to be guided by reference to Rule 1.14.

Independence from Client's Views or Activities

[5] Legal representation should not be denied to people who are unable to afford legal services, or whose cause is controversial or the subject of popular disapproval. By the same token, representing a client does not constitute approval of the client's views or activities.

Agreements Limiting Scope of Representation

[6] The scope of services to be provided by a lawyer may be limited by agreement with the client or by the terms under which the lawyer's services are made available to the client. When a lawyer has been retained by an insurer to represent an insured, for example, the representation may be limited to matters related to the insurance coverage. A limited representation may be appropriate because the client has limited objectives for the representation. In addition, the terms upon which representation is undertaken may exclude specific means that might otherwise be used to accomplish the client's objectives. Such limitations may exclude actions that the client thinks are too costly or that the lawyer regards as repugnant or imprudent.

[7] Although this Rule affords the lawyer and client substantial latitude to limit the representation, the limitation must be reasonable under the circumstances. If, for example, a client's objective is limited to securing general information about the law the client needs in order to handle a common and typically uncomplicated legal problem, the lawyer and

client may agree that the lawyer's services will be limited to a brief tele-phone consultation. Such a limitation, however, would not be reasonable if the time allotted was not sufficient to yield advice upon which the client could rely. Although an agreement for a limited representation does not exempt a lawyer from the duty to provide competent representation, the limitation is a factor to be considered when determining the legal knowledge, skill, thoroughness and preparation reasonably necessary for the representation. See Rule 1.1.

[8] All agreements concerning a lawyer's representation of a client must accord with the Rules of Professional Conduct and other law. See, e.g., Rules 1.1, 1.8 and 5.6.

Criminal, Fraudulent and Prohibited Transactions

[9] Paragraph (d) prohibits a lawyer from knowingly counseling or assisting a client to commit a crime or fraud. This prohibition, however, does not preclude the lawyer from giving an honest opinion about the actual consequences that appear likely to result from a client's conduct. Nor does the fact that a client uses advice in a course of action that is criminal or fraudulent of itself make a lawyer a party to the course of action. There is a critical distinction between presenting an analysis of legal aspects of questionable conduct and recommending the means by which a crime or fraud might be committed with impunity.

[10] When the client's course of action has already begun and is continuing, the lawyer's responsibility is especially delicate. The lawyer is required to avoid assisting the client, for example, by drafting or delivering documents that the lawyer knows are fraudulent or by suggesting how the wrongdoing might be concealed. A lawyer may not continue assisting a client in conduct that the lawyer originally supposed was legally proper but then discovers is criminal or fraudulent. The lawyer must, therefore, withdraw from the representation of the client in the matter. See Rule 1.16(a). In some cases, withdrawal alone might be insufficient. It may be necessary for the lawyer to give notice of the fact of withdrawal and to disaffirm any opinion, document, affirmation or the like. See Rule 4.1.

[11] Where the client is a fiduciary, the lawyer may be charged with special obligations in dealings with a beneficiary.

[12] Paragraph (d) applies whether or not the defrauded party is a party to the transaction. Hence, a lawyer must not participate in a transaction to effectuate criminal or fraudulent avoidance of tax liability. Paragraph (d) does not preclude undertaking a criminal defense incident to a

general retainer for legal services to a lawful enterprise. The last clause of paragraph (d) recognizes that determining the validity or interpretation of a statute or regulation may require a course of action involving disobedience of the statute or regulation or of the interpretation placed upon it by governmental authorities.

[13] If a lawyer comes to know or reasonably should know that a client expects assistance not permitted by the Rules of Professional Conduct or other law or if the lawyer intends to act contrary to the client's instructions, the lawyer must consult with the client regarding the limitations on the lawyer's conduct. See Rule 1.4(a)(5).

Definitional Cross-References

"Fraudulent" *See* Rule 1.0(d)
"Informed consent" *See* Rule 1.0(e)
"Knows" *See* Rule 1.0(f)
"Reasonable" *See* Rule 1.0(h)

RULE 1.3: DILIGENCE

A lawyer shall act with reasonable diligence and promptness in representing a client.

Comment

[1] A lawyer should pursue a matter on behalf of a client despite opposition, obstruction or personal inconvenience to the lawyer, and take whatever lawful and ethical measures are required to vindicate a client's cause or endeavor. A lawyer must also act with commitment and dedication to the interests of the client and with zeal in advocacy upon the client's behalf. A lawyer is not bound, however, to press for every advantage that might be realized for a client. For example, a lawyer may have authority to exercise professional discretion in determining the means by which a matter should be pursued. See Rule 1.2. The lawyer's duty to act with reasonable diligence does not require the use of offensive tactics or preclude the treating of all persons involved in the legal process with courtesy and respect.

[2] A lawyer's work load must be controlled so that each matter can be handled competently.

[3] Perhaps no professional shortcoming is more widely resented than procrastination. A client's interests often can be adversely affected

by the passage of time or the change of conditions; in extreme instances, as when a lawyer overlooks a statute of limitations, the client's legal position may be destroyed. Even when the client's interests are not affected in substance, however, unreasonable delay can cause a client needless anxiety and undermine confidence in the lawyer's trustworthiness. A lawyer's duty to act with reasonable promptness, however, does not preclude the lawyer from agreeing to a reasonable request for a postponement that will not prejudice the lawyer's client.

[4] Unless the relationship is terminated as provided in Rule 1.16, a lawyer should carry through to conclusion all matters undertaken for a client. If a lawyer's employment is limited to a specific matter, the relationship terminates when the matter has been resolved. If a lawyer has served a client over a substantial period in a variety of matters, the client sometimes may assume that the lawyer will continue to serve on a continuing basis unless the lawyer gives notice of withdrawal. Doubt about whether a client-lawyer relationship still exists should be clarified by the lawyer, preferably in writing, so that the client will not mistakenly suppose the lawyer is looking after the client's affairs when the lawyer has ceased to do so. For example, if a lawyer has handled a judicial or administrative proceeding that produced a result adverse to the client and the lawyer and the client have not agreed that the lawyer will handle the matter on appeal, the lawyer must consult with the client about the possibility of appeal before relinquishing responsibility for the matter. See Rule 1.4(a)(2). Whether the lawyer is obligated to prosecute the appeal for the client depends on the scope of the representation the lawyer has agreed to provide to the client. See Rule 1.2.

[5] To prevent neglect of client matters in the event of a sole practitioner's death or disability, the duty of diligence may require that each sole practitioner prepare a plan, in conformity with applicable rules, that designates another competent lawyer to review client files, notify each client of the lawyer's death or disability, and determine whether there is a need for immediate protective action. Cf. Rule 28 of the American Bar Association Model Rules for Lawyer Disciplinary Enforcement (providing for court appointment of a lawyer to inventory files and take other protective action in absence of a plan providing for another lawyer to protect the interests of the clients of a deceased or disabled lawyer).

Definitional Cross-References

"Reasonable" *See* Rule 1.0(h)

RULE 1.4: COMMUNICATION

(a) A lawyer shall:

(1) promptly inform the client of any decision or circumstance with respect to which the client's informed consent, as defined in Rule 1.0(e), is required by these Rules;

(2) reasonably consult with the client about the means by which the client's objectives are to be accomplished;

(3) keep the client reasonably informed about the status of the matter;

(4) promptly comply with reasonable requests for information; and

(5) consult with the client about any relevant limitation on the lawyer's conduct when the lawyer knows that the client expects assistance not permitted by the Rules of Professional Conduct or other law.

(b) A lawyer shall explain a matter to the extent reasonably necessary to permit the client to make informed decisions regarding the representation.

Comment

[1] Reasonable communication between the lawyer and the client is necessary for the client effectively to participate in the representation.

Communicating with Client

[2] If these Rules require that a particular decision about the representation be made by the client, paragraph (a)(1) requires that the lawyer promptly consult with and secure the client's consent prior to taking action unless prior discussions with the client have resolved what action the client wants the lawyer to take. For example, a lawyer who receives from opposing counsel an offer of settlement in a civil controversy or a proffered plea bargain in a criminal case must promptly inform the client of its substance unless the client has previously indicated that the proposal will be acceptable or unacceptable or has authorized the lawyer to accept or to reject the offer. See Rule 1.2(a).

[3] Paragraph (a)(2) requires the lawyer to reasonably consult with the client about the means to be used to accomplish the client's objectives. In some situations—depending on both the importance of the action under consideration and the feasibility of consulting with the client —this duty will require consultation prior to taking action. In other cir-

cumstances, such as during a trial when an immediate decision must be made, the exigency of the situation may require the lawyer to act without prior consultation. In such cases the lawyer must nonetheless act reasonably to inform the client of actions the lawyer has taken on the client's behalf. Additionally, paragraph (a)(3) requires that the lawyer keep the client reasonably informed about the status of the matter, such as significant developments affecting the timing or the substance of the representation.

[4] A lawyer's regular communication with clients will minimize the occasions on which a client will need to request information concerning the representation. When a client makes a reasonable request for information, however, paragraph (a)(4) requires prompt compliance with the request, or if a prompt response is not feasible, that the lawyer, or a member of the lawyer's staff, acknowledge receipt of the request and advise the client when a response may be expected. A lawyer should promptly respond to or acknowledge client communications.

Explaining Matters

[5] The client should have sufficient information to participate intelligently in decisions concerning the objectives of the representation and the means by which they are to be pursued, to the extent the client is willing and able to do so. Adequacy of communication depends in part on the kind of advice or assistance that is involved. For example, when there is time to explain a proposal made in a negotiation, the lawyer should review all important provisions with the client before proceeding to an agreement. In litigation a lawyer should explain the general strategy and prospects of success and ordinarily should consult the client on tactics that are likely to result in significant expense or to injure or coerce others. On the other hand, a lawyer ordinarily will not be expected to describe trial or negotiation strategy in detail. The guiding principle is that the lawyer should fulfill reasonable client expectations for information consistent with the duty to act in the client's best interests, and the client's overall requirements as to the character of representation. In certain circumstances, such as when a lawyer asks a client to consent to a representation affected by a conflict of interest, the client must give informed consent, as defined in Rule 1.0(e).

[6] Ordinarily, the information to be provided is that appropriate for a client who is a comprehending and responsible adult. However, fully informing the client according to this standard may be impracticable, for example, where the client is a child or suffers from diminished capacity.

See Rule 1.14. When the client is an organization or group, it is often impossible or inappropriate to inform every one of its members about its legal affairs; ordinarily, the lawyer should address communications to the appropriate officials of the organization. See Rule 1.13. Where many routine matters are involved, a system of limited or occasional reporting may be arranged with the client.

Withholding Information

[7] In some circumstances, a lawyer may be justified in delaying transmission of information when the client would be likely to react imprudently to an immediate communication. Thus, a lawyer might withhold a psychiatric diagnosis of a client when the examining psychiatrist indicates that disclosure would harm the client. A lawyer may not withhold information to serve the lawyer's own interest or convenience or the interests or convenience of another person. Rules or court orders governing litigation may provide that information supplied to a lawyer may not be disclosed to the client. Rule 3.4(c) directs compliance with such rules or orders.

Definitional Cross-References

"Informed consent" *See* Rule 1.0(e)
"Knows" *See* Rule 1.0(f)
"Reasonably" *See* Rule 1.0(h)

RULE 1.5: FEES

(a) A lawyer shall not make an agreement for, charge, or collect an unreasonable fee or an unreasonable amount for expenses. The factors to be considered in determining the reasonableness of a fee include the following:

(1) the time and labor required, the novelty and difficulty of the questions involved, and the skill requisite to perform the legal service properly;

(2) the likelihood, if apparent to the client, that the acceptance of the particular employment will preclude other employment by the lawyer;

(3) the fee customarily charged in the locality for similar legal services;

(4) the amount involved and the results obtained;

(5) the time limitations imposed by the client or by the circumstances;

(6) the nature and length of the professional relationship with the client;

(7) the experience, reputation, and ability of the lawyer or lawyers performing the services; and

(8) whether the fee is fixed or contingent.

(b) The scope of the representation and the basis or rate of the fee and expenses for which the client will be responsible shall be communicated to the client, preferably in writing, before or within a reasonable time after commencing the representation, except when the lawyer will charge a regularly represented client on the same basis or rate. Any changes in the basis or rate of the fee or expenses shall also be communicated to the client.

(c) A fee may be contingent on the outcome of the matter for which the service is rendered, except in a matter in which a contingent fee is prohibited by paragraph (d) or other law. A contingent fee agreement shall be in a writing signed by the client and shall state the method by which the fee is to be determined, including the percentage or percentages that shall accrue to the lawyer in the event of settlement, trial or appeal; litigation and other expenses to be deducted from the recovery; and whether such expenses are to be deducted before or after the contingent fee is calculated. The agreement must clearly notify the client of any expenses for which the client will be liable whether or not the client is the prevailing party. Upon conclusion of a contingent fee matter, the lawyer shall provide the client with a written statement stating the outcome of the matter and, if there is a recovery, showing the remittance to the client and the method of its determination.

(d) A lawyer shall not enter into an arrangement for, charge, or collect:

(1) any fee in a domestic relations matter, the payment or amount of which is contingent upon the securing of a divorce or upon the amount of alimony or support, or property settlement in lieu thereof; or

(2) a contingent fee for representing a defendant in a criminal case.

(e) A division of a fee between lawyers who are not in the same firm may be made only if:

(1) the division is in proportion to the services performed by each lawyer or each lawyer assumes joint responsibility for the representation;

(2) the client agrees to the arrangement, including the share each lawyer will receive, and the agreement is confirmed in writing; and

(3) the total fee is reasonable.

Comment

Reasonableness of Fee and Expenses

[1] Paragraph (a) requires that lawyers charge fees that are reasonable under the circumstances. The factors specified in (1) through (8) are not exclusive. Nor will each factor be relevant in each instance. Paragraph (a) also requires that expenses for which the client will be charged must be reasonable. A lawyer may seek reimbursement for the cost of services performed in-house, such as copying, or for other expenses incurred in-house, such as telephone charges, either by charging a reasonable amount to which the client has agreed in advance or by charging an amount that reasonably reflects the cost incurred by the lawyer.

Basis or Rate of Fee

[2] When the lawyer has regularly represented a client, they ordinarily will have evolved an understanding concerning the basis or rate of the fee and the expenses for which the client will be responsible. In a new client-lawyer relationship, however, an understanding as to fees and expenses must be promptly established. Generally, it is desirable to furnish the client with at least a simple memorandum or copy of the lawyer's customary fee arrangements that states the general nature of the legal services to be provided, the basis, rate or total amount of the fee and whether and to what extent the client will be responsible for any costs, expenses or disbursements in the course of the representation. A written statement concerning the terms of the engagement reduces the possibility of misunderstanding.

[3] Contingent fees, like any other fees, are subject to the reasonableness standard of paragraph (a) of this Rule. In determining whether a particular contingent fee is reasonable, or whether it is reasonable to charge any form of contingent fee, a lawyer must consider the factors that are relevant under the circumstances. Applicable law may impose limitations on contingent fees, such as a ceiling on the percentage allowable, or

may require a lawyer to offer clients an alternative basis for the fee. Applicable law also may apply to situations other than a contingent fee, for example, government regulations regarding fees in certain tax matters.

Terms of Payment

[4] A lawyer may require advance payment of a fee, but is obliged to return any unearned portion. See Rule 1.16(d). A lawyer may accept property in payment for services, such as an ownership interest in an enterprise, providing this does not involve acquisition of a proprietary interest in the cause of action or subject matter of the litigation contrary to Rule 1.8 (i). However, a fee paid in property instead of money may be subject to the requirements of Rule 1.8(a) because such fees often have the essential qualities of a business transaction with the client.

[5] An agreement may not be made whose terms might induce the lawyer improperly to curtail services for the client or perform them in a way contrary to the client's interest. For example, a lawyer should not enter into an agreement whereby services are to be provided only up to a stated amount when it is foreseeable that more extensive services probably will be required, unless the situation is adequately explained to the client. Otherwise, the client might have to bargain for further assistance in the midst of a proceeding or transaction. However, it is proper to define the extent of services in light of the client's ability to pay. A lawyer should not exploit a fee arrangement based primarily on hourly charges by using wasteful procedures.

Prohibited Contingent Fees

[6] Paragraph (d) prohibits a lawyer from charging a contingent fee in a domestic relations matter when payment is contingent upon the securing of a divorce or upon the amount of alimony or support or property settlement to be obtained. This provision does not preclude a contract for a contingent fee for legal representation in connection with the recovery of post-judgment balances due under support, alimony or other financial orders because such contracts do not implicate the same policy concerns.

Division of Fee

[7] A division of fee is a single billing to a client covering the fee of two or more lawyers who are not in the same firm. A division of fee facilitates association of more than one lawyer in a matter in which neither alone could serve the client as well, and most often is used when the fee

is contingent and the division is between a referring lawyer and a trial specialist. Paragraph (e) permits the lawyers to divide a fee either on the basis of the proportion of services they render or if each lawyer assumes responsibility for the representation as a whole. In addition, the client must agree to the arrangement, including the share that each lawyer is to receive, and the agreement must be confirmed in writing. Contingent fee agreements must be in a writing signed by the client and must otherwise comply with paragraph (c) of this Rule. Joint responsibility for the representation entails financial and ethical responsibility for the representation as if the lawyers were associated in a partnership. A lawyer should only refer a matter to a lawyer whom the referring lawyer reasonably believes is competent to handle the matter. See Rule 1.1.

[8] Paragraph (e) does not prohibit or regulate division of fees to be received in the future for work done when lawyers were previously associated in a law firm.

Disputes over Fees

[9] If a procedure has been established for resolution of fee disputes, such as an arbitration or mediation procedure established by the bar, the lawyer must comply with the procedure when it is mandatory, and, even when it is voluntary, the lawyer should conscientiously consider submitting to it. Law may prescribe a procedure for determining a lawyer's fee, for example, in representation of an executor or administrator, a class or a person entitled to a reasonable fee as part of the measure of damages. The lawyer entitled to such a fee and a lawyer representing another party concerned with the fee should comply with the prescribed procedure.

Definitional Cross-References

"Confirmed in writing" *See* Rule 1.0(b)
"Firm" *See* Rule 1.0(c)
"Writing" and "Written" and "Signed" *See* Rule 1.0(n)

RULE 1.6: CONFIDENTIALITY OF INFORMATION

(a) A lawyer shall not reveal information relating to the representation of a client unless the client gives informed consent, the disclosure is impliedly authorized in order to carry out the representation or the disclosure is permitted by paragraph (b).

(b) A lawyer may reveal information relating to the

representation of a client to the extent the lawyer reasonably believes necessary:

(1) to prevent reasonably certain death or substantial bodily harm;

(2) to prevent the client from committing a crime or fraud that is reasonably certain to result in substantial injury to the financial interests or property of another and in furtherance of which the client has used or is using the lawyer's services;

(3) to prevent, mitigate or rectify substantial injury to the financial interests or property of another that is reasonably certain to result or has resulted from the client's commission of a crime or fraud in furtherance of which the client has used the lawyer's services;

(4) to secure legal advice about the lawyer's compliance with these Rules;

(5) to establish a claim or defense on behalf of the lawyer in a controversy between the lawyer and the client, to establish a defense to a criminal charge or civil claim against the lawyer based upon conduct in which the client was involved, or to respond to allegations in any proceeding concerning the lawyer's representation of the client;

(6) to comply with other law or a court order; or

(7) to detect and resolve conflicts of interest arising from the lawyer's change of employment or from changes in the composition or ownership of a firm, but only if the revealed information would not compromise the attorney-client privilege or otherwise prejudice the client.

(c) A lawyer shall make reasonable efforts to prevent the inadvertent or unauthorized disclosure of, or unauthorized access to, information relating to the representation of a client.

Comment

[1] This Rule governs the disclosure by a lawyer of information relating to the representation of a client during the lawyer's representation of the client. See Rule 1.18 for the lawyer's duties with respect to information provided to the lawyer by a prospective client, Rule 1.9(c)(2) for the lawyer's duty not to reveal information relating to the lawyer's prior representation of a former client and Rules 1.8(b) and 1.9(c)(1) for the lawyer's duties with respect to the use of such information to the disadvantage of clients and former clients.

[2] A fundamental principle in the client-lawyer relationship is that, in the absence of the client's informed consent, the lawyer must not reveal information relating to the representation. See Rule 1.0(e) for the definition of informed consent. This contributes to the trust that is the hallmark of the client-lawyer relationship. The client is thereby encouraged to seek legal assistance and to communicate fully and frankly with the lawyer even as to embarrassing or legally damaging subject matter. The lawyer needs this information to represent the client effectively and, if necessary, to advise the client to refrain from wrongful conduct. Almost without exception, clients come to lawyers in order to determine their rights and what is, in the complex of laws and regulations, deemed to be legal and correct. Based upon experience, lawyers know that almost all clients follow the advice given, and the law is upheld.

[3] The principle of client-lawyer confidentiality is given effect by related bodies of law: the attorney-client privilege, the work product doctrine and the rule of confidentiality established in professional ethics. The attorney-client privilege and work product doctrine apply in judicial and other proceedings in which a lawyer may be called as a witness or otherwise required to produce evidence concerning a client. The rule of client-lawyer confidentiality applies in situations other than those where evidence is sought from the lawyer through compulsion of law. The confidentiality rule, for example, applies not only to matters communicated in confidence by the client but also to all information relating to the representation, whatever its source. A lawyer may not disclose such information except as authorized or required by the Rules of Professional Conduct or other law. See also Scope.

[4] Paragraph (a) prohibits a lawyer from revealing information relating to the representation of a client. This prohibition also applies to disclosures by a lawyer that do not in themselves reveal protected information but could reasonably lead to the discovery of such information by a third person. A lawyer's use of a hypothetical to discuss issues relating to the representation is permissible so long as there is no reasonable likelihood that the listener will be able to ascertain the identity of the client or the situation involved.

Authorized Disclosure

[5] Except to the extent that the client's instructions or special circumstances limit that authority, a lawyer is impliedly authorized to make disclosures about a client when appropriate in carrying out the represen-

tation. In some situations, for example, a lawyer may be impliedly au-thorized to admit a fact that cannot properly be disputed or to make a disclosure that facilitates a satisfactory conclusion to a matter. Lawyers in a firm may, in the course of the firm's practice, disclose to each other information relating to a client of the firm, unless the client has instructed that particular information be confined to specified lawyers.

Disclosure Adverse to Client

[6] Although the public interest is usually best served by a strict rule requiring lawyers to preserve the confidentiality of information relating to the representation of their clients, the confidentiality rule is subject to limited exceptions. Paragraph (b)(1) recognizes the overriding value of life and physical integrity and permits disclosure reasonably necessary to prevent reasonably certain death or substantial bodily harm. Such harm is reasonably certain to occur if it will be suffered imminently or if there is a present and substantial threat that a person will suffer such harm at a later date if the lawyer fails to take action necessary to eliminate the threat. Thus, a lawyer who knows that a client has accidentally dis-charged toxic waste into a town's water supply may reveal this informa-tion to the authorities if there is a present and substantial risk that a per-son who drinks the water will contract a life-threatening or debilitating disease and the lawyer's disclosure is necessary to eliminate the threat or reduce the number of victims.

[7] Paragraph (b)(2) is a limited exception to the rule of confidential-ity that permits the lawyer to reveal information to the extent necessary to enable affected persons or appropriate authorities to prevent the cli-ent from committing a crime or fraud, as defined in Rule 1.0(d), that is reasonably certain to result in substantial injury to the financial or prop-erty interests of another and in furtherance of which the client has used or is using the lawyer's services. Such a serious abuse of the client-lawyer relationship by the client forfeits the protection of this Rule. The client can, of course, prevent such disclosure by refraining from the wrongful conduct. Although paragraph (b)(2) does not require the lawyer to reveal the client's misconduct, the lawyer may not counsel or assist the client in conduct the lawyer knows is criminal or fraudulent. See Rule 1.2(d). See also Rule 1.16 with respect to the lawyer's obligation or right to withdraw from the representation of the client in such circumstances, and Rule 1.13(c), which permits the lawyer, where the client is an organization, to reveal information relating to the representation in limited circumstances.

[8] Paragraph (b)(3) addresses the situation in which the lawyer does not learn of the client's crime or fraud until after it has been consummated. Although the client no longer has the option of preventing disclosure by refraining from the wrongful conduct, there will be situations in which the loss suffered by the affected person can be prevented, rectified or mitigated. In such situations, the lawyer may disclose information relating to the representation to the extent necessary to enable the affected persons to prevent or mitigate reasonably certain losses or to attempt to recoup their losses. Paragraph (b)(3) does not apply when a person who has committed a crime or fraud thereafter employs a lawyer for representation concerning that offense.

[9] A lawyer's confidentiality obligations do not preclude a lawyer from securing confidential legal advice about the lawyer's personal responsibility to comply with these Rules. In most situations, disclosing information to secure such advice will be impliedly authorized for the lawyer to carry out the representation. Even when the disclosure is not impliedly authorized, paragraph (b)(4) permits such disclosure because of the importance of a lawyer's compliance with the Rules of Professional Conduct.

[10] Where a legal claim or disciplinary charge alleges complicity of the lawyer in a client's conduct or other misconduct of the lawyer involving representation of the client, the lawyer may respond to the extent the lawyer reasonably believes necessary to establish a defense. The same is true with respect to a claim involving the conduct or representation of a former client. Such a charge can arise in a civil, criminal, disciplinary or other proceeding and can be based on a wrong allegedly committed by the lawyer against the client or on a wrong alleged by a third person, for example, a person claiming to have been defrauded by the lawyer and client acting together. The lawyer's right to respond arises when an assertion of such complicity has been made. Paragraph (b)(5) does not require the lawyer to await the commencement of an action or proceeding that charges such complicity, so that the defense may be established by responding directly to a third party who has made such an assertion. The right to defend also applies, of course, where a proceeding has been commenced.

[11] A lawyer entitled to a fee is permitted by paragraph (b)(5) to prove the services rendered in an action to collect it. This aspect of the rule expresses the principle that the beneficiary of a fiduciary relationship may not exploit it to the detriment of the fiduciary.

[12] Other law may require that a lawyer disclose information about a client. Whether such a law supersedes Rule 1.6 is a question of law beyond the scope of these Rules. When disclosure of information relating to the representation appears to be required by other law, the lawyer must discuss the matter with the client to the extent required by Rule 1.4. If, however, the other law supersedes this Rule and requires disclosure, paragraph (b)(6) permits the lawyer to make such disclosures as are necessary to comply with the law.

Detection of Conflicts of Interest

[13] Paragraph (b)(7) recognizes that lawyers in different firms may need to disclose limited information to each other to detect and resolve conflicts of interest, such as when a lawyer is considering an association with another firm, two or more firms are considering a merger, or a lawyer is considering the purchase of a law practice. See Rule 1.17, Comment [7]. Under these circumstances, lawyers and law firms are permitted to disclose limited information, but only once substantive discussions regarding the new relationship have occurred. Any such disclosure should ordinarily include no more than the identity of the persons and entities involved in a matter, a brief summary of the general issues involved, and information about whether the matter has terminated. Even this limited information, however, should be disclosed only to the extent reasonably necessary to detect and resolve conflicts of interest that might arise from the possible new relationship. Moreover, the disclosure of any information is prohibited if it would compromise the attorney-client privilege or otherwise prejudice the client (e.g., the fact that a corporate client is seeking advice on a corporate takeover that has not been publicly announced; that a person has consulted a lawyer about the possibility of divorce before the person's intentions are known to the person's spouse; or that a person has consulted a lawyer about a criminal investigation that has not led to a public charge). Under those circumstances, paragraph (a) prohibits disclosure unless the client or former client gives informed consent. A lawyer's fiduciary duty to the lawyer's firm may also govern a lawyer's conduct when exploring an association with another firm and is beyond the scope of these Rules.

[14] Any information disclosed pursuant to paragraph (b)(7) may be used or further disclosed only to the extent necessary to detect and resolve conflicts of interest. Paragraph (b)(7) does not restrict the use of information acquired by means independent of any disclosure pursu-

ant to paragraph (b)(7). Paragraph (b)(7) also does not affect the disclosure of information within a law firm when the disclosure is otherwise authorized, see Comment [5], such as when a lawyer in a firm discloses information to another lawyer in the same firm to detect and resolve conflicts of interest that could arise in connection with undertaking a new representation.

[15] A lawyer may be ordered to reveal information relating to the representation of a client by a court or by another tribunal or governmental entity claiming authority pursuant to other law to compel the disclosure. Absent informed consent of the client to do otherwise, the lawyer should assert on behalf of the client all nonfrivolous claims that the order is not authorized by other law or that the information sought is protected against disclosure by the attorney-client privilege or other applicable law. In the event of an adverse ruling, the lawyer must consult with the client about the possibility of appeal to the extent required by Rule 1.4. Unless review is sought, however, paragraph (b)(6) permits the lawyer to comply with the court's order.

[16] Paragraph (b) permits disclosure only to the extent the lawyer reasonably believes the disclosure is necessary to accomplish one of the purposes specified. Where practicable, the lawyer should first seek to persuade the client to take suitable action to obviate the need for disclosure. In any case, a disclosure adverse to the client's interest should be no greater than the lawyer reasonably believes necessary to accomplish the purpose. If the disclosure will be made in connection with a judicial proceeding, the disclosure should be made in a manner that limits access to the information to the tribunal or other persons having a need to know it and appropriate protective orders or other arrangements should be sought by the lawyer to the fullest extent practicable.

[17] Paragraph (b) permits but does not require the disclosure of information relating to a client's representation to accomplish the purposes specified in paragraphs (b)(1) through (b)(6). In exercising the discretion conferred by this Rule, the lawyer may consider such factors as the nature of the lawyer's relationship with the client and with those who might be injured by the client, the lawyer's own involvement in the transaction and factors that may extenuate the conduct in question. A lawyer's decision not to disclose as permitted by paragraph (b) does not violate this Rule. Disclosure may be required, however, by other Rules. Some Rules require disclosure only if such disclosure would be permitted by paragraph (b). See Rules 1.2(d), 4.1(b), 8.1 and 8.3. Rule 3.3, on the other hand,

requires disclosure in some circumstances regardless of whether such disclosure is permitted by this Rule. See Rule 3.3(c).

Acting Competently to Preserve Confidentiality

[18] Paragraph (c) requires a lawyer to act competently to safeguard information relating to the representation of a client against unauthorized access by third parties and against inadvertent or unauthorized disclosure by the lawyer or other persons who are participating in the representation of the client or who are subject to the lawyer's supervision. See Rules 1.1, 5.1 and 5.3. The unauthorized access to, or the inadvertent or unauthorized disclosure of, information relating to the representation of a client does not constitute a violation of paragraph (c) if the lawyer has made reasonable efforts to prevent the access or disclosure. Factors to be considered in determining the reasonableness of the lawyer's efforts include, but are not limited to, the sensitivity of the information, the likelihood of disclosure if additional safeguards are not employed, the cost of employing additional safeguards, the difficulty of implementing the safeguards, and the extent to which the safeguards adversely affect the lawyer's ability to represent clients (e.g., by making a device or important piece of software excessively difficult to use). A client may require the lawyer to implement special security measures not required by this Rule or may give informed consent to forgo security measures that would otherwise be required by this Rule. Whether a lawyer may be required to take additional steps to safeguard a client's information in order to comply with other law, such as state and federal laws that govern data privacy or that impose notification requirements upon the loss of, or unauthorized access to, electronic information, is beyond the scope of these Rules. For a lawyer's duties when sharing information with nonlawyers outside the lawyer's own firm, see Rule 5.3, Comments [3]-[4].

[19] When transmitting a communication that includes information relating to the representation of a client, the lawyer must take reasonable precautions to prevent the information from coming into the hands of unintended recipients. This duty, however, does not require that the lawyer use special security measures if the method of communication affords a reasonable expectation of privacy. Special circumstances, however, may warrant special precautions. Factors to be considered in determining the reasonableness of the lawyer's expectation of confidentiality include the sensitivity of the information and the extent to which the privacy of the communication is protected by law or by a confidentiality agreement. A client may require the lawyer to implement special security measures

not required by this Rule or may give informed consent to the use of a means of communication that would otherwise be prohibited by this Rule. Whether a lawyer may be required to take additional steps in order to comply with other law, such as state and federal laws that govern data privacy, is beyond the scope of these Rules.

Former Client

[20] The duty of confidentiality continues after the client-lawyer relationship has terminated. See Rule 1.9(c)(2). See Rule 1.9(c)(1) for the prohibition against using such information to the disadvantage of the former client.

Definitional Cross-References

"Firm" *See* Rule 1.0(c)
"Fraud" *See* Rule 1.0(d)
"Informed consent" *See* Rule 1.0(e)
"Reasonable" and "Reasonably" *See* Rule 1.0(h)
"Reasonably believes" *See* Rule 1.0(i)
"Substantial" *See* Rule 1.0(l)

RULE 1.7: CONFLICT OF INTEREST: CURRENT CLIENTS

(a) Except as provided in paragraph (b), a lawyer shall not represent a client if the representation involves a concurrent conflict of interest. A concurrent conflict of interest exists if:

(1) the representation of one client will be directly adverse to another client; or

(2) there is a significant risk that the representation of one or more clients will be materially limited by the lawyer's responsibilities to another client, a former client or a third person or by a personal interest of the lawyer.

(b) Notwithstanding the existence of a concurrent conflict of interest under paragraph (a), a lawyer may represent a client if:

(1) the lawyer reasonably believes that the lawyer will be able to provide competent and diligent representation to each affected client;

(2) the representation is not prohibited by law;

(3) the representation does not involve the assertion of a claim by one client against another client represented by

the lawyer in the same litigation or other proceeding before a tribunal; and

(4) each affected client gives informed consent, confirmed in writing.

Comment
General Principles

[1] Loyalty and independent judgment are essential elements in the lawyer's relationship to a client. Concurrent conflicts of interest can arise from the lawyer's responsibilities to another client, a former client or a third person or from the lawyer's own interests. For specific Rules regarding certain concurrent conflicts of interest, see Rule 1.8. For former client conflicts of interest, see Rule 1.9. For conflicts of interest involving prospective clients, see Rule 1.18. For definitions of "informed consent" and "confirmed in writing," see Rule 1.0(e) and (b).

[2] Resolution of a conflict of interest problem under this Rule requires the lawyer to: 1) clearly identify the client or clients; 2) determine whether a conflict of interest exists; 3) decide whether the representation may be undertaken despite the existence of a conflict, i.e., whether the conflict is consentable; and 4) if so, consult with the clients affected under paragraph (a) and obtain their informed consent, confirmed in writing. The clients affected under paragraph (a) include both of the clients referred to in paragraph (a)(1) and the one or more clients whose representation might be materially limited under paragraph (a)(2).

[3] A conflict of interest may exist before representation is undertaken, in which event the representation must be declined, unless the lawyer obtains the informed consent of each client under the conditions of paragraph (b). To determine whether a conflict of interest exists, a lawyer should adopt reasonable procedures, appropriate for the size and type of firm and practice, to determine in both litigation and non-litigation matters the persons and issues involved. See also Comment to Rule 5.1. Ignorance caused by a failure to institute such procedures will not excuse a lawyer's violation of this Rule. As to whether a client-lawyer relationship exists or, having once been established, is continuing, see Comment to Rule 1.3 and Scope.

[4] If a conflict arises after representation has been undertaken, the lawyer ordinarily must withdraw from the representation, unless the lawyer has obtained the informed consent of the client under the conditions of paragraph (b). See Rule 1.16. Where more than one client is in-

volved, whether the lawyer may continue to represent any of the clients is determined both by the lawyer's ability to comply with duties owed to the former client and by the lawyer's ability to represent adequately the remaining client or clients, given the lawyer's duties to the former client. See Rule 1.9. See also Comments [5] and [29].

[5] Unforeseeable developments, such as changes in corporate and other organizational affiliations or the addition or realignment of parties in litigation, might create conflicts in the midst of a representation, as when a company sued by the lawyer on behalf of one client is bought by another client represented by the lawyer in an unrelated matter. Depending on the circumstances, the lawyer may have the option to withdraw from one of the representations in order to avoid the conflict. The lawyer must seek court approval where necessary and take steps to minimize harm to the clients. See Rule 1.16. The lawyer must continue to protect the confidences of the client from whose representation the lawyer has withdrawn. See Rule 1.9(c).

Identifying Conflicts of Interest: Directly Adverse

[6] Loyalty to a current client prohibits undertaking representation directly adverse to that client without that client's informed consent. Thus, absent consent, a lawyer may not act as an advocate in one matter against a person the lawyer represents in some other matter, even when the matters are wholly unrelated. The client as to whom the representation is directly adverse is likely to feel betrayed, and the resulting damage to the client-lawyer relationship is likely to impair the lawyer's ability to represent the client effectively. In addition, the client on whose behalf the adverse representation is undertaken reasonably may fear that the lawyer will pursue that client's case less effectively out of deference to the other client, i.e., that the representation may be materially limited by the lawyer's interest in retaining the current client. Similarly, a directly adverse conflict may arise when a lawyer is required to cross-examine a client who appears as a witness in a lawsuit involving another client, as when the testimony will be damaging to the client who is represented in the lawsuit. On the other hand, simultaneous representation in unrelated matters of clients whose interests are only economically adverse, such as representation of competing economic enterprises in unrelated litigation, does not ordinarily constitute a conflict of interest and thus may not require consent of the respective clients.

[7] Directly adverse conflicts can also arise in transactional matters. For example, if a lawyer is asked to represent the seller of a business in negotiations with a buyer represented by the lawyer, not in the same transaction but in another, unrelated matter, the lawyer could not undertake the representation without the informed consent of each client.

Identifying Conflicts of Interest: Material Limitation

[8] Even where there is no direct adverseness, a conflict of interest exists if there is a significant risk that a lawyer's ability to consider, recommend or carry out an appropriate course of action for the client will be materially limited as a result of the lawyer's other responsibilities or interests. For example, a lawyer asked to represent several individuals seeking to form a joint venture is likely to be materially limited in the lawyer's ability to recommend or advocate all possible positions that each might take because of the lawyer's duty of loyalty to the others. The conflict in effect forecloses alternatives that would otherwise be available to the client. The mere possibility of subsequent harm does not itself require disclosure and consent. The critical questions are the likelihood that a difference in interests will eventuate and, if it does, whether it will materially interfere with the lawyer's independent professional judgment in considering alternatives or foreclose courses of action that reasonably should be pursued on behalf of the client.

Lawyer's Responsibilities to Former Clients and Other Third Persons

[9] In addition to conflicts with other current clients, a lawyer's duties of loyalty and independence may be materially limited by responsibilities to former clients under Rule 1.9 or by the lawyer's responsibilities to other persons, such as fiduciary duties arising from a lawyer's service as a trustee, executor or corporate director.

Personal Interest Conflicts

[10] The lawyer's own interests should not be permitted to have an adverse effect on representation of a client. For example, if the probity of a lawyer's own conduct in a transaction is in serious question, it may be difficult or impossible for the lawyer to give a client detached advice. Similarly, when a lawyer has discussions concerning possible employment with an opponent of the lawyer's client, or with a law firm repre-

senting the opponent, such discussions could materially limit the lawyer's representation of the client. In addition, a lawyer may not allow related business interests to affect representation, for example, by referring clients to an enterprise in which the lawyer has an undisclosed financial interest. See Rule 1.8 for specific Rules pertaining to a number of personal interest conflicts, including business transactions with clients. See also Rule 1.10 (personal interest conflicts under Rule 1.7 ordinarily are not imputed to other lawyers in a law firm).

[11] When lawyers representing different clients in the same matter or in substantially related matters are closely related by blood or marriage, there may be a significant risk that client confidences will be revealed and that the lawyer's family relationship will interfere with both loyalty and independent professional judgment. As a result, each client is entitled to know of the existence and implications of the relationship between the lawyers before the lawyer agrees to undertake the representation. Thus, a lawyer related to another lawyer, e.g., as parent, child, sibling or spouse, ordinarily may not represent a client in a matter where that lawyer is representing another party, unless each client gives informed consent. The disqualification arising from a close family relationship is personal and ordinarily is not imputed to members of firms with whom the lawyers are associated. See Rule 1.10.

[12] A lawyer is prohibited from engaging in sexual relationships with a client unless the sexual relationship predates the formation of the client-lawyer relationship. See Rule 1.8(j).

Interest of Person Paying for a Lawyer's Service

[13] A lawyer may be paid from a source other than the client, including a co-client, if the client is informed of that fact and consents and the arrangement does not compromise the lawyer's duty of loyalty or independent judgment to the client. See Rule 1.8(f). If acceptance of the payment from any other source presents a significant risk that the lawyer's representation of the client will be materially limited by the lawyer's own interest in accommodating the person paying the lawyer's fee or by the lawyer's responsibilities to a payer who is also a co-client, then the lawyer must comply with the requirements of paragraph (b) before accepting the representation, including determining whether the conflict is consentable and, if so, that the client has adequate information about the material risks of the representation.

Prohibited Representations

[14] Ordinarily, clients may consent to representation notwithstanding a conflict. However, as indicated in paragraph (b), some conflicts are nonconsentable, meaning that the lawyer involved cannot properly ask for such agreement or provide representation on the basis of the client's consent. When the lawyer is representing more than one client, the question of consentability must be resolved as to each client.

[15] Consentability is typically determined by considering whether the interests of the clients will be adequately protected if the clients are permitted to give their informed consent to representation burdened by a conflict of interest. Thus, under paragraph (b)(1), representation is prohibited if in the circumstances the lawyer cannot reasonably conclude that the lawyer will be able to provide competent and diligent representation. See Rule 1.1 (competence) and Rule 1.3 (diligence).

[16] Paragraph (b)(2) describes conflicts that are nonconsentable because the representation is prohibited by applicable law. For example, in some states substantive law provides that the same lawyer may not represent more than one defendant in a capital case, even with the consent of the clients, and under federal criminal statutes certain representations by a former government lawyer are prohibited, despite the informed consent of the former client. In addition, decisional law in some states limits the ability of a governmental client, such as a municipality, to consent to a conflict of interest.

[17] Paragraph (b)(3) describes conflicts that are nonconsentable because of the institutional interest in vigorous development of each client's position when the clients are aligned directly against each other in the same litigation or other proceeding before a tribunal. Whether clients are aligned directly against each other within the meaning of this paragraph requires examination of the context of the proceeding. Although this paragraph does not preclude a lawyer's multiple representation of adverse parties to a mediation (because mediation is not a proceeding before a "tribunal" under Rule 1.0(m)), such representation may be precluded by paragraph (b)(1).

Informed Consent

[18] Informed consent requires that each affected client be aware of the relevant circumstances and of the material and reasonably foreseeable ways that the conflict could have adverse effects on the interests of that client. See Rule 1.0(e) (informed consent). The information required

depends on the nature of the conflict and the nature of the risks involved. When representation of multiple clients in a single matter is undertaken, the information must include the implications of the common representation, including possible effects on loyalty, confidentiality and the attorney-client privilege and the advantages and risks involved. See Comments [30] and [31] (effect of common representation on confidentiality).

[19] Under some circumstances it may be impossible to make the disclosure necessary to obtain consent. For example, when the lawyer represents different clients in related matters and one of the clients refuses to consent to the disclosure necessary to permit the other client to make an informed decision, the lawyer cannot properly ask the latter to consent. In some cases the alternative to common representation can be that each party may have to obtain separate representation with the possibility of incurring additional costs. These costs, along with the benefits of securing separate representation, are factors that may be considered by the affected client in determining whether common representation is in the client's interests.

Consent Confirmed in Writing

[20] Paragraph (b) requires the lawyer to obtain the informed consent of the client, confirmed in writing. Such a writing may consist of a document executed by the client or one that the lawyer promptly records and transmits to the client following an oral consent. See Rule 1.0(b). See also Rule 1.0(n) (writing includes electronic transmission). If it is not feasible to obtain or transmit the writing at the time the client gives informed consent, then the lawyer must obtain or transmit it within a reasonable time thereafter. See Rule 1.0(b). The requirement of a writing does not supplant the need in most cases for the lawyer to talk with the client, to explain the risks and advantages, if any, of representation burdened with a conflict of interest, as well as reasonably available alternatives, and to afford the client a reasonable opportunity to consider the risks and alternatives and to raise questions and concerns. Rather, the writing is required in order to impress upon clients the seriousness of the decision the client is being asked to make and to avoid disputes or ambiguities that might later occur in the absence of a writing.

Revoking Consent

[21] A client who has given consent to a conflict may revoke the consent and, like any other client, may terminate the lawyer's representation

at any time. Whether revoking consent to the client's own representation precludes the lawyer from continuing to represent other clients depends on the circumstances, including the nature of the conflict, whether the client revoked consent because of a material change in circumstances, the reasonable expectations of the other clients and whether material detriment to the other clients or the lawyer would result.

Consent to Future Conflict

[22] Whether a lawyer may properly request a client to waive conflicts that might arise in the future is subject to the test of paragraph (b). The effectiveness of such waivers is generally determined by the extent to which the client reasonably understands the material risks that the waiver entails. The more comprehensive the explanation of the types of future representations that might arise and the actual and reasonably foreseeable adverse consequences of those representations, the greater the likelihood that the client will have the requisite understanding. Thus, if the client agrees to consent to a particular type of conflict with which the client is already familiar, then the consent ordinarily will be effective with regard to that type of conflict. If the consent is general and open-ended, then the consent ordinarily will be ineffective, because it is not reasonably likely that the client will have understood the material risks involved. On the other hand, if the client is an experienced user of the legal services involved and is reasonably informed regarding the risk that a conflict may arise, such consent is more likely to be effective, particularly if, e.g., the client is independently represented by other counsel in giving consent and the consent is limited to future conflicts unrelated to the subject of the representation. In any case, advance consent cannot be effective if the circumstances that materialize in the future are such as would make the conflict nonconsentable under paragraph (b).

Conflicts in Litigation

[23] Paragraph (b)(3) prohibits representation of opposing parties in the same litigation, regardless of the clients' consent. On the other hand, simultaneous representation of parties whose interests in litigation may conflict, such as coplaintiffs or codefendants, is governed by paragraph (a)(2). A conflict may exist by reason of substantial discrepancy in the parties' testimony, incompatibility in positions in relation to an opposing party or the fact that there are substantially different possibilities of settlement of the claims or liabilities in question. Such conflicts can arise in

criminal cases as well as civil. The potential for conflict of interest in representing multiple defendants in a criminal case is so grave that ordinarily a lawyer should decline to represent more than one codefendant. On the other hand, common representation of persons having similar interests in civil litigation is proper if the requirements of paragraph (b) are met.

[24] Ordinarily a lawyer may take inconsistent legal positions in different tribunals at different times on behalf of different clients. The mere fact that advocating a legal position on behalf of one client might create precedent adverse to the interests of a client represented by the lawyer in an unrelated matter does not create a conflict of interest. A conflict of interest exists, however, if there is a significant risk that a lawyer's action on behalf of one client will materially limit the lawyer's effectiveness in representing another client in a different case; for example, when a decision favoring one client will create a precedent likely to seriously weaken the position taken on behalf of the other client. Factors relevant in determining whether the clients need to be advised of the risk include: where the cases are pending, whether the issue is substantive or procedural, the temporal relationship between the matters, the significance of the issue to the immediate and long-term interests of the clients involved and the clients' reasonable expectations in retaining the lawyer. If there is significant risk of material limitation, then absent informed consent of the affected clients, the lawyer must refuse one of the representations or withdraw from one or both matters.

[25] When a lawyer represents or seeks to represent a class of plaintiffs or defendants in a class-action lawsuit, unnamed members of the class are ordinarily not considered to be clients of the lawyer for purposes of applying paragraph (a)(1) of this Rule. Thus, the lawyer does not typically need to get the consent of such a person before representing a client suing the person in an unrelated matter. Similarly, a lawyer seeking to represent an opponent in a class action does not typically need the consent of an unnamed member of the class whom the lawyer represents in an unrelated matter.

Nonlitigation Conflicts

[26] Conflicts of interest under paragraphs (a)(1) and (a)(2) arise in contexts other than litigation. For a discussion of directly adverse conflicts in transactional matters, see Comment [7]. Relevant factors in determining whether there is significant potential for material limitation include the duration and intimacy of the lawyer's relationship with the

client or clients involved, the functions being performed by the lawyer, the likelihood that disagreements will arise and the likely prejudice to the client from the conflict. The question is often one of proximity and degree. See Comment [8].

[27] For example, conflict questions may arise in estate planning and estate administration. A lawyer may be called upon to prepare wills for several family members, such as husband and wife, and, depending upon the circumstances, a conflict of interest may be present. In estate administration the identity of the client may be unclear under the law of a particular jurisdiction. Under one view, the client is the fiduciary; under another view the client is the estate or trust, including its beneficiaries. In order to comply with conflict of interest rules, the lawyer should make clear the lawyer's relationship to the parties involved.

[28] Whether a conflict is consentable depends on the circumstances. For example, a lawyer may not represent multiple parties to a negotiation whose interests are fundamentally antagonistic to each other, but common representation is permissible where the clients are generally aligned in interest even though there is some difference in interest among them. Thus, a lawyer may seek to establish or adjust a relationship between clients on an amicable and mutually advantageous basis; for example, in helping to organize a business in which two or more clients are entrepreneurs, working out the financial reorganization of an enterprise in which two or more clients have an interest or arranging a property distribution in settlement of an estate. The lawyer seeks to resolve potentially adverse interests by developing the parties' mutual interests. Otherwise, each party might have to obtain separate representation, with the possibility of incurring additional cost, complication or even litigation. Given these and other relevant factors, the clients may prefer that the lawyer act for all of them.

Special Considerations in Common Representation

[29] In considering whether to represent multiple clients in the same matter, a lawyer should be mindful that if the common representation fails because the potentially adverse interests cannot be reconciled, the result can be additional cost, embarrassment and recrimination. Ordinarily, the lawyer will be forced to withdraw from representing all of the clients if the common representation fails. In some situations, the risk of failure is so great that multiple representation is plainly impossible. For example, a lawyer cannot undertake common representation of clients where

contentious litigation or negotiations between them are imminent or con-templated. Moreover, because the lawyer is required to be impartial be-tween commonly represented clients, representation of multiple clients is improper when it is unlikely that impartiality can be maintained. Gener-ally, if the relationship between the parties has already assumed antago-nism, the possibility that the clients' interests can be adequately served by common representation is not very good. Other relevant factors are whether the lawyer subsequently will represent both parties on a con-tinuing basis and whether the situation involves creating or terminating a relationship between the parties.

[30] A particularly important factor in determining the appropriate-ness of common representation is the effect on client-lawyer confidenti-ality and the attorney-client privilege. With regard to the attorney-client privilege, the prevailing rule is that, as between commonly represented clients, the privilege does not attach. Hence, it must be assumed that if litigation eventuates between the clients, the privilege will not protect any such communications, and the clients should be so advised.

[31] As to the duty of confidentiality, continued common representa-tion will almost certainly be inadequate if one client asks the lawyer not to disclose to the other client information relevant to the common repre-sentation. This is so because the lawyer has an equal duty of loyalty to each client, and each client has the right to be informed of anything bear-ing on the representation that might affect that client's interests and the right to expect that the lawyer will use that information to that client's benefit. See Rule 1.4. The lawyer should, at the outset of the common rep-resentation and as part of the process of obtaining each client's informed consent, advise each client that information will be shared and that the lawyer will have to withdraw if one client decides that some matter ma-terial to the representation should be kept from the other. In limited cir-cumstances, it may be appropriate for the lawyer to proceed with the rep-resentation when the clients have agreed, after being properly informed, that the lawyer will keep certain information confidential. For example, the lawyer may reasonably conclude that failure to disclose one client's trade secrets to another client will not adversely affect representation in-volving a joint venture between the clients and agree to keep that infor-mation confidential with the informed consent of both clients.

[32] When seeking to establish or adjust a relationship between cli-ents, the lawyer should make clear that the lawyer's role is not that of partisanship normally expected in other circumstances and, thus, that

the clients may be required to assume greater responsibility for decisions than when each client is separately represented. Any limitations on the scope of the representation made necessary as a result of the common representation should be fully explained to the clients at the outset of the representation. See Rule 1.2(c).

[33] Subject to the above limitations, each client in the common representation has the right to loyal and diligent representation and the protection of Rule 1.9 concerning the obligations to a former client. The client also has the right to discharge the lawyer as stated in Rule 1.16.

Organizational Clients

[34] A lawyer who represents a corporation or other organization does not, by virtue of that representation, necessarily represent any constituent or affiliated organization, such as a parent or subsidiary. See Rule 1.13(a). Thus, the lawyer for an organization is not barred from accepting representation adverse to an affiliate in an unrelated matter, unless the circumstances are such that the affiliate should also be considered a client of the lawyer, there is an understanding between the lawyer and the organizational client that the lawyer will avoid representation adverse to the client's affiliates, or the lawyer's obligations to either the organizational client or the new client are likely to limit materially the lawyer's representation of the other client.

[35] A lawyer for a corporation or other organization who is also a member of its board of directors should determine whether the responsibilities of the two roles may conflict. The lawyer may be called on to advise the corporation in matters involving actions of the directors. Consideration should be given to the frequency with which such situations may arise, the potential intensity of the conflict, the effect of the lawyer's resignation from the board and the possibility of the corporation's obtaining legal advice from another lawyer in such situations. If there is material risk that the dual role will compromise the lawyer's independence of professional judgment, the lawyer should not serve as a director or should cease to act as the corporation's lawyer when conflicts of interest arise. The lawyer should advise the other members of the board that in some circumstances matters discussed at board meetings while the lawyer is present in the capacity of director might not be protected by the attorney-client privilege and that conflict of interest considerations might require the lawyer's recusal as a director or might require the lawyer and the lawyer's firm to decline representation of the corporation in a matter.

Definitional Cross-References

"Confirmed in writing" *See* Rule 1.0(b)

"Informed consent" *See* Rule 1.0(e)

"Reasonably believes" *See* Rule 1.0(i)

"Tribunal" *See* Rule 1.0(m)

RULE 1.8: CONFLICT OF INTEREST: CURRENT CLIENTS: SPECIFIC RULES

(a) A lawyer shall not enter into a business transaction with a client or knowingly acquire an ownership, possessory, security or other pecuniary interest adverse to a client unless:

(1) the transaction and terms on which the lawyer acquires the interest are fair and reasonable to the client and are fully disclosed and transmitted in writing in a manner that can be reasonably understood by the client;

(2) the client is advised in writing of the desirability of seeking and is given a reasonable opportunity to seek the advice of independent legal counsel on the transaction; and

(3) the client gives informed consent, in a writing signed by the client, to the essential terms of the transaction and the lawyer's role in the transaction, including whether the lawyer is representing the client in the transaction.

(b) A lawyer shall not use information relating to representation of a client to the disadvantage of the client unless the client gives informed consent, except as permitted or required by these Rules.

(c) A lawyer shall not solicit any substantial gift from a client, including a testamentary gift, or prepare on behalf of a client an instrument giving the lawyer or a person related to the lawyer any substantial gift unless the lawyer or other recipient of the gift is related to the client. For purposes of this paragraph, related persons include a spouse, child, grandchild, parent, grandparent or other relative or individual with whom the lawyer or the client maintains a close, familial relationship.

(d) Prior to the conclusion of representation of a client, a lawyer shall not make or negotiate an agreement giving the lawyer literary or media rights to a portrayal or account based in substantial part on information relating to the representation.

(e) A lawyer shall not provide financial assistance to a client in connection with pending or contemplated litigation, except that:

(1) a lawyer may advance court costs and expenses of litigation, the repayment of which may be contingent on the outcome of the matter; and

(2) a lawyer representing an indigent client may pay court costs and expenses of litigation on behalf of the client.

(f) A lawyer shall not accept compensation for representing a client from one other than the client unless:

(1) the client gives informed consent;

(2) there is no interference with the lawyer's independence of professional judgment or with the client-lawyer relationship; and

(3) information relating to representation of a client is protected as required by Rule 1.6.

(g) A lawyer who represents two or more clients shall not participate in making an aggregate settlement of the claims of or against the clients, or in a criminal case an aggregated agreement as to guilty or nolo contendere pleas, unless each client gives informed consent, in a writing signed by the client. The lawyer's disclosure shall include the existence and nature of all the claims or pleas involved and of the participation of each person in the settlement.

(h) A lawyer shall not:

(1) make an agreement prospectively limiting the lawyer's liability to a client for malpractice unless the client is independently represented in making the agreement; or

(2) settle a claim or potential claim for such liability with an unrepresented client or former client unless that person is advised in writing of the desirability of seeking and is given a reasonable opportunity to seek the advice of independent legal counsel in connection therewith.

(i) A lawyer shall not acquire a proprietary interest in the cause of action or subject matter of litigation the lawyer is conducting for a client, except that the lawyer may:

(1) acquire a lien authorized by law to secure the lawyer's fee or expenses; and

(2) contract with a client for a reasonable contingent fee in a civil case.

(j) A lawyer shall not have sexual relations with a client unless a consensual sexual relationship existed between them when the client-lawyer relationship commenced.

(k) While lawyers are associated in a firm, a prohibition in the foregoing paragraphs (a) through (i) that applies to any one of them shall apply to all of them.

Comment

Business Transactions between Client and Lawyer

[1] A lawyer's legal skill and training, together with the relationship of trust and confidence between lawyer and client, create the possibility of overreaching when the lawyer participates in a business, property or financial transaction with a client, for example, a loan or sales transaction or a lawyer investment on behalf of a client. The requirements of paragraph (a) must be met even when the transaction is not closely related to the subject matter of the representation, as when a lawyer drafting a will for a client learns that the client needs money for unrelated expenses and offers to make a loan to the client. The Rule applies to lawyers engaged in the sale of goods or services related to the practice of law, for example, the sale of title insurance or investment services to existing clients of the lawyer's legal practice. See Rule 5.7. It also applies to lawyers purchasing property from estates they represent. It does not apply to ordinary fee arrangements between client and lawyer, which are governed by Rule 1.5, although its requirements must be met when the lawyer accepts an interest in the client's business or other nonmonetary property as payment of all or part of a fee. In addition, the Rule does not apply to standard commercial transactions between the lawyer and the client for products or services that the client generally markets to others, for example, banking or brokerage services, medical services, products manufactured or distributed by the client, and utilities' services. In such transactions, the lawyer has no advantage in dealing with the client, and the restrictions in paragraph (a) are unnecessary and impracticable.

[2] Paragraph (a)(1) requires that the transaction itself be fair to the client and that its essential terms be communicated to the client, in writing, in a manner that can be reasonably understood. Paragraph (a)(2) requires that the client also be advised, in writing, of the desirability of seeking the advice of independent legal counsel. It also requires that the client be given a reasonable opportunity to obtain such advice. Paragraph (a)(3) requires that the lawyer obtain the client's informed consent, in a

writing signed by the client, both to the essential terms of the transaction and to the lawyer's role. When necessary, the lawyer should discuss both the material risks of the proposed transaction, including any risk presented by the lawyer's involvement, and the existence of reasonably available alternatives and should explain why the advice of independent legal counsel is desirable. See Rule 1.0(e) (definition of informed consent).

[3] The risk to a client is greatest when the client expects the lawyer to represent the client in the transaction itself or when the lawyer's financial interest otherwise poses a significant risk that the lawyer's representation of the client will be materially limited by the lawyer's financial interest in the transaction. Here the lawyer's role requires that the lawyer must comply, not only with the requirements of paragraph (a), but also with the requirements of Rule 1.7. Under that Rule, the lawyer must disclose the risks associated with the lawyer's dual role as both legal adviser and participant in the transaction, such as the risk that the lawyer will structure the transaction or give legal advice in a way that favors the lawyer's interests at the expense of the client. Moreover, the lawyer must obtain the client's informed consent. In some cases, the lawyer's interest may be such that Rule 1.7 will preclude the lawyer from seeking the client's consent to the transaction.

[4] If the client is independently represented in the transaction, paragraph (a)(2) of this Rule is inapplicable, and the paragraph (a)(1) requirement for full disclosure is satisfied either by a written disclosure by the lawyer involved in the transaction or by the client's independent counsel. The fact that the client was independently represented in the transaction is relevant in determining whether the agreement was fair and reasonable to the client as paragraph (a)(1) further requires.

Use of Information Related to Representation

[5] Use of information relating to the representation to the disadvantage of the client violates the lawyer's duty of loyalty. Paragraph (b) applies when the information is used to benefit either the lawyer or a third person, such as another client or business associate of the lawyer. For example, if a lawyer learns that a client intends to purchase and develop several parcels of land, the lawyer may not use that information to purchase one of the parcels in competition with the client or to recommend that another client make such a purchase. The Rule does not prohibit uses that do not disadvantage the client. For example, a lawyer who learns a government agency's interpretation of trade legislation during the repre-

sentation of one client may properly use that information to benefit other clients. Paragraph (b) prohibits disadvantageous use of client information unless the client gives informed consent, except as permitted or required by these Rules. See Rules 1.2(d), 1.6, 1.9(c), 3.3, 4.1(b), 8.1 and 8.3.

Gifts to Lawyers

[6] A lawyer may accept a gift from a client, if the transaction meets general standards of fairness. For example, a simple gift such as a present given at a holiday or as a token of appreciation is permitted. If a client offers the lawyer a more substantial gift, paragraph (c) does not prohibit the lawyer from accepting it, although such a gift may be voidable by the client under the doctrine of undue influence, which treats client gifts as presumptively fraudulent. In any event, due to concerns about overreaching and imposition on clients, a lawyer may not suggest that a substantial gift be made to the lawyer or for the lawyer's benefit, except where the lawyer is related to the client as set forth in paragraph (c).

[7] If effectuation of a substantial gift requires preparing a legal instrument such as a will or conveyance, the client should have the detached advice that another lawyer can provide. The sole exception to this Rule is where the client is a relative of the donee.

[8] This Rule does not prohibit a lawyer from seeking to have the lawyer or a partner or associate of the lawyer named as executor of the client's estate or to another potentially lucrative fiduciary position. Nevertheless, such appointments will be subject to the general conflict of interest provision in Rule 1.7 when there is a significant risk that the lawyer's interest in obtaining the appointment will materially limit the lawyer's independent professional judgment in advising the client concerning the choice of an executor or other fiduciary. In obtaining the client's informed consent to the conflict, the lawyer should advise the client concerning the nature and extent of the lawyer's financial interest in the appointment, as well as the availability of alternative candidates for the position.

Literary Rights

[9] An agreement by which a lawyer acquires literary or media rights concerning the conduct of the representation creates a conflict between the interests of the client and the personal interests of the lawyer. Measures suitable in the representation of the client may detract from the publication value of an account of the representation. Paragraph (d) does

not prohibit a lawyer representing a client in a transaction concerning literary property from agreeing that the lawyer's fee shall consist of a share in ownership in the property, if the arrangement conforms to Rule 1.5 and paragraphs (a) and (i).

Financial Assistance

[10] Lawyers may not subsidize lawsuits or administrative proceedings brought on behalf of their clients, including making or guaranteeing loans to their clients for living expenses, because to do so would encourage clients to pursue lawsuits that might not otherwise be brought and because such assistance gives lawyers too great a financial stake in the litigation. These dangers do not warrant a prohibition on a lawyer lending a client court costs and litigation expenses, including the expenses of medical examination and the costs of obtaining and presenting evidence, because these advances are virtually indistinguishable from contingent fees and help ensure access to the courts. Similarly, an exception allowing lawyers representing indigent clients to pay court costs and litigation expenses regardless of whether these funds will be repaid is warranted.

Person Paying for a Lawyer's Services

[11] Lawyers are frequently asked to represent a client under circumstances in which a third person will compensate the lawyer, in whole or in part. The third person might be a relative or friend, an indemnitor (such as a liability insurance company) or a co-client (such as a corporation sued along with one or more of its employees). Because third-party payers frequently have interests that differ from those of the client, including interests in minimizing the amount spent on the representation and in learning how the representation is progressing, lawyers are prohibited from accepting or continuing such representations unless the lawyer determines that there will be no interference with the lawyer's independent professional judgment and there is informed consent from the client. See also Rule 5.4(c) (prohibiting interference with a lawyer's professional judgment by one who recommends, employs or pays the lawyer to render legal services for another).

[12] Sometimes, it will be sufficient for the lawyer to obtain the client's informed consent regarding the fact of the payment and the identity of the third-party payer. If, however, the fee arrangement creates a conflict of interest for the lawyer, then the lawyer must comply with Rule 1.7. The lawyer must also conform to the requirements of Rule 1.6 concern-

ing confidentiality. Under Rule 1.7(a), a conflict of interest exists if there is significant risk that the lawyer's representation of the client will be materially limited by the lawyer's own interest in the fee arrangement or by the lawyer's responsibilities to the third-party payer (for example, when the third-party payer is a co-client). Under Rule 1.7(b), the lawyer may accept or continue the representation with the informed consent of each affected client, unless the conflict is nonconsentable under that paragraph. Under Rule 1.7(b), the informed consent must be confirmed in writing.

Aggregate Settlements

[13] Differences in willingness to make or accept an offer of settlement are among the risks of common representation of multiple clients by a single lawyer. Under Rule 1.7, this is one of the risks that should be discussed before undertaking the representation, as part of the process of obtaining the clients' informed consent. In addition, Rule 1.2(a) protects each client's right to have the final say in deciding whether to accept or reject an offer of settlement and in deciding whether to enter a guilty or nolo contendere plea in a criminal case. The rule stated in this paragraph is a corollary of both these Rules and provides that, before any settlement offer or plea bargain is made or accepted on behalf of multiple clients, the lawyer must inform each of them about all the material terms of the settlement, including what the other clients will receive or pay if the settlement or plea offer is accepted. See also Rule 1.0(e) (definition of informed consent). Lawyers representing a class of plaintiffs or defendants, or those proceeding derivatively, may not have a full client-lawyer relationship with each member of the class; nevertheless, such lawyers must comply with applicable rules regulating notification of class members and other procedural requirements designed to ensure adequate protection of the entire class.

Limiting Liability and Settling Malpractice Claims

[14] Agreements prospectively limiting a lawyer's liability for malpractice are prohibited unless the client is independently represented in making the agreement because they are likely to undermine competent and diligent representation. Also, many clients are unable to evaluate the desirability of making such an agreement before a dispute has arisen, particularly if they are then represented by the lawyer seeking the agreement. This paragraph does not, however, prohibit a lawyer from entering into an agreement with the client to arbitrate legal malpractice claims,

provided such agreements are enforceable and the client is fully informed of the scope and effect of the agreement. Nor does this paragraph limit the ability of lawyers to practice in the form of a limited-liability entity, where permitted by law, provided that each lawyer remains personally liable to the client for his or her own conduct and the firm complies with any conditions required by law, such as provisions requiring client notification or maintenance of adequate liability insurance. Nor does it prohibit an agreement in accordance with Rule 1.2 that defines the scope of the representation, although a definition of scope that makes the obligations of representation illusory will amount to an attempt to limit liability.

[15] Agreements settling a claim or a potential claim for malpractice are not prohibited by this Rule. Nevertheless, in view of the danger that a lawyer will take unfair advantage of an unrepresented client or former client, the lawyer must first advise such a person in writing of the appropriateness of independent representation in connection with such a settlement. In addition, the lawyer must give the client or former client a reasonable opportunity to find and consult independent counsel.

Acquiring Proprietary Interest in Litigation

[16] Paragraph (i) states the traditional general rule that lawyers are prohibited from acquiring a proprietary interest in litigation. Like paragraph (e), the general rule has its basis in common law champerty and maintenance and is designed to avoid giving the lawyer too great an interest in the representation. In addition, when the lawyer acquires an ownership interest in the subject of the representation, it will be more difficult for a client to discharge the lawyer if the client so desires. The Rule is subject to specific exceptions developed in decisional law and continued in these Rules. The exception for certain advances of the costs of litigation is set forth in paragraph (e). In addition, paragraph (i) sets forth exceptions for liens authorized by law to secure the lawyer's fees or expenses and contracts for reasonable contingent fees. The law of each jurisdiction determines which liens are authorized by law. These may include liens granted by statute, liens originating in common law and liens acquired by contract with the client. When a lawyer acquires by contract a security interest in property other than that recovered through the lawyer's efforts in the litigation, such an acquisition is a business or financial transaction with a client and is governed by the requirements of paragraph (a). Contracts for contingent fees in civil cases are governed by Rule 1.5.

Client-Lawyer Sexual Relationships

[17] The relationship between lawyer and client is a fiduciary one in which the lawyer occupies the highest position of trust and confidence. The relationship is almost always unequal; thus, a sexual relationship between lawyer and client can involve unfair exploitation of the lawyer's fiduciary role, in violation of the lawyer's basic ethical obligation not to use the trust of the client to the client's disadvantage. In addition, such a relationship presents a significant danger that, because of the lawyer's emotional involvement, the lawyer will be unable to represent the client without impairment of the exercise of independent professional judgment. Moreover, a blurred line between the professional and personal relationships may make it difficult to predict to what extent client confidences will be protected by the attorney-client evidentiary privilege, since client confidences are protected by privilege only when they are imparted in the context of the client-lawyer relationship. Because of the significant danger of harm to client interests and because the client's own emotional involvement renders it unlikely that the client could give adequate informed consent, this Rule prohibits the lawyer from having sexual relations with a client regardless of whether the relationship is consensual and regardless of the absence of prejudice to the client.

[18] Sexual relationships that predate the client-lawyer relationship are not prohibited. Issues relating to the exploitation of the fiduciary relationship and client dependency are diminished when the sexual relationship existed prior to the commencement of the client-lawyer relationship. However, before proceeding with the representation in these circumstances, the lawyer should consider whether the lawyer's ability to represent the client will be materially limited by the relationship. See Rule 1.7(a)(2).

[19] When the client is an organization, paragraph (j) of this Rule prohibits a lawyer for the organization (whether inside counsel or outside counsel) from having a sexual relationship with a constituent of the organization who supervises, directs or regularly consults with that lawyer concerning the organization's legal matters.

Imputation of Prohibitions

[20] Under paragraph (k), a prohibition on conduct by an individual lawyer in paragraphs (a) through (i) also applies to all lawyers associated in a firm with the personally prohibited lawyer. For example, one lawyer in a firm may not enter into a business transaction with a client of

another member of the firm without complying with paragraph (a), even if the first lawyer is not personally involved in the representation of the client. The prohibition set forth in paragraph (j) is personal and is not applied to associated lawyers.

Definitional Cross-References

"Firm" *See* Rule 1.0(c)

"Informed consent" *See* Rule 1.0(e)

"Knowingly" *See* Rule 1.0(f)

"Substantial" *See* Rule 1.0(l)

"Writing" and "Signed" *See* Rule 1.0(n)

RULE 1.9: DUTIES TO FORMER CLIENTS

(a) A lawyer who has formerly represented a client in a matter shall not thereafter represent another person in the same or a substantially related matter in which that person's interests are materially adverse to the interests of the former client unless the former client gives informed consent, confirmed in writing.

(b) A lawyer shall not knowingly represent a person in the same or a substantially related matter in which a firm with which the lawyer formerly was associated had previously represented a client

(1) whose interests are materially adverse to that person; and

(2) about whom the lawyer had acquired information protected by Rules 1.6 and 1.9(c) that is material to the matter; unless the former client gives informed consent, confirmed in writing.

(c) A lawyer who has formerly represented a client in a matter or whose present or former firm has formerly represented a client in a matter shall not thereafter:

(1) use information relating to the representation to the disadvantage of the former client except as these Rules would permit or require with respect to a client, or when the information has become generally known; or

(2) reveal information relating to the representation except as these Rules would permit or require with respect to a client.

Comment

[1] After termination of a client-lawyer relationship, a lawyer has certain continuing duties with respect to confidentiality and conflicts of interest and thus may not represent another client except in conformity with this Rule. Under this Rule, for example, a lawyer could not properly seek to rescind on behalf of a new client a contract drafted on behalf of the former client. So also a lawyer who has prosecuted an accused person could not properly represent the accused in a subsequent civil action against the government concerning the same transaction. Nor could a lawyer who has represented multiple clients in a matter represent one of the clients against the others in the same or a substantially related matter after a dispute arose among the clients in that matter, unless all affected clients give informed consent. See Comment [9]. Current and former government lawyers must comply with this Rule to the extent required by Rule 1.11.

[2] The scope of a "matter" for purposes of this Rule depends on the facts of a particular situation or transaction. The lawyer's involvement in a matter can also be a question of degree. When a lawyer has been directly involved in a specific transaction, subsequent representation of other clients with materially adverse interests in that transaction clearly is prohibited. On the other hand, a lawyer who recurrently handled a type of problem for a former client is not precluded from later representing another client in a factually distinct problem of that type even though the subsequent representation involves a position adverse to the prior client. Similar considerations can apply to the reassignment of military lawyers between defense and prosecution functions within the same military jurisdictions. The underlying question is whether the lawyer was so involved in the matter that the subsequent representation can be justly regarded as a changing of sides in the matter in question.

[3] Matters are "substantially related" for purposes of this Rule if they involve the same transaction or legal dispute or if there otherwise is a substantial risk that confidential factual information as would normally have been obtained in the prior representation would materially advance the client's position in the subsequent matter. For example, a lawyer who has represented a businessperson and learned extensive private financial information about that person may not then represent that person's spouse in seeking a divorce. Similarly, a lawyer who has previously represented a client in securing environmental permits to build a shopping

center would be precluded from representing neighbors seeking to oppose rezoning of the property on the basis of environmental considerations; however, the lawyer would not be precluded, on the grounds of substantial relationship, from defending a tenant of the completed shopping center in resisting eviction for nonpayment of rent. Information that has been disclosed to the public or to other parties adverse to the former client ordinarily will not be disqualifying. Information acquired in a prior representation may have been rendered obsolete by the passage of time, a circumstance that may be relevant in determining whether two representations are substantially related. In the case of an organizational client, general knowledge of the client's policies and practices ordinarily will not preclude a subsequent representation; on the other hand, knowledge of specific facts gained in a prior representation that are relevant to the matter in question ordinarily will preclude such a representation. A former client is not required to reveal the confidential information learned by the lawyer in order to establish a substantial risk that the lawyer has confidential information to use in the subsequent matter. A conclusion about the possession of such information may be based on the nature of the services the lawyer provided the former client and information that would in ordinary practice be learned by a lawyer providing such services.

Lawyers Moving Between Firms

[4] When lawyers have been associated within a firm but then end their association, the question of whether a lawyer should undertake representation is more complicated. There are several competing considerations. First, the client previously represented by the former firm must be reasonably assured that the principle of loyalty to the client is not compromised. Second, the rule should not be so broadly cast as to preclude other persons from having reasonable choice of legal counsel. Third, the rule should not unreasonably hamper lawyers from forming new associations and taking on new clients after having left a previous association. In this connection, it should be recognized that today many lawyers practice in firms, that many lawyers to some degree limit their practice to one field or another, and that many move from one association to another several times in their careers. If the concept of imputation were applied with unqualified rigor, the result would be radical curtailment of the opportunity of lawyers to move from one practice setting to another and of the opportunity of clients to change counsel.

[5] Paragraph (b) operates to disqualify the lawyer only when the lawyer involved has actual knowledge of information protected by Rules 1.6 and 1.9(c). Thus, if a lawyer while with one firm acquired no knowledge or information relating to a particular client of the firm, and that lawyer later joined another firm, neither the lawyer individually nor the second firm is disqualified from representing another client in the same or a related matter even though the interests of the two clients conflict. See Rule 1.10(b) for the restrictions on a firm once a lawyer has terminated association with the firm.

[6] Application of paragraph (b) depends on a situation's particular facts, aided by inferences, deductions or working presumptions that reasonably may be made about the way in which lawyers work together. A lawyer may have general access to files of all clients of a law firm and may regularly participate in discussions of their affairs; it should be inferred that such a lawyer in fact is privy to all information about all the firm's clients. In contrast, another lawyer may have access to the files of only a limited number of clients and participate in discussions of the affairs of no other clients; in the absence of information to the contrary, it should be inferred that such a lawyer in fact is privy to information about the clients actually served but not those of other clients. In such an inquiry, the burden of proof should rest upon the firm whose disqualification is sought.

[7] Independent of the question of disqualification of a firm, a lawyer changing professional association has a continuing duty to preserve confidentiality of information about a client formerly represented. See Rules 1.6 and 1.9(c).

[8] Paragraph (c) provides that information acquired by the lawyer in the course of representing a client may not subsequently be used or revealed by the lawyer to the disadvantage of the client. However, the fact that a lawyer has once served a client does not preclude the lawyer from using generally known information about that client when later representing another client.

[9] The provisions of this Rule are for the protection of former clients and can be waived if the client gives informed consent, which consent must be confirmed in writing under paragraphs (a) and (b). See Rule 1.0(e). With regard to the effectiveness of an advance waiver, see Comment [22] to Rule 1.7. With regard to disqualification of a firm with which a lawyer is or was formerly associated, see Rule 1.10.

Definitional Cross-References
"Confirmed in writing" *See* Rule 1.0(b)
"Firm" *See* Rule 1.0(c)
"Informed consent" *See* Rule 1.0(e)
"Knowingly" and "Known" *See* Rule 1.0(f)
"Writing" *See* Rule 1.0(n)

RULE 1.10: IMPUTATION OF
CONFLICTS OF INTEREST: GENERAL RULE

(a) While lawyers are associated in a firm, none of them shall knowingly represent a client when any one of them practicing alone would be prohibited from doing so by Rules 1.7 or 1.9, unless

(1) the prohibition is based on a personal interest of the disqualified lawyer and does not present a significant risk of materially limiting the representation of the client by the remaining lawyers in the firm; or

(2) the prohibition is based upon Rule 1.9(a) or (b), and arises out of the disqualified lawyer's association with a prior firm, and

(i) the disqualified lawyer is timely screened from any participation in the matter and is apportioned no part of the fee therefrom;

(ii) written notice is promptly given to any affected former client to enable the former client to ascertain compliance with the provisions of this Rule, which shall include a description of the screening procedures employed; a statement of the firm's and of the screened lawyer's compliance with these Rules; a statement that review may be available before a tribunal; and an agreement by the firm to respond promptly to any written inquiries or objections by the former client about the screening procedures; and

(iii) certifications of compliance with these Rules and with the screening procedures are provided to the former client by the screened lawyer and by a partner of the firm, at reasonable intervals upon the former client's written request and upon termination of the screening procedures.

(b) When a lawyer has terminated an association with a firm, the firm is not prohibited from thereafter representing a person with interests materially adverse to those of a client represented by the formerly associated lawyer and not currently represented by the firm, unless:

(1) the matter is the same or substantially related to that in which the formerly associated lawyer represented the client; and

(2) any lawyer remaining in the firm has information protected by Rules 1.6 and 1.9(c) that is material to the matter.

(c) A disqualification prescribed by this Rule may be waived by the affected client under the conditions stated in Rule 1.7.

(d) The disqualification of lawyers associated in a firm with former or current government lawyers is governed by Rule 1.11.

Comment
Definition of "Firm"

[1] For purposes of the Rules of Professional Conduct, the term "firm" denotes lawyers in a law partnership, professional corporation, sole proprietorship or other association authorized to practice law; or lawyers employed in a legal services organization or the legal department of a corporation or other organization. See Rule 1.0(c). Whether two or more lawyers constitute a firm within this definition can depend on the specific facts. See Rule 1.0, Comments [2]–[4].

Principles of Imputed Disqualification

[2] The rule of imputed disqualification stated in paragraph (a) gives effect to the principle of loyalty to the client as it applies to lawyers who practice in a law firm. Such situations can be considered from the premise that a firm of lawyers is essentially one lawyer for purposes of the rules governing loyalty to the client, or from the premise that each lawyer is vicariously bound by the obligation of loyalty owed by each lawyer with whom the lawyer is associated. Paragraph (a)(1) operates only among the lawyers currently associated in a firm. When a lawyer moves from one firm to another, the situation is governed by Rules 1.9(b) and 1.10(a)(2) and 1.10(b).

[3] The rule in paragraph (a) does not prohibit representation where neither questions of client loyalty nor protection of confidential information are presented. Where one lawyer in a firm could not effectively represent a given client because of strong political beliefs, for example, but that lawyer will do no work on the case and the personal beliefs of the lawyer will not materially limit the representation by others in the firm,

the firm should not be disqualified. On the other hand, if an opposing party in a case were owned by a lawyer in the law firm, and others in the firm would be materially limited in pursuing the matter because of loyalty to that lawyer, the personal disqualification of the lawyer would be imputed to all others in the firm.

[4] The rule in paragraph (a) also does not prohibit representation by others in the law firm where the person prohibited from involvement in a matter is a nonlawyer, such as a paralegal or legal secretary. Nor does paragraph (a) prohibit representation if the lawyer is prohibited from acting because of events before the person became a lawyer, for example, work that the person did while a law student. Such persons, however, ordinarily must be screened from any personal participation in the matter to avoid communication to others in the firm of confidential information that both the nonlawyers and the firm have a legal duty to protect. See Rules 1.0(k) and 5.3.

[5] Rule 1.10(b) operates to permit a law firm, under certain circumstances, to represent a person with interests directly adverse to those of a client represented by a lawyer who formerly was associated with the firm. The Rule applies regardless of when the formerly associated lawyer represented the client. However, the law firm may not represent a person with interests adverse to those of a present client of the firm, which would violate Rule 1.7. Moreover, the firm may not represent the person where the matter is the same or substantially related to that in which the formerly associated lawyer represented the client and any other lawyer currently in the firm has material information protected by Rules 1.6 and 1.9(c).

[6] Rule 1.10(c) removes imputation with the informed consent of the affected client or former client under the conditions stated in Rule 1.7. The conditions stated in Rule 1.7 require the lawyer to determine that the representation is not prohibited by Rule 1.7(b) and that each affected client or former client has given informed consent to the representation, confirmed in writing. In some cases, the risk may be so severe that the conflict may not be cured by client consent. For a discussion of the effectiveness of client waivers of conflicts that might arise in the future, see Rule 1.7, Comment [22]. For a definition of informed consent, see Rule 1.0(e).

[7] Rule 1.10(a)(2) similarly removes the imputation otherwise required by Rule 1.10(a), but unlike section (c), it does so without requiring that there be informed consent by the former client. Instead, it requires that the procedures laid out in sections (a)(2)(i)-(iii) be followed. A description of effective screening mechanisms appears in Rule 1.0(k). Law-

yers should be aware, however, that, even where screening mechanisms have been adopted, tribunals may consider additional factors in ruling upon motions to disqualify a lawyer from pending litigation.

[8] Paragraph (a)(2)(i) does not prohibit the screened lawyer from receiving a salary or partnership share established by prior independent agreement, but that lawyer may not receive compensation directly related to the matter in which the lawyer is disqualified.

[9] The notice required by paragraph (a)(2)(ii) generally should include a description of the screened lawyer's prior representation and be given as soon as practicable after the need for screening becomes apparent. It also should include a statement by the screened lawyer and the firm that the client's material confidential information has not been disclosed or used in violation of the Rules. The notice is intended to enable the former client to evaluate and comment upon the effectiveness of the screening procedures.

[10] The certifications required by paragraph (a)(2)(iii) give the former client assurance that the client's material confidential information has not been disclosed or used inappropriately, either prior to timely implementation of a screen or thereafter. If compliance cannot be certified, the certificate must describe the failure to comply.

[11] Where a lawyer has joined a private firm after having represented the government, imputation is governed by Rule 1.11(b) and (c), not this Rule. Under Rule 1.11(d), where a lawyer represents the government after having served clients in private practice, nongovernmental employment or in another government agency, former-client conflicts are not imputed to government lawyers associated with the individually disqualified lawyer.

[12] Where a lawyer is prohibited from engaging in certain transactions under Rule 1.8, paragraph (k) of that Rule, and not this Rule, determines whether that prohibition also applies to other lawyers associated in a firm with the personally prohibited lawyer.

Definitional Cross-References

"Firm" *See* Rule 1.0(c)
"Knowingly" *See* Rule 1.0(f)
"Partner" *See* Rule 1.0(g)
"Screened" *See* Rule 1.0(k)
"Tribunal" *See* Rule 1.0(m)
"Written" *See* Rule 1.0(n)

RULE 1.11: SPECIAL CONFLICTS OF INTEREST FOR FORMER AND CURRENT GOVERNMENT OFFICERS AND EMPLOYEES

(a) Except as law may otherwise expressly permit, a lawyer who has formerly served as a public officer or employee of the government:

(1) is subject to Rule 1.9(c); and

(2) shall not otherwise represent a client in connection with a matter in which the lawyer participated personally and substantially as a public officer or employee, unless the appropriate government agency gives its informed consent, confirmed in writing, to the representation.

(b) When a lawyer is disqualified from representation under paragraph (a), no lawyer in a firm with which that lawyer is associated may knowingly undertake or continue representation in such a matter unless:

(1) the disqualified lawyer is timely screened from any participation in the matter and is apportioned no part of the fee therefrom; and

(2) written notice is promptly given to the appropriate government agency to enable it to ascertain compliance with the provisions of this Rule.

(c) Except as law may otherwise expressly permit, a lawyer having information that the lawyer knows is confidential government information about a person acquired when the lawyer was a public officer or employee, may not represent a private client whose interests are adverse to that person in a matter in which the information could be used to the material disadvantage of that person. As used in this Rule, the term "confidential government information" means information that has been obtained under governmental authority and which, at the time this Rule is applied, the government is prohibited by law from disclosing to the public or has a legal privilege not to disclose and which is not otherwise available to the public. A firm with which that lawyer is associated may undertake or continue representation in the matter only if the disqualified lawyer is timely screened from any participation in the matter and is apportioned no part of the fee therefrom.

(d) Except as law may otherwise expressly permit, a lawyer currently serving as a public officer or employee:

(1) is subject to Rules 1.7 and 1.9; and

(2) shall not:

(i) participate in a matter in which the lawyer participated personally and substantially while in private practice or nongovernmental employment, unless the appropriate government agency gives its informed consent, confirmed in writing; or

(ii) negotiate for private employment with any person who is involved as a party or as lawyer for a party in a matter in which the lawyer is participating personally and substantially, except that a lawyer serving as a law clerk to a judge, other adjudicative officer or arbitrator may negotiate for private employment as permitted by Rule 1.12(b) and subject to the conditions stated in Rule 1.12(b).

(e) As used in this Rule, the term "matter" includes:

(1) any judicial or other proceeding, application, request for a ruling or other determination, contract, claim, controversy, investigation, charge, accusation, arrest or other particular matter involving a specific party or parties, and

(2) any other matter covered by the conflict of interest rules of the appropriate government agency.

Comment

[1] A lawyer who has served or is currently serving as a public officer or employee is personally subject to the Rules of Professional Conduct, including the prohibition against concurrent conflicts of interest stated in Rule 1.7. In addition, such a lawyer may be subject to statutes and government regulations regarding conflict of interest. Such statutes and regulations may circumscribe the extent to which the government agency may give consent under this Rule. See Rule 1.0(e) for the definition of informed consent.

[2] Paragraphs (a)(1), (a)(2) and (d)(1) restate the obligations of an individual lawyer who has served or is currently serving as an officer or employee of the government toward a former government or private client. Rule 1.10 is not applicable to the conflicts of interest addressed by this Rule. Rather, paragraph (b) sets forth a special imputation rule for former government lawyers that provides for screening and notice. Because of the special problems raised by imputation within a government

agency, paragraph (d) does not impute the conflicts of a lawyer currently serving as an officer or employee of the government to other associated government officers or employees, although ordinarily it will be prudent to screen such lawyers.

[3] Paragraphs (a)(2) and (d)(2) apply regardless of whether a lawyer is adverse to a former client and are thus designed not only to protect the former client, but also to prevent a lawyer from exploiting public office for the advantage of another client. For example, a lawyer who has pursued a claim on behalf of the government may not pursue the same claim on behalf of a later private client after the lawyer has left government service, except when authorized to do so by the government agency under paragraph (a). Similarly, a lawyer who has pursued a claim on behalf of a private client may not pursue the claim on behalf of the government, except when authorized to do so by paragraph (d). As with paragraphs (a)(1) and (d)(1), Rule 1.10 is not applicable to the conflicts of interest addressed by these paragraphs.

[4] This Rule represents a balancing of interests. On the one hand, where the successive clients are a government agency and another client, public or private, the risk exists that power or discretion vested in that agency might be used for the special benefit of the other client. A lawyer should not be in a position where benefit to the other client might affect performance of the lawyer's professional functions on behalf of the government. Also, unfair advantage could accrue to the other client by reason of access to confidential government information about the client's adversary obtainable only through the lawyer's government service. On the other hand, the rules governing lawyers presently or formerly employed by a government agency should not be so restrictive as to inhibit transfer of employment to and from the government. The government has a legitimate need to attract qualified lawyers as well as to maintain high ethical standards. Thus a former government lawyer is disqualified only from particular matters in which the lawyer participated personally and substantially. The provisions for screening and waiver in paragraph (b) are necessary to prevent the disqualification rule from imposing too severe a deterrent against entering public service. The limitation of disqualification in paragraphs (a)(2) and (d)(2) to matters involving a specific party or parties, rather than extending disqualification to all substantive issues on which the lawyer worked, serves a similar function.

[5] When a lawyer has been employed by one government agency and then moves to a second government agency, it may be appropriate

to treat that second agency as another client for purposes of this Rule, as when a lawyer is employed by a city and subsequently is employed by a federal agency. However, because the conflict of interest is governed by paragraph (d), the latter agency is not required to screen the lawyer as paragraph (b) requires a law firm to do. The question of whether two government agencies should be regarded as the same or different clients for conflict of interest purposes is beyond the scope of these Rules. See Rule 1.13 Comment [9].

[6] Paragraphs (b) and (c) contemplate a screening arrangement. See Rule 1.0(k) (requirements for screening procedures). These paragraphs do not prohibit a lawyer from receiving a salary or partnership share established by prior independent agreement, but that lawyer may not receive compensation directly relating the lawyer's compensation to the fee in the matter in which the lawyer is disqualified.

[7] Notice, including a description of the screened lawyer's prior representation and of the screening procedures employed, generally should be given as soon as practicable after the need for screening becomes apparent.

[8] Paragraph (c) operates only when the lawyer in question has knowledge of the information, which means actual knowledge; it does not operate with respect to information that merely could be imputed to the lawyer.

[9] Paragraphs (a) and (d) do not prohibit a lawyer from jointly representing a private party and a government agency when doing so is permitted by Rule 1.7 and is not otherwise prohibited by law.

[10] For purposes of paragraph (e) of this Rule, a "matter" may continue in another form. In determining whether two particular matters are the same, the lawyer should consider the extent to which the matters involve the same basic facts, the same or related parties, and the time elapsed.

Definitional Cross-References

"Confirmed in writing" *See* Rule 1.0(b)
"Firm" *See* Rule 1.0(c)
"Informed consent" *See* Rule 1.0(e)
"Knowingly" and "Knows" *See* Rule 1.0(f)
"Screened" *See* Rule 1.0(k)
"Written" *See* Rule 1.0(n)

RULE 1.12: FORMER JUDGE, ARBITRATOR, MEDIATOR OR OTHER THIRD-PARTY NEUTRAL

(a) Except as stated in paragraph (d), a lawyer shall not represent anyone in connection with a matter in which the lawyer participated personally and substantially as a judge or other adjudicative officer or law clerk to such a person or as an arbitrator, mediator or other third-party neutral, unless all parties to the proceeding give informed consent, confirmed in writing.

(b) A lawyer shall not negotiate for employment with any person who is involved as a party or as lawyer for a party in a matter in which the lawyer is participating personally and substantially as a judge or other adjudicative officer or as an arbitrator, mediator or other third-party neutral. A lawyer serving as a law clerk to a judge or other adjudicative officer may negotiate for employment with a party or lawyer involved in a matter in which the clerk is participating personally and substantially, but only after the lawyer has notified the judge or other adjudicative officer.

(c) If a lawyer is disqualified by paragraph (a), no lawyer in a firm with which that lawyer is associated may knowingly undertake or continue representation in the matter unless:

(1) the disqualified lawyer is timely screened from any participation in the matter and is apportioned no part of the fee therefrom; and

(2) written notice is promptly given to the parties and any appropriate tribunal to enable them to ascertain compliance with the provisions of this rule.

(d) An arbitrator selected as a partisan of a party in a multimember arbitration panel is not prohibited from subsequently representing that party.

Comment

[1] This Rule generally parallels Rule 1.11. The term "personally and substantially" signifies that a judge who was a member of a multimember court, and thereafter left judicial office to practice law, is not prohibited from representing a client in a matter pending in the court, but in which the former judge did not participate. So also the fact that a former

judge exercised administrative responsibility in a court does not prevent the former judge from acting as a lawyer in a matter where the judge had previously exercised remote or incidental administrative responsibility that did not affect the merits. Compare the Comment to Rule 1.11. The term "adjudicative officer" includes such officials as judges pro tempore, referees, special masters, hearing officers and other parajudicial officers, and also lawyers who serve as part-time judges. Paragraphs C(2), D(2) and E(2) of the Application Section of the Model Code of Judicial Conduct provide that a part-time judge, judge pro tempore or retired judge recalled to active service, shall not "act as a lawyer in a proceeding in which the judge has served as a judge or in any other proceeding related thereto." Although phrased differently from this Rule, those Rules correspond in meaning.

[2] Like former judges, lawyers who have served as arbitrators, mediators or other third-party neutrals may be asked to represent a client in a matter in which the lawyer participated personally and substantially. This Rule forbids such representation unless all of the parties to the proceedings give their informed consent, confirmed in writing. See Rule 1.0(e) and (b). Other law or codes of ethics governing third-party neutrals may impose more stringent standards of personal or imputed disqualification. See Rule 2.4.

[3] Although lawyers who serve as third-party neutrals do not have information concerning the parties that is protected under Rule 1.6, they typically owe the parties an obligation of confidentiality under law or codes of ethics governing third-party neutrals. Thus, paragraph (c) provides that conflicts of the personally disqualified lawyer will be imputed to other lawyers in a law firm unless the conditions of this paragraph are met.

[4] Requirements for screening procedures are stated in Rule 1.0(k). Paragraph (c)(1) does not prohibit the screened lawyer from receiving a salary or partnership share established by prior independent agreement, but that lawyer may not receive compensation directly related to the matter in which the lawyer is disqualified.

[5] Notice, including a description of the screened lawyer's prior representation and of the screening procedures employed, generally should be given as soon as practicable after the need for screening becomes apparent.

Definitional Cross-References

"Confirmed in writing" *See* Rule 1.0(b)
"Firm" *See* Rule 1.0(c)
"Informed consent" *See* Rule 1.0(e)
"Knowingly" *See* Rule 1.0(f)
"Screened" *See* Rule 1.0(k)
"Tribunal" *See* Rule 1.0(m)
"Writing" and "Written" *See* Rule 1.0(n)

RULE 1.13: ORGANIZATION AS CLIENT

(a) A lawyer employed or retained by an organization represents the organization acting through its duly authorized constituents.

(b) If a lawyer for an organization knows that an officer, employee or other person associated with the organization is engaged in action, intends to act or refuses to act in a matter related to the representation that is a violation of a legal obligation to the organization, or a violation of law that reasonably might be imputed to the organization, and that is likely to result in substantial injury to the organization, then the lawyer shall proceed as is reasonably necessary in the best interest of the organization. Unless the lawyer reasonably believes that it is not necessary in the best interest of the organization to do so, the lawyer shall refer the matter to higher authority in the organization, including, if warranted by the circumstances, to the highest authority that can act on behalf of the organization as determined by applicable law.

(c) Except as provided in paragraph (d), if

(1) despite the lawyer's efforts in accordance with paragraph (b) the highest authority that can act on behalf of the organization insists upon or fails to address in a timely and appropriate manner an action or a refusal to act, that is clearly a violation of law; and

(2) the lawyer reasonably believes that the violation is reasonably certain to result in substantial injury to the organization,

then the lawyer may reveal information relating to the representation whether or not Rule 1.6 permits such disclosure, but only if and to the extent the lawyer reasonably believes necessary to prevent substantial injury to the organization.

(d) Paragraph (c) shall not apply with respect to information relating to a lawyer's representation of an organization to investigate an alleged violation of law, or to defend the organization or an officer, employee or other constituent associated with the organization against a claim arising out of an alleged violation of law.

(e) A lawyer who reasonably believes that he or she has been discharged because of the lawyer's actions taken pursuant to paragraphs (b) or (c), or who withdraws under circumstances that require or permit the lawyer to take action under either of those paragraphs, shall proceed as the lawyer reasonably believes necessary to assure that the organization's highest authority is informed of the lawyer's discharge or withdrawal.

(f) In dealing with an organization's directors, officers, employees, members, shareholders or other constituents, a lawyer shall explain the identity of the client when the lawyer knows or reasonably should know that the organization's interests are adverse to those of the constituents with whom the lawyer is dealing.

(g) A lawyer representing an organization may also represent any of its directors, officers, employees, members, shareholders or other constituents, subject to the provisions of Rule 1.7. If the organization's consent to the dual representation is required by Rule 1.7, the consent shall be given by an appropriate official of the organization other than the individual who is to be represented, or by the shareholders.

Comment

The Entity as the Client

[1] An organizational client is a legal entity, but it cannot act except through its officers, directors, employees, shareholders and other constituents. Officers, directors, employees and shareholders are the constituents of the corporate organizational client. The duties defined in this Comment apply equally to unincorporated associations. "Other constituents" as used in this Comment means the positions equivalent to officers, directors, employees and shareholders held by persons acting for organizational clients that are not corporations.

[2] When one of the constituents of an organizational client communicates with the organization's lawyer in that person's organizational

capacity, the communication is protected by Rule 1.6. Thus, by way of example, if an organizational client requests its lawyer to investigate allegations of wrongdoing, interviews made in the course of that investigation between the lawyer and the client's employees or other constituents are covered by Rule 1.6. This does not mean, however, that constituents of an organizational client are the clients of the lawyer. The lawyer may not disclose to such constituents information relating to the representation except for disclosures explicitly or impliedly authorized by the organizational client in order to carry out the representation or as otherwise permitted by Rule 1.6.

[3] When constituents of the organization make decisions for it, the decisions ordinarily must be accepted by the lawyer even if their utility or prudence is doubtful. Decisions concerning policy and operations, including ones entailing serious risk, are not as such in the lawyer's province. Paragraph (b) makes clear, however, that when the lawyer knows that the organization is likely to be substantially injured by action of an officer or other constituent that violates a legal obligation to the organization or is in violation of law that might be imputed to the organization, the lawyer must proceed as is reasonably necessary in the best interest of the organization. As defined in Rule 1.0(f), knowledge can be inferred from circumstances, and a lawyer cannot ignore the obvious.

[4] In determining how to proceed under paragraph (b), the lawyer should give due consideration to the seriousness of the violation and its consequences, the responsibility in the organization and the apparent motivation of the person involved, the policies of the organization concerning such matters, and any other relevant considerations. Ordinarily, referral to a higher authority would be necessary. In some circumstances, however, it may be appropriate for the lawyer to ask the constituent to reconsider the matter; for example, if the circumstances involve a constituent's innocent misunderstanding of law and subsequent acceptance of the lawyer's advice, the lawyer may reasonably conclude that the best interest of the organization does not require that the matter be referred to higher authority. If a constituent persists in conduct contrary to the lawyer's advice, it will be necessary for the lawyer to take steps to have the matter reviewed by a higher authority in the organization. If the matter is of sufficient seriousness and importance or urgency to the organization, referral to higher authority in the organization may be necessary even if the lawyer has not communicated with the constituent. Any measures taken should, to the extent practicable, minimize the risk of revealing

information relating to the representation to persons outside the organization. Even in circumstances where a lawyer is not obligated by Rule 1.13 to proceed, a lawyer may bring to the attention of an organizational client, including its highest authority, matters that the lawyer reasonably believes to be of sufficient importance to warrant doing so in the best interest of the organization.

[5] Paragraph (b) also makes clear that when it is reasonably necessary to enable the organization to address the matter in a timely and appropriate manner, the lawyer must refer the matter to higher authority, including, if warranted by the circumstances, the highest authority that can act on behalf of the organization under applicable law. The organization's highest authority to whom a matter may be referred ordinarily will be the board of directors or similar governing body. However, applicable law may prescribe that under certain conditions the highest authority reposes elsewhere, for example, in the independent directors of a corporation.

Relation to Other Rules

[6] The authority and responsibility provided in this Rule are concurrent with the authority and responsibility provided in other Rules. In particular, this Rule does not limit or expand the lawyer's responsibility under Rules 1.8, 1.16, 3.3 or 4.1. Paragraph (c) of this Rule supplements Rule 1.6(b) by providing an additional basis upon which the lawyer may reveal information relating to the representation, but does not modify, restrict, or limit the provisions of Rule 1.6(b)(1) – (6). Under paragraph (c) the lawyer may reveal such information only when the organization's highest authority insists upon or fails to address threatened or ongoing action that is clearly a violation of law, and then only to the extent the lawyer reasonably believes necessary to prevent reasonably certain substantial injury to the organization. It is not necessary that the lawyer's services be used in furtherance of the violation, but it is required that the matter be related to the lawyer's representation of the organization. If the lawyer's services are being used by an organization to further a crime or fraud by the organization, Rules 1.6(b)(2) and 1.6(b)(3) may permit the lawyer to disclose confidential information. In such circumstances Rule 1.2(d) may also be applicable, in which event, withdrawal from the representation under Rule 1.16(a)(1) may be required.

[7] Paragraph (d) makes clear that the authority of a lawyer to disclose information relating to a representation in circumstances described

in paragraph (c) does not apply with respect to information relating to a lawyer's engagement by an organization to investigate an alleged violation of law or to defend the organization or an officer, employee or other person associated with the organization against a claim arising out of an alleged violation of law. This is necessary in order to enable organizational clients to enjoy the full benefits of legal counsel in conducting an investigation or defending against a claim.

[8] A lawyer who reasonably believes that he or she has been discharged because of the lawyer's actions taken pursuant to paragraph (b) or (c), or who withdraws in circumstances that require or permit the lawyer to take action under either of these paragraphs, must proceed as the lawyer reasonably believes necessary to assure that the organization's highest authority is informed of the lawyer's discharge or withdrawal.

Government Agency

[9] The duty defined in this Rule applies to governmental organizations. Defining precisely the identity of the client and prescribing the resulting obligations of such lawyers may be more difficult in the government context and is a matter beyond the scope of these Rules. See Scope [18]. Although in some circumstances the client may be a specific agency, it may also be a branch of government, such as the executive branch, or the government as a whole. For example, if the action or failure to act involves the head of a bureau, either the department of which the bureau is a part or the relevant branch of government may be the client for purposes of this Rule. Moreover, in a matter involving the conduct of government officials, a government lawyer may have authority under applicable law to question such conduct more extensively than that of a lawyer for a private organization in similar circumstances. Thus, when the client is a governmental organization, a different balance may be appropriate between maintaining confidentiality and assuring that the wrongful act is prevented or rectified, for public business is involved. In addition, duties of lawyers employed by the government or lawyers in military service may be defined by statutes and regulation. This Rule does not limit that authority. See Scope.

Clarifying the Lawyer's Role

[10] There are times when the organization's interest may be or become adverse to those of one or more of its constituents. In such circumstances the lawyer should advise any constituent, whose interest the law-

yer finds adverse to that of the organization of the conflict or potential conflict of interest, that the lawyer cannot represent such constituent, and that such person may wish to obtain independent representation. Care must be taken to assure that the individual understands that, when there is such adversity of interest, the lawyer for the organization cannot provide legal representation for that constituent individual, and that discussions between the lawyer for the organization and the individual may not be privileged.

[11] Whether such a warning should be given by the lawyer for the organization to any constituent individual may turn on the facts of each case.

Dual Representation

[12] Paragraph (g) recognizes that a lawyer for an organization may also represent a principal officer or major shareholder.

Derivative Actions

[13] Under generally prevailing law, the shareholders or members of a corporation may bring suit to compel the directors to perform their legal obligations in the supervision of the organization. Members of unincorporated associations have essentially the same right. Such an action may be brought nominally by the organization, but usually is, in fact, a legal controversy over management of the organization.

[14] The question can arise whether counsel for the organization may defend such an action. The proposition that the organization is the lawyer's client does not alone resolve the issue. Most derivative actions are a normal incident of an organization's affairs, to be defended by the organization's lawyer like any other suit. However, if the claim involves serious charges of wrongdoing by those in control of the organization, a conflict may arise between the lawyer's duty to the organization and the lawyer's relationship with the board. In those circumstances, Rule 1.7 governs who should represent the directors and the organization.

Definitional Cross-References

"Knows" *See* Rule 1.0(f)
"Reasonably" *See* Rule 1.0(h)
"Reasonably believes" *See* Rule 1.0(i)
"Reasonably should know" *See* Rule 1.0(j)
"Substantial" *See* Rule 1.0(l)

RULE 1.14: CLIENT WITH DIMINISHED CAPACITY

(a) When a client's capacity to make adequately considered decisions in connection with a representation is diminished, whether because of minority, mental impairment or for some other reason, the lawyer shall, as far as reasonably possible, maintain a normal client-lawyer relationship with the client.

(b) When the lawyer reasonably believes that the client has diminished capacity, is at risk of substantial physical, financial or other harm unless action is taken and cannot adequately act in the client's own interest, the lawyer may take reasonably necessary protective action, including consulting with individuals or entities that have the ability to take action to protect the client and, in appropriate cases, seeking the appointment of a guardian ad litem, conservator or guardian.

(c) Information relating to the representation of a client with diminished capacity is protected by Rule 1.6. When taking protective action pursuant to paragraph (b), the lawyer is impliedly authorized under Rule 1.6(a) to reveal information about the client, but only to the extent reasonably necessary to protect the client's interests.

Comment

[1] The normal client-lawyer relationship is based on the assumption that the client, when properly advised and assisted, is capable of making decisions about important matters. When the client is a minor or suffers from a diminished mental capacity, however, maintaining the ordinary client-lawyer relationship may not be possible in all respects. In particular, a severely incapacitated person may have no power to make legally binding decisions. Nevertheless, a client with diminished capacity often has the ability to understand, deliberate upon, and reach conclusions about matters affecting the client's own well-being. For example, children as young as five or six years of age, and certainly those of ten or twelve, are regarded as having opinions that are entitled to weight in legal proceedings concerning their custody. So also, it is recognized that some persons of advanced age can be quite capable of handling routine financial matters while needing special legal protection concerning major transactions.

[2] The fact that a client suffers a disability does not diminish the

lawyer's obligation to treat the client with attention and respect. Even if the person has a legal representative, the lawyer should as far as possible accord the represented person the status of client, particularly in maintaining communication.

[3] The client may wish to have family members or other persons participate in discussions with the lawyer. When necessary to assist in the representation, the presence of such persons generally does not affect the applicability of the attorney-client evidentiary privilege. Nevertheless, the lawyer must keep the client's interests foremost and, except for protective action authorized under paragraph (b), must look to the client, and not family members, to make decisions on the client's behalf.

[4] If a legal representative has already been appointed for the client, the lawyer should ordinarily look to the representative for decisions on behalf of the client. In matters involving a minor, whether the lawyer should look to the parents as natural guardians may depend on the type of proceeding or matter in which the lawyer is representing the minor. If the lawyer represents the guardian as distinct from the ward, and is aware that the guardian is acting adversely to the ward's interest, the lawyer may have an obligation to prevent or rectify the guardian's misconduct. See Rule 1.2(d).

Taking Protective Action

[5] If a lawyer reasonably believes that a client is at risk of substantial physical, financial or other harm unless action is taken, and that a normal client-lawyer relationship cannot be maintained as provided in paragraph (a) because the client lacks sufficient capacity to communicate or to make adequately considered decisions in connection with the representation, then paragraph (b) permits the lawyer to take protective measures deemed necessary. Such measures could include: consulting with family members, using a reconsideration period to permit clarification or improvement of circumstances, using voluntary surrogate decisionmaking tools such as durable powers of attorney or consulting with support groups, professional services, adult-protective agencies or other individuals or entities that have the ability to protect the client. In taking any protective action, the lawyer should be guided by such factors as the wishes and values of the client to the extent known, the client's best interests and the goals of intruding into the client's decisionmaking autonomy to the least extent feasible, maximizing client capacities and respecting the client's family and social connections.

[6] In determining the extent of the client's diminished capacity, the lawyer should consider and balance such factors as: the client's ability to articulate reasoning leading to a decision, variability of state of mind and ability to appreciate consequences of a decision; the substantive fairness of a decision; and the consistency of a decision with the known long-term commitments and values of the client. In appropriate circumstances, the lawyer may seek guidance from an appropriate diagnostician.

[7] If a legal representative has not been appointed, the lawyer should consider whether appointment of a guardian ad litem, conservator or guardian is necessary to protect the client's interests. Thus, if a client with diminished capacity has substantial property that should be sold for the client's benefit, effective completion of the transaction may require appointment of a legal representative. In addition, rules of procedure in litigation sometimes provide that minors or persons with diminished capacity must be represented by a guardian or next friend if they do not have a general guardian. In many circumstances, however, appointment of a legal representative may be more expensive or traumatic for the client than circumstances in fact require. Evaluation of such circumstances is a matter entrusted to the professional judgment of the lawyer. In considering alternatives, however, the lawyer should be aware of any law that requires the lawyer to advocate the least restrictive action on behalf of the client.

Disclosure of the Client's Condition

[8] Disclosure of the client's diminished capacity could adversely affect the client's interests. For example, raising the question of diminished capacity could, in some circumstances, lead to proceedings for involuntary commitment. Information relating to the representation is protected by Rule 1.6. Therefore, unless authorized to do so, the lawyer may not disclose such information. When taking protective action pursuant to paragraph (b), the lawyer is impliedly authorized to make the necessary disclosures, even when the client directs the lawyer to the contrary. Nevertheless, given the risks of disclosure, paragraph (c) limits what the lawyer may disclose in consulting with other individuals or entities or seeking the appointment of a legal representative. At the very least, the lawyer should determine whether it is likely that the person or entity consulted with will act adversely to the client's interests before discussing matters related to the client. The lawyer's position in such cases is an unavoidably difficult one.

Emergency Legal Assistance

[9] In an emergency where the health, safety or a financial interest of a person with seriously diminished capacity is threatened with imminent and irreparable harm, a lawyer may take legal action on behalf of such a person even though the person is unable to establish a client-lawyer relationship or to make or express considered judgments about the matter, when the person or another acting in good faith on that person's behalf has consulted with the lawyer. Even in such an emergency, however, the lawyer should not act unless the lawyer reasonably believes that the person has no other lawyer, agent or other representative available. The lawyer should take legal action on behalf of the person only to the extent reasonably necessary to maintain the status quo or otherwise avoid imminent and irreparable harm. A lawyer who undertakes to represent a person in such an exigent situation has the same duties under these Rules as the lawyer would with respect to a client.

[10] A lawyer who acts on behalf of a person with seriously diminished capacity in an emergency should keep the confidences of the person as if dealing with a client, disclosing them only to the extent necessary to accomplish the intended protective action. The lawyer should disclose to any tribunal involved and to any other counsel involved the nature of his or her relationship with the person. The lawyer should take steps to regularize the relationship or implement other protective solutions as soon as possible. Normally, a lawyer would not seek compensation for such emergency actions taken.

Definitional Cross-References

"Reasonably" *See* Rule 1.0(h)
"Reasonably believes" *See* Rule 1.0(i)
"Substantial" *See* Rule 1.0(l)

RULE 1.15: SAFEKEEPING PROPERTY

(a) A lawyer shall hold property of clients or third persons that is in a lawyer's possession in connection with a representation separate from the lawyer's own property. Funds shall be kept in a separate account maintained in the state where the lawyer's office is situated, or elsewhere with the consent of the client or third person. Other property shall be identified as such and appropriately safeguarded. Complete records of such account funds and other property shall be kept by the lawyer and shall be preserved for a period of [five years] after termination of the representation.

(b) A lawyer may deposit the lawyer's own funds in a client trust account for the sole purpose of paying bank service charges on that account, but only in an amount necessary for that purpose.

(c) A lawyer shall deposit into a client trust account legal fees and expenses that have been paid in advance, to be withdrawn by the lawyer only as fees are earned or expenses incurred.

(d) Upon receiving funds or other property in which a client or third person has an interest, a lawyer shall promptly notify the client or third person. Except as stated in this Rule or otherwise permitted by law or by agreement with the client, a lawyer shall promptly deliver to the client or third person any funds or other property that the client or third person is entitled to receive and, upon request by the client or third person, shall promptly render a full accounting regarding such property.

(e) When in the course of representation a lawyer is in possession of property in which two or more persons (one of whom may be the lawyer) claim interests, the property shall be kept separate by the lawyer until the dispute is resolved. The lawyer shall promptly distribute all portions of the property as to which the interests are not in dispute.

Comment

[1] A lawyer should hold property of others with the care required of a professional fiduciary. Securities should be kept in a safe deposit box, except when some other form of safekeeping is warranted by special circumstances. All property that is the property of clients or third persons, including prospective clients, must be kept separate from the lawyer's business and personal property and, if monies, in one or more trust accounts. Separate trust accounts may be warranted when administering estate monies or acting in similar fiduciary capacities. A lawyer should maintain on a current basis books and records in accordance with generally accepted accounting practice and comply with any recordkeeping rules established by law or court order. See, e.g., ABA Model Rules for Client Trust Account Records.

[2] While normally it is impermissible to commingle the lawyer's own funds with client funds, paragraph (b) provides that it is permissible

when necessary to pay bank service charges on that account. Accurate records must be kept regarding which part of the funds are the lawyer's.

[3] Lawyers often receive funds from which the lawyer's fee will be paid. The lawyer is not required to remit to the client funds that the lawyer reasonably believes represent fees owed. However, a lawyer may not hold funds to coerce a client into accepting the lawyer's contention. The disputed portion of the funds must be kept in a trust account and the lawyer should suggest means for prompt resolution of the dispute, such as arbitration. The undisputed portion of the funds shall be promptly distributed.

[4] Paragraph (e) also recognizes that third parties may have lawful claims against specific funds or other property in a lawyer's custody, such as a client's creditor who has a lien on funds recovered in a personal injury action. A lawyer may have a duty under applicable law to protect such third-party claims against wrongful interference by the client. In such cases, when the third-party claim is not frivolous under applicable law, the lawyer must refuse to surrender the property to the client until the claims are resolved. A lawyer should not unilaterally assume to arbitrate a dispute between the client and the third party, but, when there are substantial grounds for dispute as to the person entitled to the funds, the lawyer may file an action to have a court resolve the dispute.

[5] The obligations of a lawyer under this Rule are independent of those arising from activity other than rendering legal services. For example, a lawyer who serves only as an escrow agent is governed by the applicable law relating to fiduciaries even though the lawyer does not render legal services in the transaction and is not governed by this Rule.

[6] A lawyers' fund for client protection provides a means through the collective efforts of the bar to reimburse persons who have lost money or property as a result of dishonest conduct of a lawyer. Where such a fund has been established, a lawyer must participate where it is mandatory, and, even when it is voluntary, the lawyer should participate.

RULE 1.16: DECLINING OR TERMINATING REPRESENTATION

(a) Except as stated in paragraph (c), a lawyer shall not represent a client or, where representation has commenced, shall withdraw from the representation of a client if:

(1) the representation will result in violation of the Rules of Professional Conduct or other law;

(2) the lawyer's physical or mental condition materially impairs the lawyer's ability to represent the client; or

(3) the lawyer is discharged.

(b) Except as stated in paragraph (c), a lawyer may withdraw from representing a client if:

(1) withdrawal can be accomplished without material adverse effect on the interests of the client;

(2) the client persists in a course of action involving the lawyer's services that the lawyer reasonably believes is criminal or fraudulent;

(3) the client has used the lawyer's services to perpetrate a crime or fraud;

(4) the client insists upon taking action that the lawyer considers repugnant or with which the lawyer has a fundamental disagreement;

(5) the client fails substantially to fulfill an obligation to the lawyer regarding the lawyer's services and has been given reasonable warning that the lawyer will withdraw unless the obligation is fulfilled;

(6) the representation will result in an unreasonable financial burden on the lawyer or has been rendered unreasonably difficult by the client; or

(7) other good cause for withdrawal exists.

(c) A lawyer must comply with applicable law requiring notice to or permission of a tribunal when terminating a representation. When ordered to do so by a tribunal, a lawyer shall continue representation notwithstanding good cause for terminating the representation.

(d) Upon termination of representation, a lawyer shall take steps to the extent reasonably practicable to protect a client's interests, such as giving reasonable notice to the client, allowing time for employment of other counsel, surrendering papers and property to which the client is entitled and refunding any advance payment of fee or expense that has not been earned or incurred. The lawyer may retain papers relating to the client to the extent permitted by other law.

Comment

[1] A lawyer should not accept representation in a matter unless it can be performed competently, promptly, without improper conflict of in-

terest and to completion. Ordinarily, a representation in a matter is completed when the agreed-upon assistance has been concluded. See Rules
1.2(c) and 6.5. See also Rule 1.3, Comment [4].

Mandatory Withdrawal

[2] A lawyer ordinarily must decline or withdraw from representation if the client demands that the lawyer engage in conduct that is illegal
or violates the Rules of Professional Conduct or other law. The lawyer
is not obliged to decline or withdraw simply because the client suggests
such a course of conduct; a client may make such a suggestion in the
hope that a lawyer will not be constrained by a professional obligation.

[3] When a lawyer has been appointed to represent a client, withdrawal ordinarily requires approval of the appointing authority. See also
Rule 6.2. Similarly, court approval or notice to the court is often required
by applicable law before a lawyer withdraws from pending litigation.
Difficulty may be encountered if withdrawal is based on the client's demand that the lawyer engage in unprofessional conduct. The court may
request an explanation for the withdrawal, while the lawyer may be
bound to keep confidential the facts that would constitute such an explanation. The lawyer's statement that professional considerations require
termination of the representation ordinarily should be accepted as sufficient. Lawyers should be mindful of their obligations to both clients and
the court under Rules 1.6 and 3.3.

Discharge

[4] A client has a right to discharge a lawyer at any time, with or
without cause, subject to liability for payment for the lawyer's services.
Where future dispute about the withdrawal may be anticipated, it may
be advisable to prepare a written statement reciting the circumstances.

[5] Whether a client can discharge appointed counsel may depend on
applicable law. A client seeking to do so should be given a full explanation of the consequences. These consequences may include a decision by
the appointing authority that appointment of successor counsel is unjustified, thus requiring self-representation by the client.

[6] If the client has severely diminished capacity, the client may lack
the legal capacity to discharge the lawyer, and in any event the discharge
may be seriously adverse to the client's interests. The lawyer should
make special effort to help the client consider the consequences and may
take reasonably necessary protective action as provided in Rule 1.14.

Optional Withdrawal

[7] A lawyer may withdraw from representation in some circumstances. The lawyer has the option to withdraw if it can be accomplished without material adverse effect on the client's interests. Withdrawal is also justified if the client persists in a course of action that the lawyer reasonably believes is criminal or fraudulent, for a lawyer is not required to be associated with such conduct even if the lawyer does not further it. Withdrawal is also permitted if the lawyer's services were misused in the past even if that would materially prejudice the client. The lawyer may also withdraw where the client insists on taking action that the lawyer considers repugnant or with which the lawyer has a fundamental disagreement.

[8] A lawyer may withdraw if the client refuses to abide by the terms of an agreement relating to the representation, such as an agreement concerning fees or court costs or an agreement limiting the objectives of the representation.

Assisting the Client upon Withdrawal

[9] Even if the lawyer has been unfairly discharged by the client, a lawyer must take all reasonable steps to mitigate the consequences to the client. The lawyer may retain papers as security for a fee only to the extent permitted by law. See Rule 1.15.

Definitional Cross-References

"Fraud" and "Fraudulent" *See* Rule 1.0(d)
"Reasonable" *See* Rule 1.0(h)
"Reasonably believes" *See* Rule 1.0(i)
"Tribunal" *See* Rule 1.0(m)

RULE 1.17: SALE OF LAW PRACTICE

A lawyer or a law firm may sell or purchase a law practice, or an area of law practice, including good will, if the following conditions are satisfied:

(a) The seller ceases to engage in the private practice of law, or in the area of practice that has been sold, [in the geographic area] [in the jurisdiction] (a jurisdiction may elect either version) in which the practice has been conducted;

(b) The entire practice, or the entire area of practice, is sold to one or more lawyers or law firms;

(c) The seller gives written notice to each of the seller's clients regarding:

(1) the proposed sale;

(2) the client's right to retain other counsel or to take possession of the file; and

(3) the fact that the client's consent to the transfer of the client's files will be presumed if the client does not take any action or does not otherwise object within ninety (90) days of receipt of the notice.

If a client cannot be given notice, the representation of that client may be transferred to the purchaser only upon entry of an order so authorizing by a court having jurisdiction. The seller may disclose to the court in camera information relating to the representation only to the extent necessary to obtain an order authorizing the transfer of a file.

(d) The fees charged clients shall not be increased by reason of the sale.

Comment

[1] The practice of law is a profession, not merely a business. Clients are not commodities that can be purchased and sold at will. Pursuant to this Rule, when a lawyer or an entire firm ceases to practice, or ceases to practice in an area of law, and other lawyers or firms take over the representation, the selling lawyer or firm may obtain compensation for the reasonable value of the practice as may withdrawing partners of law firms. See Rules 5.4 and 5.6.

Termination of Practice by the Seller

[2] The requirement that all of the private practice, or all of an area of practice, be sold is satisfied if the seller in good faith makes the entire practice, or the area of practice, available for sale to the purchasers. The fact that a number of the seller's clients decide not to be represented by the purchasers but take their matters elsewhere, therefore, does not result in a violation. Return to private practice as a result of an unanticipated change in circumstances does not necessarily result in a violation. For example, a lawyer who has sold the practice to accept an appointment to judicial office does not violate the requirement that the sale be attendant

to cessation of practice if the lawyer later resumes private practice upon being defeated in a contested or a retention election for the office or resigns from a judiciary position.

[3] The requirement that the seller cease to engage in the private practice of law does not prohibit employment as a lawyer on the staff of a public agency or a legal services entity that provides legal services to the poor, or as in-house counsel to a business.

[4] The Rule permits a sale of an entire practice attendant upon retirement from the private practice of law within the jurisdiction. Its provisions, therefore, accommodate the lawyer who sells the practice on the occasion of moving to another state. Some states are so large that a move from one locale therein to another is tantamount to leaving the jurisdiction in which the lawyer has engaged in the practice of law. To also accommodate lawyers so situated, states may permit the sale of the practice when the lawyer leaves the geographical area rather than the jurisdiction. The alternative desired should be indicated by selecting one of the two provided for in Rule 1.17(a).

[5] This Rule also permits a lawyer or law firm to sell an area of practice. If an area of practice is sold and the lawyer remains in the active practice of law, the lawyer must cease accepting any matters in the area of practice that has been sold, either as counsel or co-counsel or by assuming joint responsibility for a matter in connection with the division of a fee with another lawyer as would otherwise be permitted by Rule 1.5(e). For example, a lawyer with a substantial number of estate planning matters and a substantial number of probate administration cases may sell the estate planning portion of the practice but remain in the practice of law by concentrating on probate administration; however, that practitioner may not thereafter accept any estate planning matters. Although a lawyer who leaves a jurisdiction or geographical area typically would sell the entire practice, this Rule permits the lawyer to limit the sale to one or more areas of the practice, thereby preserving the lawyer's right to continue practice in the areas of the practice that were not sold.

Sale of Entire Practice or Entire Area of Practice

[6] The Rule requires that the seller's entire practice, or an entire area of practice, be sold. The prohibition against sale of less than an entire practice area protects those clients whose matters are less lucrative and who might find it difficult to secure other counsel if a sale could be lim-

ited to substantial fee-generating matters. The purchasers are required to undertake all client matters in the practice or practice area, subject to client consent. This requirement is satisfied, however, even if a purchaser is unable to undertake a particular client matter because of a conflict of interest.

Client Confidences, Consent and Notice

[7] Negotiations between seller and prospective purchaser prior to disclosure of information relating to a specific representation of an identifiable client no more violate the confidentiality provisions of Model Rule 1.6 than do preliminary discussions concerning the possible association of another lawyer or mergers between firms, with respect to which client consent is not required. See Rule 1.6(b)(7). Providing the purchaser access to detailed information relating to the representation, such as the client's file, however, requires client consent. The Rule provides that before such information can be disclosed by the seller to the purchaser the client must be given actual written notice of the contemplated sale, including the identity of the purchaser, and must be told that the decision to consent or make other arrangements must be made within 90 days. If nothing is heard from the client within that time, consent to the sale is presumed.

[8] A lawyer or law firm ceasing to practice cannot be required to remain in practice because some clients cannot be given actual notice of the proposed purchase. Since these clients cannot themselves consent to the purchase or direct any other disposition of their files, the Rule requires an order from a court having jurisdiction authorizing their transfer or other disposition. The court can be expected to determine whether reasonable efforts to locate the client have been exhausted, and whether the absent client's legitimate interests will be served by authorizing the transfer of the file so that the purchaser may continue the representation. Preservation of client confidences requires that the petition for a court order be considered in camera. (A procedure by which such an order can be obtained needs to be established in jurisdictions in which it presently does not exist).

[9] All elements of client autonomy, including the client's absolute right to discharge a lawyer and transfer the representation to another, survive the sale of the practice or area of practice.

Fee Arrangements Between Client and Purchaser

[10] The sale may not be financed by increases in fees charged the clients of the practice. Existing arrangements between the seller and the client as to fees and the scope of the work must be honored by the purchaser.

Other Applicable Ethical Standards

[11] Lawyers participating in the sale of a law practice or a practice area are subject to the ethical standards applicable to involving another lawyer in the representation of a client. These include, for example, the seller's obligation to exercise competence in identifying a purchaser qualified to assume the practice and the purchaser's obligation to undertake the representation competently (see Rule 1.1); the obligation to avoid disqualifying conflicts, and to secure the client's informed consent for those conflicts that can be agreed to (see Rule 1.7 regarding conflicts and Rule 1.0(e) for the definition of informed consent); and the obligation to protect information relating to the representation (see Rules 1.6 and 1.9).

[12] If approval of the substitution of the purchasing lawyer for the selling lawyer is required by the rules of any tribunal in which a matter is pending, such approval must be obtained before the matter can be included in the sale (see Rule 1.16).

Applicability of the Rule

[13] This Rule applies to the sale of a law practice of a deceased, disabled or disappeared lawyer. Thus, the seller may be represented by a non-lawyer representative not subject to these Rules. Since, however, no lawyer may participate in a sale of a law practice which does not conform to the requirements of this Rule, the representatives of the seller as well as the purchasing lawyer can be expected to see to it that they are met.

[14] Admission to or retirement from a law partnership or professional association, retirement plans and similar arrangements, and a sale of tangible assets of a law practice, do not constitute a sale or purchase governed by this Rule.

[15] This Rule does not apply to the transfers of legal representation between lawyers when such transfers are unrelated to the sale of a practice or an area of practice.

Definitional Cross-References

"Law firm" *See* Rule 1.0(c)
"Written" *See* Rule 1.0(n)

Rule 1.18: Duties to Prospective Client

(a) A person who consults with a lawyer about the possibility of forming a client-lawyer relationship with respect to a matter is a prospective client.

(b) Even when no client-lawyer relationship ensues, a lawyer who has learned information from a prospective client shall not use or reveal that information, except as Rule 1.9 would permit with respect to information of a former client.

(c) A lawyer subject to paragraph (b) shall not represent a client with interests materially adverse to those of a prospective client in the same or a substantially related matter if the lawyer received information from the prospective client that could be significantly harmful to that person in the matter, except as provided in paragraph (d). If a lawyer is disqualified from representation under this paragraph, no lawyer in a firm with which that lawyer is associated may knowingly undertake or continue representation in such a matter, except as provided in paragraph (d).

(d) When the lawyer has received disqualifying information as defined in paragraph (c), representation is permissible if:

(1) both the affected client and the prospective client have given informed consent, confirmed in writing; or:

(2) the lawyer who received the information took reasonable measures to avoid exposure to more disqualifying information than was reasonably necessary to determine whether to represent the prospective client; and

(i) the disqualified lawyer is timely screened from any participation in the matter and is apportioned no part of the fee therefrom; and

(ii) written notice is promptly given to the prospective client.

Comment

[1] Prospective clients, like clients, may disclose information to a lawyer, place documents or other property in the lawyer's custody, or rely on the lawyer's advice. A lawyer's consultations with a prospective client usually are limited in time and depth and leave both the prospective client and the lawyer free (and sometimes required) to proceed no further. Hence, prospective clients should receive some but not all of the protection afforded clients.

[2] A person becomes a prospective client by consulting with a lawyer about the possibility of forming a client-lawyer relationship with respect to a matter. Whether communications, including written, oral, or electronic communications, constitute a consultation depends on the circumstances. For example, a consultation is likely to have occurred if a lawyer, either in person or through the lawyer's advertising in any medium, specifically requests or invites the submission of information about a potential representation without clear and reasonably understandable warnings and cautionary statements that limit the lawyer's obligations, and a person provides information in response. See also Comment [4]. In contrast, a consultation does not occur if a person provides information to a lawyer in response to advertising that merely describes the lawyer's education, experience, areas of practice, and contact information, or provides legal information of general interest. Such a person communicates information unilaterally to a lawyer, without any reasonable expectation that the lawyer is willing to discuss the possibility of forming a client-lawyer relationship, and is thus not a "prospective client." Moreover, a person who communicates with a lawyer for the purpose of disqualifying the lawyer is not a "prospective client."

[3] It is often necessary for a prospective client to reveal information to the lawyer during an initial consultation prior to the decision about formation of a client-lawyer relationship. The lawyer often must learn such information to determine whether there is a conflict of interest with an existing client and whether the matter is one that the lawyer is willing to undertake. Paragraph (b) prohibits the lawyer from using or revealing that information, except as permitted by Rule 1.9, even if the client or lawyer decides not to proceed with the representation. The duty exists regardless of how brief the initial conference may be.

[4] In order to avoid acquiring disqualifying information from a prospective client, a lawyer considering whether or not to undertake a new matter should limit the initial consultation to only such information as reasonably appears necessary for that purpose. Where the information indicates that a conflict of interest or other reason for non-representation exists, the lawyer should so inform the prospective client or decline the representation. If the prospective client wishes to retain the lawyer, and if consent is possible under Rule 1.7, then consent from all affected present or former clients must be obtained before accepting the representation.

[5] A lawyer may condition a consultation with a prospective client on the person's informed consent that no information disclosed during

the consultation will prohibit the lawyer from representing a different client in the matter. See Rule 1.0(e) for the definition of informed consent. If the agreement expressly so provides, the prospective client may also consent to the lawyer's subsequent use of information received from the prospective client.

[6] Even in the absence of an agreement, under paragraph (c), the lawyer is not prohibited from representing a client with interests adverse to those of the prospective client in the same or a substantially related matter unless the lawyer has received from the prospective client information that could be significantly harmful if used in the matter.

[7] Under paragraph (c), the prohibition in this Rule is imputed to other lawyers as provided in Rule 1.10, but, under paragraph (d)(1), imputation may be avoided if the lawyer obtains the informed consent, confirmed in writing, of both the prospective and affected clients. In the alternative, imputation may be avoided if the conditions of paragraph (d)(2) are met and all disqualified lawyers are timely screened and written notice is promptly given to the prospective client. See Rule 1.0(k) (requirements for screening procedures). Paragraph (d)(2)(i) does not prohibit the screened lawyer from receiving a salary or partnership share established by prior independent agreement, but that lawyer may not receive compensation directly related to the matter in which the lawyer is disqualified.

[8] Notice, including a general description of the subject matter about which the lawyer was consulted, and of the screening procedures employed, generally should be given as soon as practicable after the need for screening becomes apparent.

[9] For the duty of competence of a lawyer who gives assistance on the merits of a matter to a prospective client, see Rule 1.1. For a lawyer's duties when a prospective client entrusts valuables or papers to the lawyer's care, see Rule 1.15.

Definitional Cross-References

"Confirmed in writing" *See* Rule 1.0(b)
"Firm" *See* Rule 1.0(c)
"Informed consent" *See* Rule 1.0(e)
"Knowingly" *See* Rule 1.0(f)
"Reasonable" and "Reasonably" *See* Rule 1.0(h)
"Screened" *See* Rule 1.0(k)
"Written" *See* Rule 1.0(n)

COUNSELOR

RULE 2.1: ADVISOR

In representing a client, a lawyer shall exercise
independent professional judgment and render candid advice.
In rendering advice, a lawyer may refer not only to law but
to other considerations such as moral, economic, social and
political factors, that may be relevant to the client's situation.

Comment

Scope of Advice

[1] A client is entitled to straightforward advice expressing the lawyer's honest assessment. Legal advice often involves unpleasant facts
and alternatives that a client may be disinclined to confront. In presenting advice, a lawyer endeavors to sustain the client's morale and may put
advice in as acceptable a form as honesty permits. However, a lawyer
should not be deterred from giving candid advice by the prospect that
the advice will be unpalatable to the client.

[2] Advice couched in narrow legal terms may be of little value to a
client, especially where practical considerations, such as cost or effects on
other people, are predominant. Purely technical legal advice, therefore,
can sometimes be inadequate. It is proper for a lawyer to refer to relevant
moral and ethical considerations in giving advice. Although a lawyer is
not a moral advisor as such, moral and ethical considerations impinge
upon most legal questions and may decisively influence how the law will
be applied.

[3] A client may expressly or impliedly ask the lawyer for purely
technical advice. When such a request is made by a client experienced in
legal matters, the lawyer may accept it at face value. When such a request
is made by a client inexperienced in legal matters, however, the lawyer's
responsibility as advisor may include indicating that more may be involved than strictly legal considerations.

[4] Matters that go beyond strictly legal questions may also be in
the domain of another profession. Family matters can involve problems
within the professional competence of psychiatry, clinical psychology
or social work; business matters can involve problems within the competence of the accounting profession or of financial specialists. Where
consultation with a professional in another field is itself something a

competent lawyer would recommend, the lawyer should make such a recommendation. At the same time, a lawyer's advice at its best often consists of recommending a course of action in the face of conflicting recommendations of experts.

Offering Advice

[5] In general, a lawyer is not expected to give advice until asked by the client. However, when a lawyer knows that a client proposes a course of action that is likely to result in substantial adverse legal consequences to the client, the lawyer's duty to the client under Rule 1.4 may require that the lawyer offer advice if the client's course of action is related to the representation. Similarly, when a matter is likely to involve litigation, it may be necessary under Rule 1.4 to inform the client of forms of dispute resolution that might constitute reasonable alternatives to litigation. A lawyer ordinarily has no duty to initiate investigation of a client's affairs or to give advice that the client has indicated is unwanted, but a lawyer may initiate advice to a client when doing so appears to be in the client's interest.

RULE 2.2 (DELETED 2002)

RULE 2.3: EVALUATION FOR USE BY THIRD PERSONS

(a) A lawyer may provide an evaluation of a matter affecting a client for the use of someone other than the client if the lawyer reasonably believes that making the evaluation is compatible with other aspects of the lawyer's relationship with the client.

(b) When the lawyer knows or reasonably should know that the evaluation is likely to affect the client's interests materially and adversely, the lawyer shall not provide the evaluation unless the client gives informed consent.

(c) Except as disclosure is authorized in connection with a report of an evaluation, information relating to the evaluation is otherwise protected by Rule 1.6.

Comment
Definition

[1] An evaluation may be performed at the client's direction or when impliedly authorized in order to carry out the representation. See Rule 1.2. Such an evaluation may be for the primary purpose of establishing information for the benefit of third parties; for example, an opinion concerning the title of property rendered at the behest of a vendor for the information of a prospective purchaser, or at the behest of a borrower for the information of a prospective lender. In some situations, the evaluation may be required by a government agency; for example, an opinion concerning the legality of the securities registered for sale under the securities laws. In other instances, the evaluation may be required by a third person, such as a purchaser of a business.

[2] A legal evaluation should be distinguished from an investigation of a person with whom the lawyer does not have a client-lawyer relationship. For example, a lawyer retained by a purchaser to analyze a vendor's title to property does not have a client-lawyer relationship with the vendor. So also, an investigation into a person's affairs by a government lawyer or by special counsel employed by the government, is not an evaluation as that term is used in this Rule. The question is whether the lawyer is retained by the person whose affairs are being examined. When the lawyer is retained by that person, the general rules concerning loyalty to client and preservation of confidences apply, which is not the case if the lawyer is retained by someone else. For this reason, it is essential to identify the person by whom the lawyer is retained. This should be made clear not only to the person under examination, but also to others to whom the results are to be made available.

Duties Owed to Third Person and Client

[3] When the evaluation is intended for the information or use of a third person, a legal duty to that person may or may not arise. That legal question is beyond the scope of this Rule. However, since such an evaluation involves a departure from the normal client-lawyer relationship, careful analysis of the situation is required. The lawyer must be satisfied as a matter of professional judgment that making the evaluation is compatible with other functions undertaken in behalf of the client. For example, if the lawyer is acting as advocate in defending the client against charges of fraud, it would normally be incompatible with that responsi-

bility for the lawyer to perform an evaluation for others concerning the same or a related transaction. Assuming no such impediment is apparent, however, the lawyer should advise the client of the implications of the evaluation, particularly the lawyer's responsibilities to third persons and the duty to disseminate the findings.

Access to and Disclosure of Information

[4] The quality of an evaluation depends on the freedom and extent of the investigation upon which it is based. Ordinarily a lawyer should have whatever latitude of investigation seems necessary as a matter of professional judgment. Under some circumstances, however, the terms of the evaluation may be limited. For example, certain issues or sources may be categorically excluded, or the scope of search may be limited by time constraints or the noncooperation of persons having relevant information. Any such limitations that are material to the evaluation should be described in the report. If after a lawyer has commenced an evaluation, the client refuses to comply with the terms upon which it was understood the evaluation was to have been made, the lawyer's obligations are determined by law, having reference to the terms of the client's agreement and the surrounding circumstances. In no circumstances is the lawyer permitted to knowingly make a false statement of material fact or law in providing an evaluation under this Rule. See Rule 4.1.

Obtaining Client's Informed Consent

[5] Information relating to an evaluation is protected by Rule 1.6. In many situations, providing an evaluation to a third party poses no significant risk to the client; thus, the lawyer may be impliedly authorized to disclose information to carry out the representation. See Rule 1.6(a). Where, however, it is reasonably likely that providing the evaluation will affect the client's interests materially and adversely, the lawyer must first obtain the client's consent after the client has been adequately informed concerning the important possible effects on the client's interests. See Rules 1.6(a) and 1.0(e).

Financial Auditors' Requests for Information

[6] When a question concerning the legal situation of a client arises at the instance of the client's financial auditor and the question is referred to the lawyer, the lawyer's response may be made in accordance with procedures recognized in the legal profession. Such a procedure is set forth

in the American Bar Association Statement of Policy Regarding Lawyers' Responses to Auditors' Requests for Information, adopted in 1975.

Definitional Cross-References

"Informed consent" *See* Rule 1.0(e)
"Knows" *See* Rule 1.0(f)
"Reasonably believes" *See* Rule 1.0(i)
"Reasonably should know" *See* Rule 1.0(j)

RULE 2.4: LAWYER SERVING AS THIRD-PARTY NEUTRAL

(a) A lawyer serves as a third-party neutral when the lawyer assists two or more persons who are not clients of the lawyer to reach a resolution of a dispute or other matter that has arisen between them. Service as a third-party neutral may include service as an arbitrator, a mediator or in such other capacity as will enable the lawyer to assist the parties to resolve the matter.

(b) A lawyer serving as a third-party neutral shall inform unrepresented parties that the lawyer is not representing them. When the lawyer knows or reasonably should know that a party does not understand the lawyer's role in the matter, the lawyer shall explain the difference between the lawyer's role as a third-party neutral and a lawyer's role as one who represents a client.

Comment

[1] Alternative dispute resolution has become a substantial part of the civil justice system. Aside from representing clients in dispute-resolution processes, lawyers often serve as third-party neutrals. A third-party neutral is a person, such as a mediator, arbitrator, conciliator or evaluator, who assists the parties, represented or unrepresented, in the resolution of a dispute or in the arrangement of a transaction. Whether a third-party neutral serves primarily as a facilitator, evaluator or decisionmaker depends on the particular process that is either selected by the parties or mandated by a court.

[2] The role of a third-party neutral is not unique to lawyers, although, in some court-connected contexts, only lawyers are allowed to serve in this role or to handle certain types of cases. In performing this role, the lawyer may be subject to court rules or other law that apply ei-

ther to third-party neutrals generally or to lawyers serving as third-party neutrals. Lawyer-neutrals may also be subject to various codes of ethics, such as the Code of Ethics for Arbitrators in Commercial Disputes prepared by a joint committee of the American Bar Association and the American Arbitration Association or the Model Standards of Conduct for Mediators jointly prepared by the American Bar Association, the American Arbitration Association and the Society of Professionals in Dispute Resolution.

[3] Unlike nonlawyers who serve as third-party neutrals, lawyers serving in this role may experience unique problems as a result of differences between the role of a third-party neutral and a lawyer's service as a client representative. The potential for confusion is significant when the parties are unrepresented in the process. Thus, paragraph (b) requires a lawyer-neutral to inform unrepresented parties that the lawyer is not representing them. For some parties, particularly parties who frequently use dispute-resolution processes, this information will be sufficient. For others, particularly those who are using the process for the first time, more information will be required. Where appropriate, the lawyer should inform unrepresented parties of the important differences between the lawyer's role as third-party neutral and a lawyer's role as a client representative, including the inapplicability of the attorney-client evidentiary privilege. The extent of disclosure required under this paragraph will depend on the particular parties involved and the subject matter of the proceeding, as well as the particular features of the dispute-resolution process selected.

[4] A lawyer who serves as a third-party neutral subsequently may be asked to serve as a lawyer representing a client in the same matter. The conflicts of interest that arise for both the individual lawyer and the lawyer's law firm are addressed in Rule 1.12.

[5] Lawyers who represent clients in alternative dispute-resolution processes are governed by the Rules of Professional Conduct. When the dispute-resolution process takes place before a tribunal, as in binding arbitration (see Rule 1.0(m)), the lawyer's duty of candor is governed by Rule 3.3. Otherwise, the lawyer's duty of candor toward both the third-party neutral and other parties is governed by Rule 4.1.

Definitional Cross-References
"Knows" *See* Rule 1.0(f)
"Reasonably should know" *See* Rule 1.0(j)

ADVOCATE

RULE 3.1: MERITORIOUS CLAIMS AND CONTENTIONS

A lawyer shall not bring or defend a proceeding, or assert or controvert an issue therein, unless there is a basis in law and fact for doing so that is not frivolous, which includes a good faith argument for an extension, modification or reversal of existing law. A lawyer for the defendant in a criminal proceeding, or the respondent in a proceeding that could result in incarceration, may nevertheless so defend the proceeding as to require that every element of the case be established.

Comment

[1] The advocate has a duty to use legal procedure for the fullest benefit of the client's cause, but also a duty not to abuse legal procedure. The law, both procedural and substantive, establishes the limits within which an advocate may proceed. However, the law is not always clear and never is static. Accordingly, in determining the proper scope of advocacy, account must be taken of the law's ambiguities and potential for change.

[2] The filing of an action or defense or similar action taken for a client is not frivolous merely because the facts have not first been fully substantiated or because the lawyer expects to develop vital evidence only by discovery. What is required of lawyers, however, is that they inform themselves about the facts of their clients' cases and the applicable law and determine that they can make good faith arguments in support of their clients' positions. Such action is not frivolous even though the lawyer believes that the client's position ultimately will not prevail. The action is frivolous, however, if the lawyer is unable either to make a good faith argument on the merits of the action taken or to support the action taken by a good faith argument for an extension, modification or reversal of existing law.

[3] The lawyer's obligations under this Rule are subordinate to federal or state constitutional law that entitles a defendant in a criminal matter to the assistance of counsel in presenting a claim or contention that otherwise would be prohibited by this Rule.

RULE 3.2: EXPEDITING LITIGATION

A lawyer shall make reasonable efforts to expedite litigation consistent with the interests of the client.

Comment

[1] Dilatory practices bring the administration of justice into disrepute. Although there will be occasions when a lawyer may properly seek a postponement for personal reasons, it is not proper for a lawyer to routinely fail to expedite litigation solely for the convenience of the advocates. Nor will a failure to expedite be reasonable if done for the purpose of frustrating an opposing party's attempt to obtain rightful redress or repose. It is not a justification that similar conduct is often tolerated by the bench and bar. The question is whether a competent lawyer acting in good faith would regard the course of action as having some substantial purpose other than delay. Realizing financial or other benefit from otherwise improper delay in litigation is not a legitimate interest of the client.

Definitional Cross-References

"Reasonable" *See* Rule 1.0(h)

RULE 3.3: CANDOR TOWARD THE TRIBUNAL

(a) A lawyer shall not knowingly:

(1) make a false statement of fact or law to a tribunal or fail to correct a false statement of material fact or law previously made to the tribunal by the lawyer;

(2) fail to disclose to the tribunal legal authority in the controlling jurisdiction known to the lawyer to be directly adverse to the position of the client and not disclosed by opposing counsel; or

(3) offer evidence that the lawyer knows to be false. If a lawyer, the lawyer's client, or a witness called by the lawyer, has offered material evidence and the lawyer comes to know of its falsity, the lawyer shall take reasonable remedial measures, including, if necessary, disclosure to the tribunal. A lawyer may refuse to offer evidence, other than the testimony of a defendant in a criminal matter, that the lawyer reasonably believes is false.

(b) A lawyer who represents a client in an adjudicative proceeding and who knows that a person intends to engage, is engaging or has engaged in criminal or fraudulent conduct related to the proceeding shall take reasonable remedial measures, including, if necessary, disclosure to the tribunal.

(c) The duties stated in paragraphs (a) and (b) continue to the conclusion of the proceeding, and apply even if compliance requires disclosure of information otherwise protected by Rule 1.6.

(d) In an ex parte proceeding, a lawyer shall inform the tribunal of all material facts known to the lawyer that will enable the tribunal to make an informed decision, whether or not the facts are adverse.

Comment

[1] This Rule governs the conduct of a lawyer who is representing a client in the proceedings of a tribunal. See Rule 1.0(m) for the definition of "tribunal." It also applies when the lawyer is representing a client in an ancillary proceeding conducted pursuant to the tribunal's adjudicative authority, such as a deposition. Thus, for example, paragraph (a) (3) requires a lawyer to take reasonable remedial measures if the lawyer comes to know that a client who is testifying in a deposition has offered evidence that is false.

[2] This Rule sets forth the special duties of lawyers as officers of the court to avoid conduct that undermines the integrity of the adjudicative process. A lawyer acting as an advocate in an adjudicative proceeding has an obligation to present the client's case with persuasive force. Performance of that duty while maintaining confidences of the client, however, is qualified by the advocate's duty of candor to the tribunal. Consequently, although a lawyer in an adversary proceeding is not required to present an impartial exposition of the law or to vouch for the evidence submitted in a cause, the lawyer must not allow the tribunal to be misled by false statements of law or fact or evidence that the lawyer knows to be false.

Representations by a Lawyer

[3] An advocate is responsible for pleadings and other documents prepared for litigation, but is usually not required to have personal knowledge of matters asserted therein, for litigation documents ordinarily present assertions by the client, or by someone on the client's behalf,

and not assertions by the lawyer. Compare Rule 3.1. However, an assertion purporting to be on the lawyer's own knowledge, as in an affidavit by the lawyer or in a statement in open court, may properly be made only when the lawyer knows the assertion is true or believes it to be true on the basis of a reasonably diligent inquiry. There are circumstances where failure to make a disclosure is the equivalent of an affirmative misrepresentation. The obligation prescribed in Rule 1.2(d) not to counsel a client to commit or assist the client in committing a fraud applies in litigation. Regarding compliance with Rule 1.2(d), see the Comment to that Rule. See also the Comment to Rule 8.4(b).

Legal Argument

[4] Legal argument based on a knowingly false representation of law constitutes dishonesty toward the tribunal. A lawyer is not required to make a disinterested exposition of the law, but must recognize the existence of pertinent legal authorities. Furthermore, as stated in paragraph (a)(2), an advocate has a duty to disclose directly adverse authority in the controlling jurisdiction that has not been disclosed by the opposing party. The underlying concept is that legal argument is a discussion seeking to determine the legal premises properly applicable to the case.

Offering Evidence

[5] Paragraph (a)(3) requires that the lawyer refuse to offer evidence that the lawyer knows to be false, regardless of the client's wishes. This duty is premised on the lawyer's obligation as an officer of the court to prevent the trier of fact from being misled by false evidence. A lawyer does not violate this Rule if the lawyer offers the evidence for the purpose of establishing its falsity.

[6] If a lawyer knows that the client intends to testify falsely or wants the lawyer to introduce false evidence, the lawyer should seek to persuade the client that the evidence should not be offered. If the persuasion is ineffective and the lawyer continues to represent the client, the lawyer must refuse to offer the false evidence. If only a portion of a witness's testimony will be false, the lawyer may call the witness to testify but may not elicit or otherwise permit the witness to present the testimony that the lawyer knows is false.

[7] The duties stated in paragraphs (a) and (b) apply to all lawyers, including defense counsel in criminal cases. In some jurisdictions, however, courts have required counsel to present the accused as a witness

or to give a narrative statement if the accused so desires, even if counsel knows that the testimony or statement will be false. The obligation of the advocate under the Rules of Professional Conduct is subordinate to such requirements. See also Comment [9].

[8] The prohibition against offering false evidence only applies if the lawyer knows that the evidence is false. A lawyer's reasonable belief that evidence is false does not preclude its presentation to the trier of fact. A lawyer's knowledge that evidence is false, however, can be inferred from the circumstances. See Rule 1.0(f). Thus, although a lawyer should resolve doubts about the veracity of testimony or other evidence in favor of the client, the lawyer cannot ignore an obvious falsehood.

[9] Although paragraph (a)(3) only prohibits a lawyer from offering evidence the lawyer knows to be false, it permits the lawyer to refuse to offer testimony or other proof that the lawyer reasonably believes is false. Offering such proof may reflect adversely on the lawyer's ability to discriminate in the quality of evidence and thus impair the lawyer's effectiveness as an advocate. Because of the special protections historically provided criminal defendants, however, this Rule does not permit a lawyer to refuse to offer the testimony of such a client where the lawyer reasonably believes but does not know that the testimony will be false. Unless the lawyer knows the testimony will be false, the lawyer must honor the client's decision to testify. See also Comment [7].

Remedial Measures

[10] Having offered material evidence in the belief that it was true, a lawyer may subsequently come to know that the evidence is false. Or, a lawyer may be surprised when the lawyer's client, or another witness called by the lawyer, offers testimony the lawyer knows to be false, either during the lawyer's direct examination or in response to cross-examination by the opposing lawyer. In such situations or if the lawyer knows of the falsity of testimony elicited from the client during a deposition, the lawyer must take reasonable remedial measures. In such situations, the advocate's proper course is to remonstrate with the client confidentially, advise the client of the lawyer's duty of candor to the tribunal and seek the client's cooperation with respect to the withdrawal or correction of the false statements or evidence. If that fails, the advocate must take further remedial action. If withdrawal from the representation is not permitted or will not undo the effect of the false evidence, the advocate must make such disclosure to the tribunal as is reasonably necessary to remedy

the situation, even if doing so requires the lawyer to reveal information that otherwise would be protected by Rule 1.6. It is for the tribunal then to determine what should be done—making a statement about the matter to the trier of fact, ordering a mistrial or perhaps nothing.

[11] The disclosure of a client's false testimony can result in grave consequences to the client, including not only a sense of betrayal but also loss of the case and perhaps a prosecution for perjury. But the alternative is that the lawyer cooperate in deceiving the court, thereby subverting the truth-finding process which the adversary system is designed to implement. See Rule 1.2(d). Furthermore, unless it is clearly understood that the lawyer will act upon the duty to disclose the existence of false evidence, the client can simply reject the lawyer's advice to reveal the false evidence and insist that the lawyer keep silent. Thus the client could in effect coerce the lawyer into being a party to fraud on the court.

Preserving Integrity of Adjudicative Process

[12] Lawyers have a special obligation to protect a tribunal against criminal or fraudulent conduct that undermines the integrity of the adjudicative process, such as bribing, intimidating or otherwise unlawfully communicating with a witness, juror, court official or other participant in the proceeding, unlawfully destroying or concealing documents or other evidence or failing to disclose information to the tribunal when required by law to do so. Thus, paragraph (b) requires a lawyer to take reasonable remedial measures, including disclosure if necessary, whenever the lawyer knows that a person, including the lawyer's client, intends to engage, is engaging or has engaged in criminal or fraudulent conduct related to the proceeding.

Duration of Obligation

[13] A practical time limit on the obligation to rectify false evidence or false statements of law and fact has to be established. The conclusion of the proceeding is a reasonably definite point for the termination of the obligation. A proceeding has concluded within the meaning of this Rule when a final judgment in the proceeding has been affirmed on appeal or the time for review has passed.

Ex Parte Proceedings

[14] Ordinarily, an advocate has the limited responsibility of presenting one side of the matters that a tribunal should consider in reaching a

decision; the conflicting position is expected to be presented by the opposing party. However, in any ex parte proceeding, such as an application for a temporary restraining order, there is no balance of presentation by opposing advocates. The object of an ex parte proceeding is nevertheless to yield a substantially just result. The judge has an affirmative responsibility to accord the absent party just consideration. The lawyer for the represented party has the correlative duty to make disclosures of material facts known to the lawyer and that the lawyer reasonably believes are necessary to an informed decision.

Withdrawal

[15] Normally, a lawyer's compliance with the duty of candor imposed by this Rule does not require that the lawyer withdraw from the representation of a client whose interests will be or have been adversely affected by the lawyer's disclosure. The lawyer may, however, be required by Rule 1.16(a) to seek permission of the tribunal to withdraw if the lawyer's compliance with this Rule's duty of candor results in such an extreme deterioration of the client-lawyer relationship that the lawyer can no longer competently represent the client. Also see Rule 1.16(b) for the circumstances in which a lawyer will be permitted to seek a tribunal's permission to withdraw. In connection with a request for permission to withdraw that is premised on a client's misconduct, a lawyer may reveal information relating to the representation only to the extent reasonably necessary to comply with this Rule or as otherwise permitted by Rule 1.6.

Definitional Cross-References

"Fraudulent" *See* Rule 1.0(d)
"Knowingly" and "Known" and "Knows" *See* Rule 1.0(f)
"Reasonable" *See* Rule 1.0(h)
"Reasonably believes" *See* Rule 1.0(i)
"Tribunal" *See* Rule 1.0(m)

RULE 3.4: FAIRNESS TO OPPOSING PARTY AND COUNSEL

A lawyer shall not:
(a) unlawfully obstruct another party's access to evidence or unlawfully alter, destroy or conceal a document or other material

having potential evidentiary value. A lawyer shall not counsel or assist another person to do any such act;

(b) falsify evidence, counsel or assist a witness to testify falsely, or offer an inducement to a witness that is prohibited by law;

(c) knowingly disobey an obligation under the rules of a tribunal, except for an open refusal based on an assertion that no valid obligation exists;

(d) in pretrial procedure, make a frivolous discovery request or fail to make reasonably diligent effort to comply with a legally proper discovery request by an opposing party;

(e) in trial, allude to any matter that the lawyer does not reasonably believe is relevant or that will not be supported by admissible evidence, assert personal knowledge of facts in issue except when testifying as a witness, or state a personal opinion as to the justness of a cause, the credibility of a witness, the culpability of a civil litigant or the guilt or innocence of an accused; or

(f) request a person other than a client to refrain from voluntarily giving relevant information to another party unless:

(1) the person is a relative or an employee or other agent of a client; and

(2) the lawyer reasonably believes that the person's interests will not be adversely affected by refraining from giving such information.

Comment

[1] The procedure of the adversary system contemplates that the evidence in a case is to be marshalled competitively by the contending parties. Fair competition in the adversary system is secured by prohibitions against destruction or concealment of evidence, improperly influencing witnesses, obstructive tactics in discovery procedure, and the like.

[2] Documents and other items of evidence are often essential to establish a claim or defense. Subject to evidentiary privileges, the right of an opposing party, including the government, to obtain evidence through discovery or subpoena is an important procedural right. The exercise of that right can be frustrated if relevant material is altered, concealed or destroyed. Applicable law in many jurisdictions makes it an offense to destroy material for purpose of impairing its availability in a pending proceeding or one whose commencement can be foreseen. Falsifying evi-

dence is also generally a criminal offense. Paragraph (a) applies to evidentiary material generally, including computerized information. Applicable law may permit a lawyer to take temporary possession of physical evidence of client crimes for the purpose of conducting a limited examination that will not alter or destroy material characteristics of the evidence. In such a case, applicable law may require the lawyer to turn the evidence over to the police or other prosecuting authority, depending on the circumstances.

[3] With regard to paragraph (b), it is not improper to pay a witness's expenses or to compensate an expert witness on terms permitted by law. The common law rule in most jurisdictions is that it is improper to pay an occurrence witness any fee for testifying and that it is improper to pay an expert witness a contingent fee.

[4] Paragraph (f) permits a lawyer to advise employees of a client to refrain from giving information to another party, for the employees may identify their interests with those of the client. See also Rule 4.2.

Definitional Cross-References

"Knowingly" *See* Rule 1.0(f)
"Reasonably" *See* Rule 1.0(h)
"Reasonably believes" *See* Rule 1.0(i)
"Tribunal" *See* Rule 1.0(m)

RULE 3.5: IMPARTIALITY AND DECORUM OF THE TRIBUNAL

A lawyer shall not:

(a) seek to influence a judge, juror, prospective juror or other official by means prohibited by law;

(b) communicate ex parte with such a person during the proceeding unless authorized to do so by law or court order;

(c) communicate with a juror or prospective juror after discharge of the jury if:

(1) the communication is prohibited by law or court order;

(2) the juror has made known to the lawyer a desire not to communicate; or

(3) the communication involves misrepresentation, coercion, duress or harassment; or

(d) engage in conduct intended to disrupt a tribunal.

Comment

[1] Many forms of improper influence upon a tribunal are proscribed by criminal law. Others are specified in the ABA Model Code of Judicial Conduct, with which an advocate should be familiar. A lawyer is required to avoid contributing to a violation of such provisions.

[2] During a proceeding a lawyer may not communicate ex parte with persons serving in an official capacity in the proceeding, such as judges, masters or jurors, unless authorized to do so by law or court order.

[3] A lawyer may on occasion want to communicate with a juror or prospective juror after the jury has been discharged. The lawyer may do so unless the communication is prohibited by law or a court order but must respect the desire of the juror not to talk with the lawyer. The lawyer may not engage in improper conduct during the communication.

[4] The advocate's function is to present evidence and argument so that the cause may be decided according to law. Refraining from abusive or obstreperous conduct is a corollary of the advocate's right to speak on behalf of litigants. A lawyer may stand firm against abuse by a judge but should avoid reciprocation; the judge's default is no justification for similar dereliction by an advocate. An advocate can present the cause, protect the record for subsequent review and preserve professional integrity by patient firmness no less effectively than by belligerence or theatrics.

[5] The duty to refrain from disruptive conduct applies to any proceeding of a tribunal, including a deposition. See Rule 1.0(m).

Definitional Cross-References

"Known" *See* Rule 1.0(f)
"Tribunal" *See* Rule 1.0(m)

RULE 3.6: TRIAL PUBLICITY

(a) A lawyer who is participating or has participated in the investigation or litigation of a matter shall not make an extrajudicial statement that the lawyer knows or reasonably should know will be disseminated by means of public communication and will have a substantial likelihood of materially prejudicing an adjudicative proceeding in the matter.

(b) Notwithstanding paragraph (a), a lawyer may state:

(1) the claim, offense or defense involved and, except when prohibited by law, the identity of the persons involved;

(2) information contained in a public record;

(3) that an investigation of a matter is in progress;

(4) the scheduling or result of any step in litigation;

(5) a request for assistance in obtaining evidence and information necessary thereto;

(6) a warning of danger concerning the behavior of a person involved, when there is reason to believe that there exists the likelihood of substantial harm to an individual or to the public interest; and

(7) in a criminal case, in addition to subparagraphs (1) through (6):

    (i) the identity, residence, occupation and family status of the accused;

    (ii) if the accused has not been apprehended, information necessary to aid in apprehension of that person;

    (iii) the fact, time and place of arrest; and

    (iv) the identity of investigating and arresting officers or agencies and the length of the investigation.

(c) Notwithstanding paragraph (a), a lawyer may make a statement that a reasonable lawyer would believe is required to protect a client from the substantial undue prejudicial effect of recent publicity not initiated by the lawyer or the lawyer's client. A statement made pursuant to this paragraph shall be limited to such information as is necessary to mitigate the recent adverse publicity.

(d) No lawyer associated in a firm or government agency with a lawyer subject to paragraph (a) shall make a statement prohibited by paragraph (a).

Comment

[1] It is difficult to strike a balance between protecting the right to a fair trial and safeguarding the right of free expression. Preserving the right to a fair trial necessarily entails some curtailment of the information that may be disseminated about a party prior to trial, particularly where trial by jury is involved. If there were no such limits, the result would be the practical nullification of the protective effect of the rules of forensic decorum and the exclusionary rules of evidence. On the other hand, there are vital social interests served by the free dissemination of information about events having legal consequences and about legal proceedings

themselves. The public has a right to know about threats to its safety and measures aimed at assuring its security. It also has a legitimate interest in the conduct of judicial proceedings, particularly in matters of general public concern. Furthermore, the subject matter of legal proceedings is often of direct significance in debate and deliberation over questions of public policy.

[2] Special rules of confidentiality may validly govern proceedings in juvenile, domestic relations and mental disability proceedings, and perhaps other types of litigation. Rule 3.4(c) requires compliance with such rules.

[3] The Rule sets forth a basic general prohibition against a lawyer's making statements that the lawyer knows or should know will have a substantial likelihood of materially prejudicing an adjudicative proceeding. Recognizing that the public value of informed commentary is great and the likelihood of prejudice to a proceeding by the commentary of a lawyer who is not involved in the proceeding is small, the Rule applies only to lawyers who are, or who have been involved in the investigation or litigation of a case, and their associates.

[4] Paragraph (b) identifies specific matters about which a lawyer's statements would not ordinarily be considered to present a substantial likelihood of material prejudice, and should not in any event be considered prohibited by the general prohibition of paragraph (a). Paragraph (b) is not intended to be an exhaustive listing of the subjects upon which a lawyer may make a statement, but statements on other matters may be subject to paragraph (a).

[5] There are, on the other hand, certain subjects that are more likely than not to have a material prejudicial effect on a proceeding, particularly when they refer to a civil matter triable to a jury, a criminal matter, or any other proceeding that could result in incarceration. These subjects relate to:

(1) the character, credibility, reputation or criminal record of a party, suspect in a criminal investigation or witness, or the identity of a witness, or the expected testimony of a party or witness;

(2) in a criminal case or proceeding that could result in incarceration, the possibility of a plea of guilty to the offense or the existence or contents of any confession, admission, or statement given by a defendant or suspect or that person's refusal or failure to make a statement;

(3) the performance or results of any examination or test or the re-

fusal or failure of a person to submit to an examination or test, or the identity or nature of physical evidence expected to be presented;

(4) any opinion as to the guilt or innocence of a defendant or suspect in a criminal case or proceeding that could result in incarceration;

(5) information that the lawyer knows or reasonably should know is likely to be inadmissible as evidence in a trial and that would, if disclosed, create a substantial risk of prejudicing an impartial trial; or

(6) the fact that a defendant has been charged with a crime, unless there is included therein a statement explaining that the charge is merely an accusation and that the defendant is presumed innocent until and unless proven guilty.

[6] Another relevant factor in determining prejudice is the nature of the proceeding involved. Criminal jury trials will be most sensitive to extrajudicial speech. Civil trials may be less sensitive. Non-jury hearings and arbitration proceedings may be even less affected. The Rule will still place limitations on prejudicial comments in these cases, but the likelihood of prejudice may be different depending on the type of proceeding.

[7] Finally, extrajudicial statements that might otherwise raise a question under this Rule may be permissible when they are made in response to statements made publicly by another party, another party's lawyer, or third persons, where a reasonable lawyer would believe a public response is required in order to avoid prejudice to the lawyer's client. When prejudicial statements have been publicly made by others, responsive statements may have the salutary effect of lessening any resulting adverse impact on the adjudicative proceeding. Such responsive statements should be limited to contain only such information as is necessary to mitigate undue prejudice created by the statements made by others.

[8] See Rule 3.8(f) for additional duties of prosecutors in connection with extrajudicial statements about criminal proceedings.

Definitional Cross-References

"Firm" *See* Rule 1.0(c)
"Knows" *See* Rule 1.0(f)
"Reasonable" *See* Rule 1.0(h)
"Reasonably should know" *See* Rule 1.0(j)
"Substantial" *See* Rule 1.0(l)

RULE 3.7: LAWYER AS WITNESS

(a) A lawyer shall not act as advocate at a trial in which the lawyer is likely to be a necessary witness unless:

(1) the testimony relates to an uncontested issue;

(2) the testimony relates to the nature and value of legal services rendered in the case; or

(3) disqualification of the lawyer would work substantial hardship on the client.

(b) A lawyer may act as advocate in a trial in which another lawyer in the lawyer's firm is likely to be called as a witness unless precluded from doing so by Rule 1.7 or Rule 1.9.

Comment

[1] Combining the roles of advocate and witness can prejudice the tribunal and the opposing party and can also involve a conflict of interest between the lawyer and client.

Advocate-Witness Rule

[2] The tribunal has proper objection when the trier of fact may be confused or misled by a lawyer serving as both advocate and witness. The opposing party has proper objection where the combination of roles may prejudice that party's rights in the litigation. A witness is required to testify on the basis of personal knowledge, while an advocate is expected to explain and comment on evidence given by others. It may not be clear whether a statement by an advocate-witness should be taken as proof or as an analysis of the proof.

[3] To protect the tribunal, paragraph (a) prohibits a lawyer from simultaneously serving as advocate and necessary witness except in those circumstances specified in paragraphs (a)(1) through (a)(3). Paragraph (a)(1) recognizes that if the testimony will be uncontested, the ambiguities in the dual role are purely theoretical. Paragraph (a)(2) recognizes that where the testimony concerns the extent and value of legal services rendered in the action in which the testimony is offered, permitting the lawyers to testify avoids the need for a second trial with new counsel to resolve that issue. Moreover, in such a situation the judge has firsthand knowledge of the matter in issue; hence, there is less dependence on the adversary process to test the credibility of the testimony.

[4] Apart from these two exceptions, paragraph (a)(3) recognizes that a balancing is required between the interests of the client and those of

the tribunal and the opposing party. Whether the tribunal is likely to be misled or the opposing party is likely to suffer prejudice depends on the nature of the case, the importance and probable tenor of the lawyer's testimony, and the probability that the lawyer's testimony will conflict with that of other witnesses. Even if there is risk of such prejudice, in determining whether the lawyer should be disqualified, due regard must be given to the effect of disqualification on the lawyer's client. It is relevant that one or both parties could reasonably foresee that the lawyer would probably be a witness. The conflict of interest principles stated in Rules 1.7, 1.9 and 1.10 have no application to this aspect of the problem.

[5] Because the tribunal is not likely to be misled when a lawyer acts as advocate in a trial in which another lawyer in the lawyer's firm will testify as a necessary witness, paragraph (b) permits the lawyer to do so except in situations involving a conflict of interest.

Conflict of Interest

[6] In determining if it is permissible to act as advocate in a trial in which the lawyer will be a necessary witness, the lawyer must also consider that the dual role may give rise to a conflict of interest that will require compliance with Rules 1.7 or 1.9. For example, if there is likely to be substantial conflict between the testimony of the client and that of the lawyer the representation involves a conflict of interest that requires compliance with Rule 1.7. This would be true even though the lawyer might not be prohibited by paragraph (a) from simultaneously serving as advocate and witness because the lawyer's disqualification would work a substantial hardship on the client. Similarly, a lawyer who might be permitted to simultaneously serve as an advocate and a witness by paragraph (a)(3) might be precluded from doing so by Rule 1.9. The problem can arise whether the lawyer is called as a witness on behalf of the client or is called by the opposing party. Determining whether or not such a conflict exists is primarily the responsibility of the lawyer involved. If there is a conflict of interest, the lawyer must secure the client's informed consent, confirmed in writing. In some cases, the lawyer will be precluded from seeking the client's consent. See Rule 1.7. See Rule 1.0(b) for the definition of "confirmed in writing" and Rule 1.0(e) for the definition of "informed consent."

[7] Paragraph (b) provides that a lawyer is not disqualified from serving as an advocate because a lawyer with whom the lawyer is associated in a firm is precluded from doing so by paragraph (a). If, however,

the testifying lawyer would also be disqualified by Rule 1.7 or Rule 1.9 from representing the client in the matter, other lawyers in the firm will be precluded from representing the client by Rule 1.10 unless the client gives informed consent under the conditions stated in Rule 1.7.

Definitional Cross-References

"Firm" *See* Rule 1.0(c)
"Substantial" *See* Rule 1.0(l)

RULE 3.8: SPECIAL RESPONSIBILITIES OF A PROSECUTOR

The prosecutor in a criminal case shall:

(a) refrain from prosecuting a charge that the prosecutor knows is not supported by probable cause;

(b) make reasonable efforts to assure that the accused has been advised of the right to, and the procedure for obtaining, counsel and has been given reasonable opportunity to obtain counsel;

(c) not seek to obtain from an unrepresented accused a waiver of important pretrial rights, such as the right to a preliminary hearing;

(d) make timely disclosure to the defense of all evidence or information known to the prosecutor that tends to negate the guilt of the accused or mitigates the offense, and, in connection with sentencing, disclose to the defense and to the tribunal all unprivileged mitigating information known to the prosecutor, except when the prosecutor is relieved of this responsibility by a protective order of the tribunal;

(e) not subpoena a lawyer in a grand jury or other criminal proceeding to present evidence about a past or present client unless the prosecutor reasonably believes:

(1) the information sought is not protected from disclosure by any applicable privilege;

(2) the evidence sought is essential to the successful completion of an ongoing investigation or prosecution; and

(3) there is no other feasible alternative to obtain the information;

(f) except for statements that are necessary to inform the public of the nature and extent of the prosecutor's action and that serve a legitimate law enforcement purpose, refrain from making extrajudicial comments that have a substantial likelihood of heightening public condemnation of the accused and exercise reasonable care to prevent investigators, law enforcement personnel, employees or other persons assisting or associated with the prosecutor in a criminal case from making an extrajudicial statement that the prosecutor would be prohibited from making under Rule 3.6 or this Rule.

(g) When a prosecutor knows of new, credible and material evidence creating a reasonable likelihood that a convicted defendant did not commit an offense of which the defendant was convicted, the prosecutor shall:

> (1) promptly disclose that evidence to an appropriate court or authority, and

> (2) if the conviction was obtained in the prosecutor's jurisdiction,

>> (i) promptly disclose that evidence to the defendant unless a court authorizes delay, and

>> (ii) undertake further investigation, or make reasonable efforts to cause an investigation, to determine whether the defendant was convicted of an offense that the defendant did not commit.

(h) When a prosecutor knows of clear and convincing evidence establishing that a defendant in the prosecutor's jurisdiction was convicted of an offense that the defendant did not commit, the prosecutor shall seek to remedy the conviction.

Comment

[1] A prosecutor has the responsibility of a minister of justice and not simply that of an advocate. This responsibility carries with it specific obligations to see that the defendant is accorded procedural justice, that guilt is decided upon the basis of sufficient evidence, and that special precautions are taken to prevent and to rectify the conviction of innocent persons. The extent of mandated remedial action is a matter of debate and varies in different jurisdictions. Many jurisdictions have adopted the ABA Standards for Criminal Justice Relating to the Prosecution Function, which are the product of prolonged and careful deliberation by lawyers experienced in both criminal prosecution and defense. Competent representation of the sovereignty may require a prosecutor to undertake some procedural and remedial measures as a matter of obligation. Applicable

law may require other measures by the prosecutor and knowing disregard of those obligations or a systematic abuse of prosecutorial discretion could constitute a violation of Rule 8.4.

[2] In some jurisdictions, a defendant may waive a preliminary hearing and thereby lose a valuable opportunity to challenge probable cause. Accordingly, prosecutors should not seek to obtain waivers of preliminary hearings or other important pretrial rights from unrepresented accused persons. Paragraph (c) does not apply, however, to an accused appearing *pro se* with the approval of the tribunal. Nor does it forbid the lawful questioning of an uncharged suspect who has knowingly waived the rights to counsel and silence.

[3] The exception in paragraph (d) recognizes that a prosecutor may seek an appropriate protective order from the tribunal if disclosure of information to the defense could result in substantial harm to an individual or to the public interest.

[4] Paragraph (e) is intended to limit the issuance of lawyer subpoenas in grand jury and other criminal proceedings to those situations in which there is a genuine need to intrude into the client-lawyer relationship.

[5] Paragraph (f) supplements Rule 3.6, which prohibits extrajudicial statements that have a substantial likelihood of prejudicing an adjudicatory proceeding. In the context of a criminal prosecution, a prosecutor's extrajudicial statement can create the additional problem of increasing public condemnation of the accused. Although the announcement of an indictment, for example, will necessarily have severe consequences for the accused, a prosecutor can, and should, avoid comments which have no legitimate law enforcement purpose and have a substantial likelihood of increasing public opprobrium of the accused. Nothing in this Comment is intended to restrict the statements which a prosecutor may make which comply with Rule 3.6(b) or 3.6(c).

[6] Like other lawyers, prosecutors are subject to Rules 5.1 and 5.3, which relate to responsibilities regarding lawyers and nonlawyers who work for or are associated with the lawyer's office. Paragraph (f) reminds the prosecutor of the importance of these obligations in connection with the unique dangers of improper extrajudicial statements in a criminal case. In addition, paragraph (f) requires a prosecutor to exercise reasonable care to prevent persons assisting or associated with the prosecutor from making improper extrajudicial statements, even when such persons are not under the direct supervision of the prosecutor. Ordinarily,

the reasonable care standard will be satisfied if the prosecutor issues the appropriate cautions to law enforcement personnel and other relevant individuals.

[7] When a prosecutor knows of new, credible and material evidence creating a reasonable likelihood that a person outside the prosecutor's jurisdiction was convicted of a crime that the person did not commit, paragraph (g) requires prompt disclosure to the court or other appropriate authority, such as the chief prosecutor of the jurisdiction where the conviction occurred. If the conviction was obtained in the prosecutor's jurisdiction, paragraph (g) requires the prosecutor to examine the evidence and undertake further investigation to determine whether the defendant is in fact innocent or make reasonable efforts to cause another appropriate authority to undertake the necessary investigation, and to promptly disclose the evidence to the court and, absent court-authorized delay, to the defendant. Consistent with the objectives of Rules 4.2 and 4.3, disclosure to a represented defendant must be made through the defendant's counsel, and, in the case of an unrepresented defendant, would ordinarily be accompanied by a request to a court for the appointment of counsel to assist the defendant in taking such legal measures as may be appropriate.

[8] Under paragraph (h), once the prosecutor knows of clear and convincing evidence that the defendant was convicted of an offense that the defendant did not commit, the prosecutor must seek to remedy the conviction. Necessary steps may include disclosure of the evidence to the defendant, requesting that the court appoint counsel for an unrepresented indigent defendant and, where appropriate, notifying the court that the prosecutor has knowledge that the defendant did not commit the offense of which the defendant was convicted.

[9] A prosecutor's independent judgment, made in good faith, that the new evidence is not of such nature as to trigger the obligations of sections (g) and (h), though subsequently determined to have been erroneous, does not constitute a violation of this Rule.

Definitional Cross-References

"Known" and "Knows" *See* Rule 1.0(f)
"Reasonable" *See* Rule 1.0(h)
"Reasonably believes" *See* Rule 1.0(i)
"Substantial" *See* Rule 1.0(l)
"Tribunal" *See* Rule 1.0(m)

RULE 3.9: ADVOCATE IN NONADJUDICATIVE PROCEEDINGS

A lawyer representing a client before a legislative body or administrative agency in a nonadjudicative proceeding shall disclose that the appearance is in a representative capacity and shall conform to the provisions of Rules 3.3(a) through (c), 3.4(a) through (c), and 3.5.

Comment

[1] In representation before bodies such as legislatures, municipal councils, and executive and administrative agencies acting in a rule-making or policy-making capacity, lawyers present facts, formulate issues and advance argument in the matters under consideration. The decision-making body, like a court, should be able to rely on the integrity of the submissions made to it. A lawyer appearing before such a body must deal with it honestly and in conformity with applicable rules of procedure. See Rules 3.3(a) through (c), 3.4(a) through (c) and 3.5.

[2] Lawyers have no exclusive right to appear before nonadjudicative bodies, as they do before a court. The requirements of this Rule therefore may subject lawyers to regulations inapplicable to advocates who are not lawyers. However, legislatures and administrative agencies have a right to expect lawyers to deal with them as they deal with courts.

[3] This Rule only applies when a lawyer represents a client in connection with an official hearing or meeting of a governmental agency or a legislative body to which the lawyer or the lawyer's client is presenting evidence or argument. It does not apply to representation of a client in a negotiation or other bilateral transaction with a governmental agency or in connection with an application for a license or other privilege or the client's compliance with generally applicable reporting requirements, such as the filing of income-tax returns. Nor does it apply to the representation of a client in connection with an investigation or examination of the client's affairs conducted by government investigators or examiners. Representation in such matters is governed by Rules 4.1 through 4.4.

TRANSACTIONS WITH PERSONS OTHER THAN CLIENTS

RULE 4.1: TRUTHFULNESS IN STATEMENTS TO OTHERS

In the course of representing a client a lawyer shall not knowingly:

(a) make a false statement of material fact or law to a third person; or

(b) fail to disclose a material fact when disclosure is necessary to avoid assisting a criminal or fraudulent act by a client, unless disclosure is prohibited by Rule 1.6.

Comment

Misrepresentation

[1] A lawyer is required to be truthful when dealing with others on a client's behalf, but generally has no affirmative duty to inform an opposing party of relevant facts. A misrepresentation can occur if the lawyer incorporates or affirms a statement of another person that the lawyer knows is false. Misrepresentations can also occur by partially true but misleading statements or omissions that are the equivalent of affirmative false statements. For dishonest conduct that does not amount to a false statement or for misrepresentations by a lawyer other than in the course of representing a client, see Rule 8.4.

Statements of Fact

[2] This Rule refers to statements of fact. Whether a particular statement should be regarded as one of fact can depend on the circumstances. Under generally accepted conventions in negotiation, certain types of statements ordinarily are not taken as statements of material fact. Estimates of price or value placed on the subject of a transaction and a party's intentions as to an acceptable settlement of a claim are ordinarily in this category, and so is the existence of an undisclosed principal except where nondisclosure of the principal would constitute fraud. Lawyers should be mindful of their obligations under applicable law to avoid criminal and tortious misrepresentation.

Crime or Fraud by Client

[3] Under Rule 1.2(d), a lawyer is prohibited from counseling or assisting a client in conduct that the lawyer knows is criminal or fraudulent. Paragraph (b) states a specific application of the principle set forth in Rule 1.2(d) and addresses the situation where a client's crime or fraud takes the form of a lie or misrepresentation. Ordinarily, a lawyer can avoid assisting a client's crime or fraud by withdrawing from the representation. Sometimes it may be necessary for the lawyer to give notice of the fact of withdrawal and to disaffirm an opinion, document, affirmation or the like. In extreme cases, substantive law may require a lawyer to disclose information relating to the representation to avoid being deemed to have assisted the client's crime or fraud. If the lawyer can avoid assisting a client's crime or fraud only by disclosing this information, then under paragraph (b) the lawyer is required to do so, unless the disclosure is prohibited by Rule 1.6.

Definitional Cross-References

"Fraudulent" *See* Rule 1.0(d)
"Knowingly" *See* Rule 1.0(f)

RULE 4.2: COMMUNICATION WITH PERSON REPRESENTED BY COUNSEL

In representing a client, a lawyer shall not communicate about the subject of the representation with a person the lawyer knows to be represented by another lawyer in the matter, unless the lawyer has the consent of the other lawyer or is authorized to do so by law or a court order.

Comment

[1] This Rule contributes to the proper functioning of the legal system by protecting a person who has chosen to be represented by a lawyer in a matter against possible overreaching by other lawyers who are participating in the matter, interference by those lawyers with the client-lawyer relationship and the uncounselled disclosure of information relating to the representation.

[2] This Rule applies to communications with any person who is represented by counsel concerning the matter to which the communication relates.

[3] The Rule applies even though the represented person initiates or consents to the communication. A lawyer must immediately terminate communication with a person if, after commencing communication, the lawyer learns that the person is one with whom communication is not permitted by this Rule.

[4] This Rule does not prohibit communication with a represented person, or an employee or agent of such a person, concerning matters outside the representation. For example, the existence of a controversy between a government agency and a private party, or between two organizations, does not prohibit a lawyer for either from communicating with nonlawyer representatives of the other regarding a separate matter. Nor does this Rule preclude communication with a represented person who is seeking advice from a lawyer who is not otherwise representing a client in the matter. A lawyer may not make a communication prohibited by this Rule through the acts of another. See Rule 8.4(a). Parties to a matter may communicate directly with each other, and a lawyer is not prohibited from advising a client concerning a communication that the client is legally entitled to make. Also, a lawyer having independent justification or legal authorization for communicating with a represented person is permitted to do so.

[5] Communications authorized by law may include communications by a lawyer on behalf of a client who is exercising a constitutional or other legal right to communicate with the government. Communications authorized by law may also include investigative activities of lawyers representing governmental entities, directly or through investigative agents, prior to the commencement of criminal or civil enforcement proceedings. When communicating with the accused in a criminal matter, a government lawyer must comply with this Rule in addition to honoring the constitutional rights of the accused. The fact that a communication does not violate a state or federal constitutional right is insufficient to establish that the communication is permissible under this Rule.

[6] A lawyer who is uncertain whether a communication with a represented person is permissible may seek a court order. A lawyer may also seek a court order in exceptional circumstances to authorize a communication that would otherwise be prohibited by this Rule, for example, where communication with a person represented by counsel is necessary to avoid reasonably certain injury.

[7] In the case of a represented organization, this Rule prohibits communications with a constituent of the organization who supervises, di-

rects or regularly consults with the organization's lawyer concerning the matter or has authority to obligate the organization with respect to the matter or whose act or omission in connection with the matter may be imputed to the organization for purposes of civil or criminal liability. Consent of the organization's lawyer is not required for communication with a former constituent. If a constituent of the organization is represented in the matter by his or her own counsel, the consent by that counsel to a communication will be sufficient for purposes of this Rule. Compare Rule 3.4(f). In communicating with a current or former constituent of an organization, a lawyer must not use methods of obtaining evidence that violate the legal rights of the organization. See Rule 4.4.

[8] The prohibition on communications with a represented person only applies in circumstances where the lawyer knows that the person is in fact represented in the matter to be discussed. This means that the lawyer has actual knowledge of the fact of the representation; but such actual knowledge may be inferred from the circumstances. See Rule 1.0(f). Thus, the lawyer cannot evade the requirement of obtaining the consent of counsel by closing eyes to the obvious.

[9] In the event the person with whom the lawyer communicates is not known to be represented by counsel in the matter, the lawyer's communications are subject to Rule 4.3.

Definitional Cross-References

"Knows" *See* Rule 1.0(f)

RULE 4.3: DEALING WITH UNREPRESENTED PERSON

In dealing on behalf of a client with a person who is not represented by counsel, a lawyer shall not state or imply that the lawyer is disinterested. When the lawyer knows or reasonably should know that the unrepresented person misunderstands the lawyer's role in the matter, the lawyer shall make reasonable efforts to correct the misunderstanding. The lawyer shall not give legal advice to an unrepresented person, other than the advice to secure counsel, if the lawyer knows or reasonably should know that the interests of such a person are or have a reasonable possibility of being in conflict with the interests of the client.

Comment

[1] An unrepresented person, particularly one not experienced in dealing with legal matters, might assume that a lawyer is disinterested in loyalties or is a disinterested authority on the law even when the lawyer represents a client. In order to avoid a misunderstanding, a lawyer will typically need to identify the lawyer's client and, where necessary, explain that the client has interests opposed to those of the unrepresented person. For misunderstandings that sometimes arise when a lawyer for an organization deals with an unrepresented constituent, see Rule 1.13(f).

[2] The Rule distinguishes between situations involving unrepresented persons whose interests may be adverse to those of the lawyer's client and those in which the person's interests are not in conflict with the client's. In the former situation, the possibility that the lawyer will compromise the unrepresented person's interests is so great that the Rule prohibits the giving of any advice, apart from the advice to obtain counsel. Whether a lawyer is giving impermissible advice may depend on the experience and sophistication of the unrepresented person, as well as the setting in which the behavior and comments occur. This Rule does not prohibit a lawyer from negotiating the terms of a transaction or settling a dispute with an unrepresented person. So long as the lawyer has explained that the lawyer represents an adverse party and is not representing the person, the lawyer may inform the person of the terms on which the lawyer's client will enter into an agreement or settle a matter, prepare documents that require the person's signature and explain the lawyer's own view of the meaning of the document or the lawyer's view of the underlying legal obligations.

Definitional Cross-References

"Knows" *See* Rule 1.0(f)
"Reasonable" *See* Rule 1.0(h)
"Reasonably should know" *See* Rule 1.0(j)

RULE 4.4: RESPECT FOR RIGHTS OF THIRD PERSONS

(a) In representing a client, a lawyer shall not use means that have no substantial purpose other than to embarrass, delay, or burden a third person, or use methods of obtaining evidence that violate the legal rights of such a person.

(b) A lawyer who receives a document or electronically stored information relating to the representation of the lawyer's client and knows or reasonably should know that the document or electronically stored information was inadvertently sent shall promptly notify the sender.

Comment

[1] Responsibility to a client requires a lawyer to subordinate the interests of others to those of the client, but that responsibility does not imply that a lawyer may disregard the rights of third persons. It is impractical to catalogue all such rights, but they include legal restrictions on methods of obtaining evidence from third persons and unwarranted intrusions into privileged relationships, such as the client-lawyer relationship.

[2] Paragraph (b) recognizes that lawyers sometimes receive a document or electronically stored information that was mistakenly sent or produced by opposing parties or their lawyers. A document or electronically stored information is inadvertently sent when it is accidentally transmitted, such as when an email or letter is misaddressed or a document or electronically stored information is accidentally included with information that was intentionally transmitted. If a lawyer knows or reasonably should know that such a document or electronically stored information was sent inadvertently, then this Rule requires the lawyer to promptly notify the sender in order to permit that person to take protective measures. Whether the lawyer is required to take additional steps, such as returning the document or deleting electronically stored information, is a matter of law beyond the scope of these Rules, as is the question of whether the privileged status of a document or electronically stored information has been waived. Similarly, this Rule does not address the legal duties of a lawyer who receives a document or electronically stored information that the lawyer knows or reasonably should know may have been inappropriately obtained by the sending person. For purposes of this Rule, "document or electronically stored information" includes, in addition to paper documents, email and other forms of electronically stored information, including embedded data (commonly referred to as "metadata"), that is subject to being read or put into readable form. Metadata in electronic documents creates an obligation under this Rule only if the receiving lawyer knows or reasonably should know that the metadata was inadvertently sent to the receiving lawyer.

[3] Some lawyers may choose to return a document or delete electronically stored information unread, for example, when the lawyer learns before receiving it that it was inadvertently sent. Where a lawyer is not required by applicable law to do so, the decision to voluntarily return such a document or delete electronically stored information is a matter of professional judgment ordinarily reserved to the lawyer. See Rules 1.2 and 1.4.

Definitional Cross-References
"Knows" *See* Rule 1.0(f)
"Reasonably should know" *See* Rule 1.0(j)
"Substantial" *See* Rule 1.0(l)

LAW FIRMS AND ASSOCIATIONS

RULE 5.1: RESPONSIBILITIES OF PARTNERS, MANAGERS, AND SUPERVISORY LAWYERS

(a) A partner in a law firm, and a lawyer who individually or together with other lawyers possesses comparable managerial authority in a law firm, shall make reasonable efforts to ensure that the firm has in effect measures giving reasonable assurance that all lawyers in the firm conform to the Rules of Professional Conduct.

(b) A lawyer having direct supervisory authority over another lawyer shall make reasonable efforts to ensure that the other lawyer conforms to the Rules of Professional Conduct.

(c) A lawyer shall be responsible for another lawyer's violation of the Rules of Professional Conduct if:

(1) the lawyer orders or, with knowledge of the specific conduct, ratifies the conduct involved; or

(2) the lawyer is a partner or has comparable managerial authority in the law firm in which the other lawyer practices, or has direct supervisory authority over the other lawyer, and knows of the conduct at a time when its consequences can be avoided or mitigated but fails to take reasonable remedial action.

Comment

[1] Paragraph (a) applies to lawyers who have managerial authority over the professional work of a firm. See Rule 1.0(c). This includes mem-

bers of a partnership, the shareholders in a law firm organized as a professional corporation, and members of other associations authorized to practice law; lawyers having comparable managerial authority in a legal services organization or a law department of an enterprise or government agency; and lawyers who have intermediate managerial responsibilities in a firm. Paragraph (b) applies to lawyers who have supervisory authority over the work of other lawyers in a firm.

[2] Paragraph (a) requires lawyers with managerial authority within a firm to make reasonable efforts to establish internal policies and procedures designed to provide reasonable assurance that all lawyers in the firm will conform to the Rules of Professional Conduct. Such policies and procedures include those designed to detect and resolve conflicts of interest, identify dates by which actions must be taken in pending matters, account for client funds and property and ensure that inexperienced lawyers are properly supervised.

[3] Other measures that may be required to fulfill the responsibility prescribed in paragraph (a) can depend on the firm's structure and the nature of its practice. In a small firm of experienced lawyers, informal supervision and periodic review of compliance with the required systems ordinarily will suffice. In a large firm, or in practice situations in which difficult ethical problems frequently arise, more elaborate measures may be necessary. Some firms, for example, have a procedure whereby junior lawyers can make confidential referral of ethical problems directly to a designated senior partner or special committee. See Rule 5.2. Firms, whether large or small, may also rely on continuing legal education in professional ethics. In any event, the ethical atmosphere of a firm can influence the conduct of all its members, and the partners may not assume that all lawyers associated with the firm will inevitably conform to the Rules.

[4] Paragraph (c) expresses a general principle of personal responsibility for acts of another. See also Rule 8.4(a).

[5] Paragraph (c)(2) defines the duty of a partner or other lawyer having comparable managerial authority in a law firm, as well as a lawyer who has direct supervisory authority over performance of specific legal work by another lawyer. Whether a lawyer has supervisory authority in particular circumstances is a question of fact. Partners and lawyers with comparable authority have at least indirect responsibility for all work being done by the firm, while a partner or manager in charge of a particular matter ordinarily also has supervisory responsibility for the work of other firm lawyers engaged in the matter. Appropriate remedial

action by a partner or managing lawyer would depend on the immediacy of that lawyer's involvement and the seriousness of the misconduct. A supervisor is required to intervene to prevent avoidable consequences of misconduct if the supervisor knows that the misconduct occurred. Thus, if a supervising lawyer knows that a subordinate misrepresented a matter to an opposing party in negotiation, the supervisor as well as the subordinate has a duty to correct the resulting misapprehension.

[6] Professional misconduct by a lawyer under supervision could reveal a violation of paragraph (b) on the part of the supervisory lawyer even though it does not entail a violation of paragraph (c) because there was no direction, ratification or knowledge of the violation.

[7] Apart from this Rule and Rule 8.4(a), a lawyer does not have disciplinary liability for the conduct of a partner, associate or subordinate. Whether a lawyer may be liable civilly or criminally for another lawyer's conduct is a question of law beyond the scope of these Rules.

[8] The duties imposed by this Rule on managing and supervising lawyers do not alter the personal duty of each lawyer in a firm to abide by the Rules of Professional Conduct. See Rule 5.2(a).

Definitional Cross-References

"Firm" and "Law firm" *See* Rule 1.0(c)
"Knows" *See* Rule 1.0(f)
"Partner" *See* Rule 1.0(g)
"Reasonable" *See* Rule 1.0(h)

RULE 5.2: RESPONSIBILITIES OF A SUBORDINATE LAWYER

(a) A lawyer is bound by the Rules of Professional Conduct notwithstanding that the lawyer acted at the direction of another person.

(b) A subordinate lawyer does not violate the Rules of Professional Conduct if that lawyer acts in accordance with a supervisory lawyer's reasonable resolution of an arguable question of professional duty.

Comment

[1] Although a lawyer is not relieved of responsibility for a violation by the fact that the lawyer acted at the direction of a supervisor, that fact

may be relevant in determining whether a lawyer had the knowledge required to render conduct a violation of the Rules. For example, if a subordinate filed a frivolous pleading at the direction of a supervisor, the subordinate would not be guilty of a professional violation unless the subordinate knew of the document's frivolous character.

[2] When lawyers in a supervisor-subordinate relationship encounter a matter involving professional judgment as to ethical duty, the supervisor may assume responsibility for making the judgment. Otherwise a consistent course of action or position could not be taken. If the question can reasonably be answered only one way, the duty of both lawyers is clear and they are equally responsible for fulfilling it. However, if the question is reasonably arguable, someone has to decide upon the course of action. That authority ordinarily reposes in the supervisor, and a subordinate may be guided accordingly. For example, if a question arises whether the interests of two clients conflict under Rule 1.7, the supervisor's reasonable resolution of the question should protect the subordinate professionally if the resolution is subsequently challenged.

Definitional Cross-References

"Reasonable" *See* Rule 1.0(h)

RULE 5.3: RESPONSIBILITIES REGARDING NONLAWYER ASSISTANCE

With respect to a nonlawyer employed or retained by or associated with a lawyer:

(a) a partner, and a lawyer who individually or together with other lawyers possesses comparable managerial authority in a law firm shall make reasonable efforts to ensure that the firm has in effect measures giving reasonable assurance that the person's conduct is compatible with the professional obligations of the lawyer;

(b) a lawyer having direct supervisory authority over the nonlawyer shall make reasonable efforts to ensure that the person's conduct is compatible with the professional obligations of the lawyer; and

(c) a lawyer shall be responsible for conduct of such a person that would be a violation of the Rules of Professional Conduct if engaged in by a lawyer if:

(1) the lawyer orders or, with the knowledge of the specific conduct, ratifies the conduct involved; or

(2) the lawyer is a partner or has comparable managerial authority in the law firm in which the person is employed, or has direct supervisory authority over the person, and knows of the conduct at a time when its consequences can be avoided or mitigated but fails to take reasonable remedial action.

Comment

[1] Paragraph (a) requires lawyers with managerial authority within a law firm to make reasonable efforts to ensure that the firm has in effect measures giving reasonable assurance that nonlawyers in the firm and nonlawyers outside the firm who work on firm matters act in a way compatible with the professional obligations of the lawyer. See Comment [6] to Rule 1.1 (retaining lawyers outside the firm) and Comment [1] to Rule 5.1 (responsibilities with respect to lawyers within a firm). Paragraph (b) applies to lawyers who have supervisory authority over such nonlawyers within or outside the firm. Paragraph (c) specifies the circumstances in which a lawyer is responsible for the conduct of such nonlawyers within or outside the firm that would be a violation of the Rules of Professional Conduct if engaged in by a lawyer.

Nonlawyers Within the Firm

[2] Lawyers generally employ assistants in their practice, including secretaries, investigators, law student interns, and paraprofessionals. Such assistants, whether employees or independent contractors, act for the lawyer in rendition of the lawyer's professional services. A lawyer must give such assistants appropriate instruction and supervision concerning the ethical aspects of their employment, particularly regarding the obligation not to disclose information relating to representation of the client, and should be responsible for their work product. The measures employed in supervising nonlawyers should take account of the fact that they do not have legal training and are not subject to professional discipline.

Nonlawyers Outside the Firm

[3] A lawyer may use nonlawyers outside the firm to assist the lawyer in rendering legal services to the client. Examples include the retention of an investigative or paraprofessional service, hiring a document

management company to create and maintain a database for complex litigation, sending client documents to a third party for printing or scanning, and using an Internet-based service to store client information. When using such services outside the firm, a lawyer must make reasonable efforts to ensure that the services are provided in a manner that is compatible with the lawyer's professional obligations. The extent of this obligation will depend upon the circumstances, including the education, experience and reputation of the nonlawyer; the nature of the services involved; the terms of any arrangements concerning the protection of client information; and the legal and ethical environments of the jurisdictions in which the services will be performed, particularly with regard to confidentiality. See also Rules 1.1 (competence), 1.2 (allocation of authority), 1.4 (communication with client), 1.6 (confidentiality), 5.4(a) (professional independence of the lawyer), and 5.5(a) (unauthorized practice of law). When retaining or directing a nonlawyer outside the firm, a lawyer should communicate directions appropriate under the circumstances to give reasonable assurance that the nonlawyer's conduct is compatible with the professional obligations of the lawyer.

[4] Where the client directs the selection of a particular nonlawyer service provider outside the firm, the lawyer ordinarily should agree with the client concerning the allocation of responsibility for monitoring as between the client and the lawyer. See Rule 1.2. When making such an allocation in a matter pending before a tribunal, lawyers and parties may have additional obligations that are a matter of law beyond the scope of these Rules.

Definitional Cross-References
"Firm" and "Law firm" *See* Rule 1.0(c)
"Knows" *See* Rule 1.0(f)
"Partner" *See* Rule 1.0(g)
"Reasonable" *See* Rule 1.0(h)

RULE 5.4: PROFESSIONAL INDEPENDENCE OF A LAWYER

(a) A lawyer or law firm shall not share legal fees with a nonlawyer, except that:

(1) an agreement by a lawyer with the lawyer's firm, partner, or associate may provide for the payment of money,

over a reasonable period of time after the lawyer's death, to the lawyer's estate or to one or more specified persons;

(2) a lawyer who purchases the practice of a deceased, disabled, or disappeared lawyer may, pursuant to the provisions of Rule 1.17, pay to the estate or other representative of that lawyer the agreed-upon purchase price;

(3) a lawyer or law firm may include nonlawyer employees in a compensation or retirement plan, even though the plan is based in whole or in part on a profit-sharing arrangement; and

(4) a lawyer may share court-awarded legal fees with a nonprofit organization that employed, retained or recommended employment of the lawyer in the matter.

(b) A lawyer shall not form a partnership with a nonlawyer if any of the activities of the partnership consist of the practice of law.

(c) A lawyer shall not permit a person who recommends, employs, or pays the lawyer to render legal services for another to direct or regulate the lawyer's professional judgment in rendering such legal services.

(d) A lawyer shall not practice with or in the form of a professional corporation or association authorized to practice law for a profit, if:

(1) a nonlawyer owns any interest therein, except that a fiduciary representative of the estate of a lawyer may hold the stock or interest of the lawyer for a reasonable time during administration;

(2) a nonlawyer is a corporate director or officer thereof or occupies the position of similar responsibility in any form of association other than a corporation ; or

(3) a nonlawyer has the right to direct or control the professional judgment of a lawyer.

Comment

[1] The provisions of this Rule express traditional limitations on sharing fees. These limitations are to protect the lawyer's professional independence of judgment. Where someone other than the client pays the lawyer's fee or salary, or recommends employment of the lawyer, that arrangement does not modify the lawyer's obligation to the client. As stated in paragraph (c), such arrangements should not interfere with the lawyer's professional judgment.

[2] This Rule also expresses traditional limitations on permitting a third party to direct or regulate the lawyer's professional judgment in rendering legal services to another. See also Rule 1.8(f) (lawyer may accept compensation from a third party as long as there is no interference with the lawyer's independent professional judgment and the client gives informed consent).

Definitional Cross-References
"Firm" and "Law firm" *See* Rule 1.0(c)
"Partner" *See* Rule 1.0(g)

RULE 5.5: UNAUTHORIZED PRACTICE OF LAW; MULTIJURISDICTIONAL PRACTICE OF LAW

(a) A lawyer shall not practice law in a jurisdiction in violation of the regulation of the legal profession in that jurisdiction, or assist another in doing so.

(b) A lawyer who is not admitted to practice in this jurisdiction shall not:

(1) except as authorized by these Rules or other law, establish an office or other systematic and continuous presence in this jurisdiction for the practice of law; or

(2) hold out to the public or otherwise represent that the lawyer is admitted to practice law in this jurisdiction.

(c) A lawyer admitted in another United States jurisdiction, and not disbarred or suspended from practice in any jurisdiction, may provide legal services on a temporary basis in this jurisdiction that:

(1) are undertaken in association with a lawyer who is admitted to practice in this jurisdiction and who actively participates in the matter;

(2) are in or reasonably related to a pending or potential proceeding before a tribunal in this or another jurisdiction, if the lawyer, or a person the lawyer is assisting, is authorized by law or order to appear in such proceeding or reasonably expects to be so authorized;

(3) are in or reasonably related to a pending or potential arbitration, mediation, or other alternative dispute resolution proceeding in this or another jurisdiction, if the services arise out of or are reasonably related to the lawyer's practice in a

jurisdiction in which the lawyer is admitted to practice and are not services for which the forum requires pro hac vice admission; or

(4) are not within paragraphs (c)(2) or (c)(3) and arise out of or are reasonably related to the lawyer's practice in a jurisdiction in which the lawyer is admitted to practice.

(d) A lawyer admitted in another United States jurisdiction or in a foreign jurisdiction, and not disbarred or suspended from practice in any jurisdiction or the equivalent thereof, may provide legal services through an office or other systematic and continuous presence in this jurisdiction that:

(1) are provided to the lawyer's employer or its organizational affiliates; are not services for which the forum requires pro hac vice admission; and, when performed by a foreign lawyer and requires advice on the law of this or another jurisdiction or of the United States, such advice shall be based upon the advice of a lawyer who is duly licensed and authorized by the jurisdiction to provide such advice; or

(2) are services that the lawyer is authorized by federal law or other law or rule to provide in this jurisdiction.

(e) For purposes of paragraph (d), the foreign lawyer must be a member in good standing of a recognized legal profession in a foreign jurisdiction, the members of which are admitted to practice as lawyers or counselors at law or the equivalent, and are subject to effective regulation and discipline by a duly constituted professional body or a public authority.

Comment

[1] A lawyer may practice law only in a jurisdiction in which the lawyer is authorized to practice. A lawyer may be admitted to practice law in a jurisdiction on a regular basis or may be authorized by court rule or order or by law to practice for a limited purpose or on a restricted basis. Paragraph (a) applies to unauthorized practice of law by a lawyer, whether through the lawyer's direct action or by the lawyer assisting another person. For example, a lawyer may not assist a person in practicing law in violation of the rules governing professional conduct in that person's jurisdiction.

[2] The definition of the practice of law is established by law and varies from one jurisdiction to another. Whatever the definition, limiting the practice of law to members of the bar protects the public against rendi-

tion of legal services by unqualified persons. This Rule does not prohibit a lawyer from employing the services of paraprofessionals and delegating functions to them, so long as the lawyer supervises the delegated work and retains responsibility for their work. See Rule 5.3.

[3] A lawyer may provide professional advice and instruction to non-lawyers whose employment requires knowledge of the law; for example, claims adjusters, employees of financial or commercial institutions, social workers, accountants and persons employed in government agencies. Lawyers also may assist independent nonlawyers, such as paraprofessionals, who are authorized by the law of a jurisdiction to provide particular law-related services. In addition, a lawyer may counsel nonlawyers who wish to proceed pro se.

[4] Other than as authorized by law or this Rule, a lawyer who is not admitted to practice generally in this jurisdiction violates paragraph (b)(1) if the lawyer establishes an office or other systematic and continuous presence in this jurisdiction for the practice of law. Presence may be systematic and continuous even if the lawyer is not physically present here. Such a lawyer must not hold out to the public or otherwise represent that the lawyer is admitted to practice law in this jurisdiction. See also Rules 7.1(a) and 7.5(b).

[5] There are occasions in which a lawyer admitted to practice in another United States jurisdiction, and not disbarred or suspended from practice in any jurisdiction, may provide legal services on a temporary basis in this jurisdiction under circumstances that do not create an unreasonable risk to the interests of their clients, the public or the courts. Paragraph (c) identifies four such circumstances. The fact that conduct is not so identified does not imply that the conduct is or is not authorized. With the exception of paragraphs (d)(1) and (d)(2), this Rule does not authorize a U.S. or foreign lawyer to establish an office or other systematic and continuous presence in this jurisdiction without being admitted to practice generally here.

[6] There is no single test to determine whether a lawyer's services are provided on a "temporary basis" in this jurisdiction, and may therefore be permissible under paragraph (c). Services may be "temporary" even though the lawyer provides services in this jurisdiction on a recurring basis, or for an extended period of time, as when the lawyer is representing a client in a single lengthy negotiation or litigation.

[7] Paragraphs (c) and (d) apply to lawyers who are admitted to practice law in any United States jurisdiction, which includes the District of

Columbia and any state, territory or commonwealth of the United States. Paragraph (d) also applies to lawyers admitted in a foreign jurisdiction. The word "admitted" in paragraphs (c), (d) and (e) contemplates that the lawyer is authorized to practice in the jurisdiction in which the lawyer is admitted and excludes a lawyer who while technically admitted is not authorized to practice, because, for example, the lawyer is on inactive status.

[8] Paragraph (c)(1) recognizes that the interests of clients and the public are protected if a lawyer admitted only in another jurisdiction associates with a lawyer licensed to practice in this jurisdiction. For this paragraph to apply, however, the lawyer admitted to practice in this jurisdiction must actively participate in and share responsibility for the representation of the client.

[9] Lawyers not admitted to practice generally in a jurisdiction may be authorized by law or order of a tribunal or an administrative agency to appear before the tribunal or agency. This authority may be granted pursuant to formal rules governing admission pro hac vice or pursuant to informal practice of the tribunal or agency. Under paragraph (c)(2), a lawyer does not violate this Rule when the lawyer appears before a tribunal or agency pursuant to such authority. To the extent that a court rule or other law of this jurisdiction requires a lawyer who is not admitted to practice in this jurisdiction to obtain admission pro hac vice before appearing before a tribunal or administrative agency, this Rule requires the lawyer to obtain that authority.

[10] Paragraph (c)(2) also provides that a lawyer rendering services in this jurisdiction on a temporary basis does not violate this Rule when the lawyer engages in conduct in anticipation of a proceeding or hearing in a jurisdiction in which the lawyer is authorized to practice law or in which the lawyer reasonably expects to be admitted pro hac vice. Examples of such conduct include meetings with the client, interviews of potential witnesses, and the review of documents. Similarly, a lawyer admitted only in another jurisdiction may engage in conduct temporarily in this jurisdiction in connection with pending litigation in another jurisdiction in which the lawyer is or reasonably expects to be authorized to appear, including taking depositions in this jurisdiction.

[11] When a lawyer has been or reasonably expects to be admitted to appear before a court or administrative agency, paragraph (c)(2) also permits conduct by lawyers who are associated with that lawyer in the matter, but who do not expect to appear before the court or administrative

agency. For example, subordinate lawyers may conduct research, review documents, and attend meetings with witnesses in support of the lawyer responsible for the litigation.

[12] Paragraph (c)(3) permits a lawyer admitted to practice law in another jurisdiction to perform services on a temporary basis in this jurisdiction if those services are in or reasonably related to a pending or potential arbitration, mediation, or other alternative dispute resolution proceeding in this or another jurisdiction, if the services arise out of or are reasonably related to the lawyer's practice in a jurisdiction in which the lawyer is admitted to practice. The lawyer, however, must obtain admission pro hac vice in the case of a court-annexed arbitration or mediation or otherwise if court rules or law so require.

[13] Paragraph (c)(4) permits a lawyer admitted in another jurisdiction to provide certain legal services on a temporary basis in this jurisdiction that arise out of or are reasonably related to the lawyer's practice in a jurisdiction in which the lawyer is admitted but are not within paragraphs (c)(2) or (c)(3). These services include both legal services and services that nonlawyers may perform but that are considered the practice of law when performed by lawyers.

[14] Paragraphs (c)(3) and (c)(4) require that the services arise out of or be reasonably related to the lawyer's practice in a jurisdiction in which the lawyer is admitted. A variety of factors evidence such a relationship. The lawyer's client may have been previously represented by the lawyer, or may be resident in or have substantial contacts with the jurisdiction in which the lawyer is admitted. The matter, although involving other jurisdictions, may have a significant connection with that jurisdiction. In other cases, significant aspects of the lawyer's work might be conducted in that jurisdiction or a significant aspect of the matter may involve the law of that jurisdiction. The necessary relationship might arise when the client's activities or the legal issues involve multiple jurisdictions, such as when the officers of a multinational corporation survey potential business sites and seek the services of their lawyer in assessing the relative merits of each. In addition, the services may draw on the lawyer's recognized expertise developed through the regular practice of law on behalf of clients in matters involving a particular body of federal, nationally-uniform, foreign, or international law. Lawyers desiring to provide pro bono legal services on a temporary basis in a jurisdiction that has been affected by a major disaster, but in which they are not otherwise authorized to practice law, as well as lawyers from the affected jurisdiction who seek to practice

law temporarily in another jurisdiction, but in which they are not otherwise authorized to practice law, should consult the [*Model Court Rule on Provision of Legal Services Following Determination of Major Disaster*].

[15] Paragraph (d) identifies two circumstances in which a lawyer who is admitted to practice in another United States or a foreign jurisdiction, and is not disbarred or suspended from practice in any jurisdiction, or the equivalent thereof, may establish an office or other systematic and continuous presence in this jurisdiction for the practice of law. Pursuant to paragraph (c) of this Rule, a lawyer admitted in any U.S. jurisdiction may also provide legal services in this jurisdiction on a temporary basis. See also *Model Rule on Temporary Practice by Foreign Lawyers*. Except as provided in paragraphs (d)(1) and (d)(2), a lawyer who is admitted to practice law in another United States or foreign jurisdiction and who establishes an office or other systematic or continuous presence in this jurisdiction must become admitted to practice law generally in this jurisdiction.

[16] Paragraph (d)(1) applies to a U.S. or foreign lawyer who is employed by a client to provide legal services to the client or its organizational affiliates, i.e., entities that control, are controlled by, or are under common control with the employer. This paragraph does not authorize the provision of personal legal services to the employer's officers or employees. The paragraph applies to in-house corporate lawyers, government lawyers and others who are employed to render legal services to the employer. The lawyer's ability to represent the employer outside the jurisdiction in which the lawyer is licensed generally serves the interests of the employer and does not create an unreasonable risk to the client and others because the employer is well situated to assess the lawyer's qualifications and the quality of the lawyer's work. To further decrease any risk to the client, when advising on the domestic law of a United States jurisdiction or on the law of the United States, the foreign lawyer authorized to practice under paragraph (d)(1) of this Rule needs to base that advice on the advice of a lawyer licensed and authorized by the jurisdiction to provide it.

[17] If an employed lawyer establishes an office or other systematic presence in this jurisdiction for the purpose of rendering legal services to the employer, the lawyer may be subject to registration or other requirements, including assessments for client protection funds and mandatory continuing legal education. See *Model Rule for Registration of In-House Counsel*.

[18] Paragraph (d)(2) recognizes that a U.S. or foreign lawyer may provide legal services in a jurisdiction in which the lawyer is not licensed when authorized to do so by federal or other law, which includes statute, court rule, executive regulation or judicial precedent. See, e.g., *Model Rule on Practice Pending Admission.*

[19] A lawyer who practices law in this jurisdiction pursuant to paragraphs (c) or (d) or otherwise is subject to the disciplinary authority of this jurisdiction. See Rule 8.5(a).

[20] In some circumstances, a lawyer who practices law in this jurisdiction pursuant to paragraphs (c) or (d) may have to inform the client that the lawyer is not licensed to practice law in this jurisdiction. For example, that may be required when the representation occurs primarily in this jurisdiction and requires knowledge of the law of this jurisdiction. See Rule 1.4(b).

[21] Paragraphs (c) and (d) do not authorize communications advertising legal services in this jurisdiction by lawyers who are admitted to practice in other jurisdictions. Whether and how lawyers may communicate the availability of their services in this jurisdiction is governed by Rules 7.1 to 7.5.

Definitional Cross-References

"Reasonably" *See* Rule 1.0(h)
"Tribunal" *See* Rule 1.0(m)

RULE 5.6: RESTRICTIONS ON RIGHT TO PRACTICE

A lawyer shall not participate in offering or making:

(a) a partnership, shareholders, operating, employment, or other similar type of agreement that restricts the right of a lawyer to practice after termination of the relationship, except an agreement concerning benefits upon retirement; or

(b) an agreement in which a restriction on the lawyer's right to practice is part of the settlement of a client controversy.

Comment

[1] An agreement restricting the right of lawyers to practice after leaving a firm not only limits their professional autonomy but also limits the freedom of clients to choose a lawyer. Paragraph (a) prohibits such

agreements except for restrictions incident to provisions concerning retirement benefits for service with the firm.

[2] Paragraph (b) prohibits a lawyer from agreeing not to represent other persons in connection with settling a claim on behalf of a client.

[3] This Rule does not apply to prohibit restrictions that may be included in the terms of the sale of a law practice pursuant to Rule 1.17.

RULE 5.7: RESPONSIBILITIES REGARDING LAW-RELATED SERVICES

(a) A lawyer shall be subject to the Rules of Professional Conduct with respect to the provision of law-related services, as defined in paragraph (b), if the law-related services are provided:

(1) by the lawyer in circumstances that are not distinct from the lawyer's provision of legal services to clients; or

(2) in other circumstances by an entity controlled by the lawyer individually or with others if the lawyer fails to take reasonable measures to assure that a person obtaining the law-related services knows that the services are not legal services and that the protections of the client-lawyer relationship do not exist.

(b) The term "law-related services" denotes services that might reasonably be performed in conjunction with and in substance are related to the provision of legal services, and that are not prohibited as unauthorized practice of law when provided by a nonlawyer.

Comment

[1] When a lawyer performs law-related services or controls an organization that does so, there exists the potential for ethical problems. Principal among these is the possibility that the person for whom the law-related services are performed fails to understand that the services may not carry with them the protections normally afforded as part of the client-lawyer relationship. The recipient of the law-related services may expect, for example, that the protection of client confidences, prohibitions against representation of persons with conflicting interests, and obligations of a lawyer to maintain professional independence apply to the provision of law-related services when that may not be the case.

[2] Rule 5.7 applies to the provision of law-related services by a lawyer even when the lawyer does not provide any legal services to the person for whom the law-related services are performed and whether the law-related services are performed through a law firm or a separate entity. The Rule identifies the circumstances in which all of the Rules of Professional Conduct apply to the provision of law-related services. Even when those circumstances do not exist, however, the conduct of a lawyer involved in the provision of law-related services is subject to those Rules that apply generally to lawyer conduct, regardless of whether the conduct involves the provision of legal services. See, e.g., Rule 8.4.

[3] When law-related services are provided by a lawyer under circumstances that are not distinct from the lawyer's provision of legal services to clients, the lawyer in providing the law-related services must adhere to the requirements of the Rules of Professional Conduct as provided in paragraph (a)(1). Even when the law-related and legal services are provided in circumstances that are distinct from each other, for example through separate entities or different support staff within the law firm, the Rules of Professional Conduct apply to the lawyer as provided in paragraph (a)(2) unless the lawyer takes reasonable measures to assure that the recipient of the law-related services knows that the services are not legal services and that the protections of the client-lawyer relationship do not apply.

[4] Law-related services also may be provided through an entity that is distinct from that through which the lawyer provides legal services. If the lawyer individually or with others has control of such an entity's operations, the Rule requires the lawyer to take reasonable measures to assure that each person using the services of the entity knows that the services provided by the entity are not legal services and that the Rules of Professional Conduct that relate to the client-lawyer relationship do not apply. A lawyer's control of an entity extends to the ability to direct its operation. Whether a lawyer has such control will depend upon the circumstances of the particular case.

[5] When a client-lawyer relationship exists with a person who is referred by a lawyer to a separate law-related service entity controlled by the lawyer, individually or with others, the lawyer must comply with Rule 1.8(a).

[6] In taking the reasonable measures referred to in paragraph (a)(2) to assure that a person using law-related services understands the practical effect or significance of the inapplicability of the Rules of Professional

Conduct, the lawyer should communicate to the person receiving the law-related services, in a manner sufficient to assure that the person understands the significance of the fact, that the relationship of the person to the business entity will not be a client-lawyer relationship. The communication should be made before entering into an agreement for provision of or providing law-related services, and preferably should be in writing.

[7] The burden is upon the lawyer to show that the lawyer has taken reasonable measures under the circumstances to communicate the desired understanding. For instance, a sophisticated user of law-related services, such as a publicly held corporation, may require a lesser explanation than someone unaccustomed to making distinctions between legal services and law-related services, such as an individual seeking tax advice from a lawyer-accountant or investigative services in connection with a lawsuit.

[8] Regardless of the sophistication of potential recipients of law-related services, a lawyer should take special care to keep separate the provision of law-related and legal services in order to minimize the risk that the recipient will assume that the law-related services are legal services. The risk of such confusion is especially acute when the lawyer renders both types of services with respect to the same matter. Under some circumstances the legal and law-related services may be so closely entwined that they cannot be distinguished from each other, and the requirement of disclosure and consultation imposed by paragraph (a)(2) of the Rule cannot be met. In such a case a lawyer will be responsible for assuring that both the lawyer's conduct and, to the extent required by Rule 5.3, that of nonlawyer employees in the distinct entity that the lawyer controls complies in all respects with the Rules of Professional Conduct.

[9] A broad range of economic and other interests of clients may be served by lawyers' engaging in the delivery of law-related services. Examples of law-related services include providing title insurance, financial planning, accounting, trust services, real estate counseling, legislative lobbying, economic analysis, social work, psychological counseling, tax preparation, and patent, medical or environmental consulting.

[10] When a lawyer is obliged to accord the recipients of such services the protections of those Rules that apply to the client-lawyer relationship, the lawyer must take special care to heed the proscriptions of the Rules addressing conflict of interest (Rules 1.7 through 1.11, espe-

cially Rules 1.7(a)(2) and 1.8(a), (b) and (f)), and to scrupulously adhere to the requirements of Rule 1.6 relating to disclosure of confidential information. The promotion of the law-related services must also in all respects comply with Rules 7.1 through 7.3, dealing with advertising and solicitation. In that regard, lawyers should take special care to identify the obligations that may be imposed as a result of a jurisdiction's decisional law.

[11] When the full protections of all of the Rules of Professional Conduct do not apply to the provision of law-related services, principles of law external to the Rules, for example, the law of principal and agent, govern the legal duties owed to those receiving the services. Those other legal principles may establish a different degree of protection for the recipient with respect to confidentiality of information, conflicts of interest and permissible business relationships with clients. See also Rule 8.4 (Misconduct).

Definitional Cross-References
"Knows" *See* Rule 1.0(f)
"Reasonable" *See* Rule 1.0(h)

PUBLIC SERVICE

RULE 6.1: VOLUNTARY PRO BONO PUBLICO SERVICE

Every lawyer has a professional responsibility to provide legal services to those unable to pay. A lawyer should aspire to render at least (50) hours of pro bono publico legal services per year. In fulfilling this responsibility, the lawyer should:

(a) provide a substantial majority of the (50) hours of legal services without fee or expectation of fee to:

(1) persons of limited means; or

(2) charitable, religious, civic, community, governmental and educational organizations in matters that are designed primarily to address the needs of persons of limited means; and

(b) provide any additional services through:

(1) delivery of legal services at no fee or substantially reduced fee to individuals, groups or organizations seeking to secure or protect civil rights, civil liberties or public rights,

or charitable, religious, civic, community, governmental and educational organizations in matters in furtherance of their organizational purposes, where the payment of standard legal fees would significantly deplete the organization's economic resources or would be otherwise inappropriate;

(2) delivery of legal services at a substantially reduced fee to persons of limited means; or

(3) participation in activities for improving the law, the legal system or the legal profession.

In addition, a lawyer should voluntarily contribute financial support to organizations that provide legal services to persons of limited means.

Comment

[1] Every lawyer, regardless of professional prominence or professional work load, has a responsibility to provide legal services to those unable to pay, and personal involvement in the problems of the disadvantaged can be one of the most rewarding experiences in the life of a lawyer. The American Bar Association urges all lawyers to provide a minimum of 50 hours of pro bono services annually. States, however, may decide to choose a higher or lower number of hours of annual service (which may be expressed as a percentage of a lawyer's professional time) depending upon local needs and local conditions. It is recognized that in some years a lawyer may render greater or fewer hours than the annual standard specified, but during the course of his or her legal career, each lawyer should render on average per year, the number of hours set forth in this Rule. Services can be performed in civil matters or in criminal or quasi-criminal matters for which there is no government obligation to provide funds for legal representation, such as post-conviction death penalty appeal cases.

[2] Paragraphs (a)(1) and (2) recognize the critical need for legal services that exists among persons of limited means by providing that a substantial majority of the legal services rendered annually to the disadvantaged be furnished without fee or expectation of fee. Legal services under these paragraphs consist of a full range of activities, including individual and class representation, the provision of legal advice, legislative lobbying, administrative rule making and the provision of free training or mentoring to those who represent persons of limited means. The variety of these activities should facilitate participation by government

lawyers, even when restrictions exist on their engaging in the outside practice of law.

[3] Persons eligible for legal services under paragraphs (a)(1) and (2) are those who qualify for participation in programs funded by the Legal Services Corporation and those whose incomes and financial resources are slightly above the guidelines utilized by such programs but nevertheless, cannot afford counsel. Legal services can be rendered to individuals or to organizations such as homeless shelters, battered women's centers and food pantries that serve those of limited means. The term "governmental organizations" includes, but is not limited to, public protection programs and sections of governmental or public sector agencies.

[4] Because service must be provided without fee or expectation of fee, the intent of the lawyer to render free legal services is essential for the work performed to fall within the meaning of paragraphs (a)(1) and (2). Accordingly, services rendered cannot be considered pro bono if an anticipated fee is uncollected, but the award of statutory attorneys' fees in a case originally accepted as pro bono would not disqualify such services from inclusion under this section. Lawyers who do receive fees in such cases are encouraged to contribute an appropriate portion of such fees to organizations or projects that benefit persons of limited means.

[5] While it is possible for a lawyer to fulfill the annual responsibility to perform pro bono services exclusively through activities described in paragraphs (a)(1) and (2), to the extent that any hours of service remained unfulfilled, the remaining commitment can be met in a variety of ways as set forth in paragraph (b). Constitutional, statutory or regulatory restrictions may prohibit or impede government and public sector lawyers and judges from performing the pro bono services outlined in paragraphs (a)(1) and (2). Accordingly, where those restrictions apply, government and public sector lawyers and judges may fulfill their pro bono responsibility by performing services outlined in paragraph (b).

[6] Paragraph (b)(1) includes the provision of certain types of legal services to those whose incomes and financial resources place them above limited means. It also permits the pro bono lawyer to accept a substantially reduced fee for services. Examples of the types of issues that may be addressed under this paragraph include First Amendment claims, Title VII claims and environmental protection claims. Additionally, a wide range of organizations may be represented, including social service, medical research, cultural and religious groups.

[7] Paragraph (b)(2) covers instances in which lawyers agree to and receive a modest fee for furnishing legal services to persons of limited means. Participation in judicare programs and acceptance of court appointments in which the fee is substantially below a lawyer's usual rate are encouraged under this section.

[8] Paragraph (b)(3) recognizes the value of lawyers engaging in activities that improve the law, the legal system or the legal profession. Serving on bar association committees, serving on boards of pro bono or legal services programs, taking part in Law Day activities, acting as a continuing legal education instructor, a mediator or an arbitrator and engaging in legislative lobbying to improve the law, the legal system or the profession are a few examples of the many activities that fall within this paragraph.

[9] Because the provision of pro bono services is a professional responsibility, it is the individual ethical commitment of each lawyer. Nevertheless, there may be times when it is not feasible for a lawyer to engage in pro bono services. At such times a lawyer may discharge the pro bono responsibility by providing financial support to organizations providing free legal services to persons of limited means. Such financial support should be reasonably equivalent to the value of the hours of service that would have otherwise been provided. In addition, at times it may be more feasible to satisfy the pro bono responsibility collectively, as by a firm's aggregate pro bono activities.

[10] Because the efforts of individual lawyers are not enough to meet the need for free legal services that exists among persons of limited means, the government and the profession have instituted additional programs to provide those services. Every lawyer should financially support such programs, in addition to either providing direct pro bono services or making financial contributions when pro bono service is not feasible.

[11] Law firms should act reasonably to enable and encourage all lawyers in the firm to provide the pro bono legal services called for by this Rule.

[12] The responsibility set forth in this Rule is not intended to be enforced through disciplinary process.

Definitional Cross-References

"Substantial" *See* Rule 1.0(l)

RULE 6.2: ACCEPTING APPOINTMENTS

A lawyer shall not seek to avoid appointment by a tribunal to represent a person except for good cause, such as:

(a) representing the client is likely to result in violation of the Rules of Professional Conduct or other law;

(b) representing the client is likely to result in an unreasonable financial burden on the lawyer; or

(c) the client or the cause is so repugnant to the lawyer as to be likely to impair the client-lawyer relationship or the lawyer's ability to represent the client.

Comment

[1] A lawyer ordinarily is not obliged to accept a client whose character or cause the lawyer regards as repugnant. The lawyer's freedom to select clients is, however, qualified. All lawyers have a responsibility to assist in providing pro bono publico service. See Rule 6.1. An individual lawyer fulfills this responsibility by accepting a fair share of unpopular matters or indigent or unpopular clients. A lawyer may also be subject to appointment by a court to serve unpopular clients or persons unable to afford legal services.

Appointed Counsel

[2] For good cause a lawyer may seek to decline an appointment to represent a person who cannot afford to retain counsel or whose cause is unpopular. Good cause exists if the lawyer could not handle the matter competently, see Rule 1.1, or if undertaking the representation would result in an improper conflict of interest, for example, when the client or the cause is so repugnant to the lawyer as to be likely to impair the client-lawyer relationship or the lawyer's ability to represent the client. A lawyer may also seek to decline an appointment if acceptance would be unreasonably burdensome, for example, when it would impose a financial sacrifice so great as to be unjust.

[3] An appointed lawyer has the same obligations to the client as retained counsel, including the obligations of loyalty and confidentiality, and is subject to the same limitations on the client-lawyer relationship, such as the obligation to refrain from assisting the client in violation of the Rules.

Definitional Cross-References

"Tribunal" *See* Rule 1.0(m)

RULE 6.3: MEMBERSHIP IN LEGAL SERVICES ORGANIZATION

A lawyer may serve as a director, officer or member of a legal services organization, apart from the law firm in which the lawyer practices, notwithstanding that the organization serves persons having interests adverse to a client of the lawyer. The lawyer shall not knowingly participate in a decision or action of the organization:

(a) if participating in the decision or action would be incompatible with the lawyer's obligations to a client under Rule 1.7; or

(b) where the decision or action could have a material adverse effect on the representation of a client of the organization whose interests are adverse to a client of the lawyer.

Comment

[1] Lawyers should be encouraged to support and participate in legal service organizations. A lawyer who is an officer or a member of such an organization does not thereby have a client-lawyer relationship with persons served by the organization. However, there is potential conflict between the interests of such persons and the interests of the lawyer's clients. If the possibility of such conflict disqualified a lawyer from serving on the board of a legal services organization, the profession's involvement in such organizations would be severely curtailed.

[2] It may be necessary in appropriate cases to reassure a client of the organization that the representation will not be affected by conflicting loyalties of a member of the board. Established, written policies in this respect can enhance the credibility of such assurances.

Definitional Cross-References

"Law firm" *See* Rule 1.0(c)
"Knowingly" *See* Rule 1.0(f)

RULE 6.4: LAW REFORM ACTIVITIES AFFECTING CLIENT INTERESTS

A lawyer may serve as a director, officer or member of an organization involved in reform of the law or its administration notwithstanding that the reform may affect the interests of a client of the lawyer. When the lawyer knows that the interests of a client may be materially benefitted by a decision in which the lawyer participates, the lawyer shall disclose that fact but need not identify the client.

Comment

[1] Lawyers involved in organizations seeking law reform generally do not have a client-lawyer relationship with the organization. Otherwise, it might follow that a lawyer could not be involved in a bar association law reform program that might indirectly affect a client. See also Rule 1.2(b). For example, a lawyer specializing in antitrust litigation might be regarded as disqualified from participating in drafting revisions of rules governing that subject. In determining the nature and scope of participation in such activities, a lawyer should be mindful of obligations to clients under other Rules, particularly Rule 1.7. A lawyer is professionally obligated to protect the integrity of the program by making an appropriate disclosure within the organization when the lawyer knows a private client might be materially benefitted.

Definitional Cross-References

"Knows" *See* Rule 1.0(f)

RULE 6.5: NONPROFIT AND COURT-ANNEXED LIMITED LEGAL SERVICES PROGRAMS

(a) A lawyer who, under the auspices of a program sponsored by a nonprofit organization or court, provides short-term limited legal services to a client without expectation by either the lawyer or the client that the lawyer will provide continuing representation in the matter:

(1) is subject to Rules 1.7 and 1.9(a) only if the lawyer knows that the representation of the client involves a conflict of interest; and

(2) is subject to Rule 1.10 only if the lawyer knows that another lawyer associated with the lawyer in a law firm is disqualified by Rule 1.7 or 1.9(a) with respect to the matter.

(b) Except as provided in paragraph (a)(2), Rule 1.10 is inapplicable to a representation governed by this Rule.

Comment

[1] Legal services organizations, courts and various nonprofit organizations have established programs through which lawyers provide short-term limited legal services—such as advice or the completion of legal forms—that will assist persons to address their legal problems without further representation by a lawyer. In these programs, such as legal-advice hotlines, advice-only clinics or pro se counseling programs, a client-lawyer relationship is established, but there is no expectation that the lawyer's representation of the client will continue beyond the limited consultation. Such programs are normally operated under circumstances in which it is not feasible for a lawyer to systematically screen for conflicts of interest as is generally required before undertaking a representation. See, e.g., Rules 1.7, 1.9 and 1.10.

[2] A lawyer who provides short-term limited legal services pursuant to this Rule must secure the client's informed consent to the limited scope of the representation. See Rule 1.2(c). If a short-term limited representation would not be reasonable under the circumstances, the lawyer may offer advice to the client but must also advise the client of the need for further assistance of counsel. Except as provided in this Rule, the Rules of Professional Conduct, including Rules 1.6 and 1.9(c), are applicable to the limited representation.

[3] Because a lawyer who is representing a client in the circumstances addressed by this Rule ordinarily is not able to check systematically for conflicts of interest, paragraph (a) requires compliance with Rules 1.7 or 1.9(a) only if the lawyer knows that the representation presents a conflict of interest for the lawyer, and with Rule 1.10 only if the lawyer knows that another lawyer in the lawyer's firm is disqualified by Rules 1.7 or 1.9(a) in the matter.

[4] Because the limited nature of the services significantly reduces the risk of conflicts of interest with other matters being handled by the lawyer's firm, paragraph (b) provides that Rule 1.10 is inapplicable to a representation governed by this Rule except as provided by paragraph (a)(2). Paragraph (a)(2) requires the participating lawyer to comply with Rule 1.10 when the lawyer knows that the lawyer's firm is disqualified by Rules 1.7 or 1.9(a). By virtue of paragraph (b), however, a lawyer's participation in a short-term limited legal services program will not preclude the lawyer's firm from undertaking or continuing the representation of a client with interests adverse to a client being represented under

the program's auspices. Nor will the personal disqualification of a lawyer participating in the program be imputed to other lawyers participating in the program.

[5] If, after commencing a short-term limited representation in accordance with this Rule, a lawyer undertakes to represent the client in the matter on an ongoing basis, Rules 1.7, 1.9(a) and 1.10 become applicable.

Definitional Cross-References

"Law firm" *See* Rule 1.0(c)
"Knows" *See* Rule 1.0(f)

INFORMATION ABOUT LEGAL SERVICES

RULE 7.1: COMMUNICATIONS CONCERNING A LAWYER'S SERVICES

A lawyer shall not make a false or misleading communication about the lawyer or the lawyer's services. A communication is false or misleading if it contains a material misrepresentation of fact or law, or omits a fact necessary to make the statement considered as a whole not materially misleading.

Comment

[1] This Rule governs all communications about a lawyer's services, including advertising permitted by Rule 7.2. Whatever means are used to make known a lawyer's services, statements about them must be truthful.

[2] Truthful statements that are misleading are also prohibited by this Rule. A truthful statement is misleading if it omits a fact necessary to make the lawyer's communication considered as a whole not materially misleading. A truthful statement is also misleading if there is a substantial likelihood that it will lead a reasonable person to formulate a specific conclusion about the lawyer or the lawyer's services for which there is no reasonable factual foundation.

[3] An advertisement that truthfully reports a lawyer's achievements on behalf of clients or former clients may be misleading if presented so as to lead a reasonable person to form an unjustified expectation that the same results could be obtained for other clients in similar matters without reference to the specific factual and legal circumstances of each client's case. Similarly, an unsubstantiated comparison of the lawyer's ser-

vices or fees with the services or fees of other lawyers may be misleading if presented with such specificity as would lead a reasonable person to conclude that the comparison can be substantiated. The inclusion of an appropriate disclaimer or qualifying language may preclude a finding that a statement is likely to create unjustified expectations or otherwise mislead the public.

[4] See also Rule 8.4(e) for the prohibition against stating or implying an ability to influence improperly a government agency or official or to achieve results by means that violate the Rules of Professional Conduct or other law.

RULE 7.2: ADVERTISING

(a) Subject to the requirements of Rules 7.1 and 7.3, a lawyer may advertise services through written, recorded or electronic communication, including public media.

(b) A lawyer shall not give anything of value to a person for recommending the lawyer's services except that a lawyer may

(1) pay the reasonable costs of advertisements or communications permitted by this Rule;

(2) pay the usual charges of a legal service plan or a not-for-profit or qualified lawyer referral service. A qualified lawyer referral service is a lawyer referral service that has been approved by an appropriate regulatory authority;

(3) pay for a law practice in accordance with Rule 1.17; and

(4) refer clients to another lawyer or a nonlawyer professional pursuant to an agreement not otherwise prohibited under these Rules that provides for the other person to refer clients or customers to the lawyer, if:

(i) the reciprocal referral agreement is not exclusive; and

(ii) the client is informed of the existence and nature of the agreement.

(c) Any communication made pursuant to this Rule shall include the name and office address of at least one lawyer or law firm responsible for its content.

Comment

[1] To assist the public in learning about and obtaining legal services, lawyers should be allowed to make known their services not only through reputation but also through organized information campaigns in

the form of advertising. Advertising involves an active quest for clients, contrary to the tradition that a lawyer should not seek clientele. However, the public's need to know about legal services can be fulfilled in part through advertising. This need is particularly acute in the case of persons of moderate means who have not made extensive use of legal services. The interest in expanding public information about legal services ought to prevail over considerations of tradition. Nevertheless, advertising by lawyers entails the risk of practices that are misleading or overreaching.

[2] This Rule permits public dissemination of information concerning a lawyer's name or firm name, address, email address, website, and telephone number; the kinds of services the lawyer will undertake; the basis on which the lawyer's fees are determined, including prices for specific services and payment and credit arrangements; a lawyer's foreign language ability; names of references and, with their consent, names of clients regularly represented; and other information that might invite the attention of those seeking legal assistance.

[3] Questions of effectiveness and taste in advertising are matters of speculation and subjective judgment. Some jurisdictions have had extensive prohibitions against television and other forms of advertising, against advertising going beyond specified facts about a lawyer, or against "undignified" advertising. Television, the Internet, and other forms of electronic communication are now among the most powerful media for getting information to the public, particularly persons of low and moderate income; prohibiting television, Internet, and other forms of electronic advertising, therefore, would impede the flow of information about legal services to many sectors of the public. Limiting the information that may be advertised has a similar effect and assumes that the bar can accurately forecast the kind of information that the public would regard as relevant. But seé Rule 7.3(a) for the prohibition against a solicitation through a real-time electronic exchange initiated by the lawyer.

[4] Neither this Rule nor Rule 7.3 prohibits communications authorized by law, such as notice to members of a class in class action litigation.

Paying Others to Recommend a Lawyer

[5] Except as permitted under paragraphs (b)(1)-(b)(4), lawyers are not permitted to pay others for recommending the lawyer's services or for channeling professional work in a manner that violates Rule 7.3. A communication contains a recommendation if it endorses or vouches for a lawyer's credentials, abilities, competence, character, or other pro-

fessional qualities. Paragraph (b)(1), however, allows a lawyer to pay for advertising and communications permitted by this Rule, including the costs of print directory listings, on-line directory listings, newspaper ads, television and radio airtime, domain-name registrations, sponsorship fees, Internet-based advertisements, and group advertising. A lawyer may compensate employees, agents and vendors who are engaged to provide marketing or client development services, such as publicists, public-relations personnel, business-development staff and website designers. Moreover, a lawyer may pay others for generating client leads, such as Internet-based client leads, as long as the lead generator does not recommend the lawyer, any payment to the lead generator is consistent with Rules 1.5(e) (division of fees) and 5.4 (professional independence of the lawyer), and the lead generator's communications are consistent with Rule 7.1 (communications concerning a lawyer's services). To comply with Rule 7.1, a lawyer must not pay a lead generator that states, implies, or creates a reasonable impression that it is recommending the lawyer, is making the referral without payment from the lawyer, or has analyzed a person's legal problems when determining which lawyer should receive the referral. See also Rule 5.3 (duties of lawyers and law firms with respect to the conduct of nonlawyers); Rule 8.4(a) (duty to avoid violating the Rules through the acts of another).

[6] A lawyer may pay the usual charges of a legal service plan or a not-for-profit or qualified lawyer referral service. A legal service plan is a prepaid or group legal service plan or a similar delivery system that assists people who seek to secure legal representation. A lawyer referral service, on the other hand, is any organization that holds itself out to the public as a lawyer referral service. Such referral services are understood by the public to be consumer-oriented organizations that provide unbiased referrals to lawyers with appropriate experience in the subject matter of the representation and afford other client protections, such as complaint procedures or malpractice insurance requirements. Consequently, this Rule only permits a lawyer to pay the usual charges of a not-for-profit or qualified lawyer referral service. A qualified lawyer referral service is one that is approved by an appropriate regulatory authority as affording adequate protections for the public. See, e.g., the American Bar Association's Model Supreme Court Rules Governing Lawyer Referral Services and Model Lawyer Referral and Information Service Quality Assurance Act (requiring that organizations that are identified as lawyer referral services (i) permit the participation of all lawyers who are licensed

and eligible to practice in the jurisdiction and who meet reasonable objective eligibility requirements as may be established by the referral service for the protection of the public; (ii) require each participating lawyer to carry reasonably adequate malpractice insurance; (iii) act reasonably to assess client satisfaction and address client complaints; and (iv) do not make referrals to lawyers who own, operate or are employed by the referral service.)

[7] A lawyer who accepts assignments or referrals from a legal service plan or referrals from a lawyer referral service must act reasonably to assure that the activities of the plan or service are compatible with the lawyer's professional obligations. See Rule 5.3. Legal service plans and lawyer referral services may communicate with the public, but such communication must be in conformity with these Rules. Thus, advertising must not be false or misleading, as would be the case if the communications of a group advertising program or a group legal services plan would mislead the public to think that it was a lawyer referral service sponsored by a state agency or bar association. Nor could the lawyer allow in-person, telephonic, or real-time contacts that would violate Rule 7.3.

[8] A lawyer also may agree to refer clients to another lawyer or a nonlawyer professional, in return for the undertaking of that person to refer clients or customers to the lawyer. Such reciprocal referral arrangements must not interfere with the lawyer's professional judgment as to making referrals or as to providing substantive legal services. See Rules 2.1 and 5.4(c). Except as provided in Rule 1.5(e), a lawyer who receives referrals from a lawyer or nonlawyer professional must not pay anything solely for the referral, but the lawyer does not violate paragraph (b) of this Rule by agreeing to refer clients to the other lawyer or nonlawyer professional, so long as the reciprocal referral agreement is not exclusive and the client is informed of the referral agreement. Conflicts of interest created by such arrangements are governed by Rule 1.7. Reciprocal referral agreements should not be of indefinite duration and should be reviewed periodically to determine whether they comply with these Rules. This Rule does not restrict referrals or divisions of revenues or net income among lawyers within firms comprised of multiple entities.

Definitional Cross-References

"Law firm" *See* Rule 1.0(c)
"Written" *See* Rule 1.0(n)

RULE 7.3: SOLICITATION OF CLIENTS

(a) A lawyer shall not by in-person, live telephone or real-time electronic contact solicit professional employment when a significant motive for the lawyer's doing so is the lawyer's pecuniary gain, unless the person contacted:

(1) is a lawyer; or

(2) has a family, close personal, or prior professional relationship with the lawyer.

(b) A lawyer shall not solicit professional employment by written, recorded or electronic communication or by in-person, telephone or real-time electronic contact even when not otherwise prohibited by paragraph (a), if:

(1) the target of the solicitation has made known to the lawyer a desire not to be solicited by the lawyer; or

(2) the solicitation involves coercion, duress or harassment.

(c) Every written, recorded or electronic communication from a lawyer soliciting professional employment from anyone known to be in need of legal services in a particular matter shall include the words "Advertising Material" on the outside envelope, if any, and at the beginning and ending of any recorded or electronic communication, unless the recipient of the communication is a person specified in paragraphs (a)(1) or (a)(2).

(d) Notwithstanding the prohibitions in paragraph (a), a lawyer may participate with a prepaid or group legal service plan operated by an organization not owned or directed by the lawyer that uses in-person or telephone contact to solicit memberships or subscriptions for the plan from persons who are not known to need legal services in a particular matter covered by the plan.

Comment

[1] A solicitation is a targeted communication initiated by the lawyer that is directed to a specific person and that offers to provide, or can reasonably be understood as offering to provide, legal services. In contrast, a lawyer's communication typically does not constitute a solicitation if it is directed to the general public, such as through a billboard, an Internet banner advertisement, a website or a television commercial, or if it is in response to a request for information or is automatically generated in response to Internet searches.

[2] There is a potential for abuse when a solicitation involves direct

in-person, live telephone or real-time electronic contact by a lawyer with someone known to need legal services. These forms of contact subject a person to the private importuning of the trained advocate in a direct interpersonal encounter. The person, who may already feel overwhelmed by the circumstances giving rise to the need for legal services, may find it difficult fully to evaluate all available alternatives with reasoned judgment and appropriate self-interest in the face of the lawyer's presence and insistence upon being retained immediately. The situation is fraught with the possibility of undue influence, intimidation, and over-reaching.

[3] This potential for abuse inherent in direct in-person, live telephone or real-time electronic solicitation justifies its prohibition, particularly since lawyers have alternative means of conveying necessary information to those who may be in need of legal services. In particular, communications can be mailed or transmitted by email or other electronic means that do not involve real-time contact and do not violate other laws governing solicitations. These forms of communications and solicitations make it possible for the public to be informed about the need for legal services, and about the qualifications of available lawyers and law firms, without subjecting the public to direct in-person, telephone or real-time electronic persuasion that may overwhelm a person's judgment.

[4] The use of general advertising and written, recorded or electronic communications to transmit information from lawyer to the public, rather than direct in-person, live telephone or real-time electronic contact, will help to assure that the information flows cleanly as well as freely. The contents of advertisements and communications permitted under Rule 7.2 can be permanently recorded so that they cannot be disputed and may be shared with others who know the lawyer. This potential for informal review is itself likely to help guard against statements and claims that might constitute false and misleading communications, in violation of Rule 7.1. The contents of direct in-person, live telephone or real-time electronic contact can be disputed and may not be subject to third-party scrutiny. Consequently, they are much more likely to approach (and occasionally cross) the dividing line between accurate representations and those that are false and misleading.

[5] There is far less likelihood that a lawyer would engage in abusive practices against a former client, or a person with whom the lawyer has a close personal or family relationship, or in situations in which the lawyer is motivated by considerations other than the lawyer's pecuniary gain. Nor is there a serious potential for abuse when the person contacted

is a lawyer. Consequently, the general prohibition in Rule 7.3(a) and the requirements of Rule 7.3(c) are not applicable in those situations. Also, paragraph (a) is not intended to prohibit a lawyer from participating in constitutionally protected activities of public or charitable legal-service organizations or bona fide political, social, civic, fraternal, employee or trade organizations whose purposes include providing or recommending legal services to their members or beneficiaries.

[6] But even permitted forms of solicitation can be abused. Thus, any solicitation which contains information which is false or misleading within the meaning of Rule 7.1, which involves coercion, duress or harassment within the meaning of Rule 7.3(b)(2), or which involves contact with someone who has made known to the lawyer a desire not to be solicited by the lawyer within the meaning of Rule 7.3(b)(1) is prohibited. Moreover, if after sending a letter or other communication as permitted by Rule 7.2 the lawyer receives no response, any further effort to communicate with the recipient of the communication may violate the provisions of Rule 7.3(b).

[7] This Rule is not intended to prohibit a lawyer from contacting representatives of organizations or groups that may be interested in establishing a group or prepaid legal plan for their members, insureds, beneficiaries or other third parties for the purpose of informing such entities of the availability of and details concerning the plan or arrangement which the lawyer or lawyer's firm is willing to offer. This form of communication is not directed to people who are seeking legal services for themselves. Rather, it is usually addressed to an individual acting in a fiduciary capacity seeking a supplier of legal services for others who may, if they choose, become prospective clients of the lawyer. Under these circumstances, the activity which the lawyer undertakes in communicating with such representatives and the type of information transmitted to the individual are functionally similar to and serve the same purpose as advertising permitted under Rule 7.2.

[8] The requirement in Rule 7.3(c) that certain communications be marked "Advertising Material" does not apply to communications sent in response to requests of potential clients or their spokespersons or sponsors. General announcements by lawyers, including changes in personnel or office location, do not constitute communications soliciting professional employment from a client known to be in need of legal services within the meaning of this Rule.

[9] Paragraph (d) of this Rule permits a lawyer to participate with an

organization which uses personal contact to solicit members for its group or prepaid legal service plan, provided that the personal contact is not undertaken by any lawyer who would be a provider of legal services through the plan. The organization must not be owned by or directed (whether as manager or otherwise) by any lawyer or law firm that participates in the plan. For example, paragraph (d) would not permit a lawyer to create an organization controlled directly or indirectly by the lawyer and use the organization for the in-person or telephone solicitation of legal employment of the lawyer through memberships in the plan or otherwise. The communication permitted by these organizations also must not be directed to a person known to need legal services in a particular matter, but is to be designed to inform potential plan members generally of another means of affordable legal services. Lawyers who participate in a legal service plan must reasonably assure that the plan sponsors are in compliance with Rules 7.1, 7.2 and 7.3(b). See 8.4(a).

Definitional Cross-References
"Known" *See* Rule 1.0(f)
"Written" *See* Rule 1.0(n)

RULE 7.4: COMMUNICATION OF FIELDS OF PRACTICE AND SPECIALIZATION

(a) A lawyer may communicate the fact that the lawyer does or does not practice in particular fields of law.

(b) A lawyer admitted to engage in patent practice before the United States Patent and Trademark Office may use the designation "Patent Attorney" or a substantially similar designation.

(c) A lawyer engaged in Admiralty practice may use the designation "Admiralty," "Proctor in Admiralty" or a substantially similar designation.

(d) A lawyer shall not state or imply that a lawyer is certified as a specialist in a particular field of law, unless:

(1) the lawyer has been certified as a specialist by an organization that has been approved by an appropriate state authority or that has been accredited by the American Bar Association; and

(2) the name of the certifying organization is clearly identified in the communication.

Comment

[1] Paragraph (a) of this Rule permits a lawyer to indicate areas of practice in communications about the lawyer's services. If a lawyer practices only in certain fields, or will not accept matters except in a specified field or fields, the lawyer is permitted to so indicate. A lawyer is generally permitted to state that the lawyer is a "specialist," practices a "specialty," or "specializes in" particular fields, but such communications are subject to the "false and misleading" standard applied in Rule 7.1 to communications concerning a lawyer's services.

[2] Paragraph (b) recognizes the long-established policy of the Patent and Trademark Office for the designation of lawyers practicing before the Office. Paragraph (c) recognizes that designation of Admiralty practice has a long historical tradition associated with maritime commerce and the federal courts.

[3] Paragraph (d) permits a lawyer to state that the lawyer is certified as a specialist in a field of law if such certification is granted by an organization approved by an appropriate state authority or accredited by the American Bar Association or another organization, such as a state bar association, that has been approved by the state authority to accredit organizations that certify lawyers as specialists. Certification signifies that an objective entity has recognized an advanced degree of knowledge and experience in the specialty area greater than is suggested by general licensure to practice law. Certifying organizations may be expected to apply standards of experience, knowledge and proficiency to insure that a lawyer's recognition as a specialist is meaningful and reliable. In order to insure that consumers can obtain access to useful information about an organization granting certification, the name of the certifying organization must be included in any communication regarding the certification.

RULE 7.5: FIRM NAMES
AND LETTERHEADS

(a) A lawyer shall not use a firm name, letterhead or other professional designation that violates Rule 7.1. A trade name may be used by a lawyer in private practice if it does not imply a connection with a government agency or with a public or charitable legal services organization and is not otherwise in violation of Rule 7.1.

(b) A law firm with offices in more than one jurisdiction may use the same name or other professional designation in each jurisdiction, but identification of the lawyers in an office of the firm shall indicate the jurisdictional limitations on those not licensed to practice in the jurisdiction where the office is located.

(c) The name of a lawyer holding a public office shall not be used in the name of a law firm, or in communications on its behalf, during any substantial period in which the lawyer is not actively and regularly practicing with the firm.

(d) Lawyers may state or imply that they practice in a partnership or other organization only when that is the fact.

Comment

[1] A firm may be designated by the names of all or some of its members, by the names of deceased members where there has been a continuing succession in the firm's identity or by a trade name such as the "ABC Legal Clinic." A lawyer or law firm may also be designated by a distinctive website address or comparable professional designation. Although the United States Supreme Court has held that legislation may prohibit the use of trade names in professional practice, use of such names in law practice is acceptable so long as it is not misleading. If a private firm uses a trade name that includes a geographical name such as "Springfield Legal Clinic," an express disclaimer that it is a public legal aid agency may be required to avoid a misleading implication. It may be observed that any firm name including the name of a deceased partner is, strictly speaking, a trade name. The use of such names to designate law firms has proven a useful means of identification. However, it is misleading to use the name of a lawyer not associated with the firm or a predecessor of the firm, or the name of a nonlawyer.

[2] With regard to paragraph (d), lawyers sharing office facilities, but who are not in fact associated with each other in a law firm, may not denominate themselves as, for example, "Smith and Jones," for that title suggests that they are practicing law together in a firm.

Definitional Cross-References

"Firm" and "Law firm" *See* Rule 1.0(c)
"Substantial" *See* Rule 1.0(l)

RULE 7.6: POLITICAL CONTRIBUTIONS TO OBTAIN GOVERNMENT LEGAL ENGAGEMENTS OR APPOINTMENTS BY JUDGES

A lawyer or law firm shall not accept a government legal engagement or an appointment by a judge if the lawyer or law firm makes a political contribution or solicits political contributions for the purpose of obtaining or being considered for that type of legal engagement or appointment.

Comment

[1] Lawyers have a right to participate fully in the political process, which includes making and soliciting political contributions to candidates for judicial and other public office. Nevertheless, when lawyers make or solicit political contributions in order to obtain an engagement for legal work awarded by a government agency, or to obtain appointment by a judge, the public may legitimately question whether the lawyers engaged to perform the work are selected on the basis of competence and merit. In such a circumstance, the integrity of the profession is undermined.

[2] The term "political contribution" denotes any gift, subscription, loan, advance or deposit of anything of value made directly or indirectly to a candidate, incumbent, political party or campaign committee to influence or provide financial support for election to or retention in judicial or other government office. Political contributions in initiative and referendum elections are not included. For purposes of this Rule, the term "political contribution" does not include uncompensated services.

[3] Subject to the exceptions below, (i) the term "government legal engagement" denotes any engagement to provide legal services that a public official has the direct or indirect power to award; and (ii) the term "appointment by a judge" denotes an appointment to a position such as referee, commissioner, special master, receiver, guardian or other similar position that is made by a judge. Those terms do not, however, include (a) substantially uncompensated services; (b) engagements or appointments made on the basis of experience, expertise, professional qualifications and cost following a request for proposal or other process that is free from influence based upon political contributions; and (c) engagements or appointments made on a rotational basis from a list compiled without regard to political contributions.

[4] The term "lawyer or law firm" includes a political action committee or other entity owned or controlled by a lawyer or law firm.

[5] Political contributions are for the purpose of obtaining or being considered for a government legal engagement or appointment by a judge if, but for the desire to be considered for the legal engagement or appointment, the lawyer or law firm would not have made or solicited the contributions. The purpose may be determined by an examination of the circumstances in which the contributions occur. For example, one or more contributions that in the aggregate are substantial in relation to other contributions by lawyers or law firms, made for the benefit of an official in a position to influence award of a government legal engagement, and followed by an award of the legal engagement to the contributing or soliciting lawyer or the lawyer's firm would support an inference that the purpose of the contributions was to obtain the engagement, absent other factors that weigh against existence of the proscribed purpose. Those factors may include among others that the contribution or solicitation was made to further a political, social, or economic interest or because of an existing personal, family, or professional relationship with a candidate.

[6] If a lawyer makes or solicits a political contribution under circumstances that constitute bribery or another crime, Rule 8.4(b) is implicated.

Definitional Cross-References

"Law firm" *See* Rule 1.0(c)

MAINTAINING THE INTEGRITY OF THE PROFESSION

RULE 8.1: BAR ADMISSION AND DISCIPLINARY MATTERS

An applicant for admission to the bar, or a lawyer in connection with a bar admission application or in connection with a disciplinary matter, shall not:

(a) knowingly make a false statement of material fact; or

(b) fail to disclose a fact necessary to correct a misapprehension known by the person to have arisen in the matter, or knowingly fail to respond to a lawful demand for information from an admissions or disciplinary authority, except that this Rule does not require disclosure of information otherwise protected by Rule 1.6.

Comment

[1] The duty imposed by this Rule extends to persons seeking admission to the bar as well as to lawyers. Hence, if a person makes a material false statement in connection with an application for admission, it may be the basis for subsequent disciplinary action if the person is admitted, and in any event may be relevant in a subsequent admission application. The duty imposed by this Rule applies to a lawyer's own admission or discipline as well as that of others. Thus, it is a separate professional offense for a lawyer to knowingly make a misrepresentation or omission in connection with a disciplinary investigation of the lawyer's own conduct. Paragraph (b) of this Rule also requires correction of any prior misstatement in the matter that the applicant or lawyer may have made and affirmative clarification of any misunderstanding on the part of the admissions or disciplinary authority of which the person involved becomes aware.

[2] This Rule is subject to the provisions of the Fifth Amendment of the United States Constitution and corresponding provisions of state constitutions. A person relying on such a provision in response to a question, however, should do so openly and not use the right of nondisclosure as a justification for failure to comply with this Rule.

[3] A lawyer representing an applicant for admission to the bar, or representing a lawyer who is the subject of a disciplinary inquiry or proceeding, is governed by the Rules applicable to the client-lawyer relationship, including Rule 1.6 and, in some cases, Rule 3.3.

Definitional Cross-References

"Knowingly" and "Known" *See* Rule 1.0(f)

RULE 8.2: JUDICIAL AND LEGAL OFFICIALS

(a) A lawyer shall not make a statement that the lawyer knows to be false or with reckless disregard as to its truth or falsity concerning the qualifications or integrity of a judge, adjudicatory officer or public legal officer, or of a candidate for election or appointment to judicial or legal office.

(b) A lawyer who is a candidate for judicial office shall comply with the applicable provisions of the Code of Judicial Conduct.

Comment

[1] Assessments by lawyers are relied on in evaluating the professional or personal fitness of persons being considered for election or appointment to judicial office and to public legal offices, such as attorney general, prosecuting attorney and public defender. Expressing honest and candid opinions on such matters contributes to improving the administration of justice. Conversely, false statements by a lawyer can unfairly undermine public confidence in the administration of justice.

[2] When a lawyer seeks judicial office, the lawyer should be bound by applicable limitations on political activity.

[3] To maintain the fair and independent administration of justice, lawyers are encouraged to continue traditional efforts to defend judges and courts unjustly criticized.

Definitional Cross-References

"Knows" *See* Rule 1.0(f)

RULE 8.3: REPORTING
PROFESSIONAL MISCONDUCT

(a) A lawyer who knows that another lawyer has committed a violation of the Rules of Professional Conduct that raises a substantial question as to that lawyer's honesty, trustworthiness or fitness as a lawyer in other respects, shall inform the appropriate professional authority.

(b) A lawyer who knows that a judge has committed a violation of applicable rules of judicial conduct that raises a substantial question as to the judge's fitness for office shall inform the appropriate authority.

(c) This Rule does not require disclosure of information otherwise protected by Rule 1.6 or information gained by a lawyer or judge while participating in an approved lawyers assistance program.

Comment

[1] Self-regulation of the legal profession requires that members of the profession initiate disciplinary investigation when they know of a violation of the Rules of Professional Conduct. Lawyers have a similar obligation with respect to judicial misconduct. An apparently isolated

violation may indicate a pattern of misconduct that only a disciplinary investigation can uncover. Reporting a violation is especially important where the victim is unlikely to discover the offense.

[2] A report about misconduct is not required where it would involve violation of Rule 1.6. However, a lawyer should encourage a client to consent to disclosure where prosecution would not substantially prejudice the client's interests.

[3] If a lawyer were obliged to report every violation of the Rules, the failure to report any violation would itself be a professional offense. Such a requirement existed in many jurisdictions but proved to be unenforceable. This Rule limits the reporting obligation to those offenses that a self-regulating profession must vigorously endeavor to prevent. A measure of judgment is, therefore, required in complying with the provisions of this Rule. The term "substantial" refers to the seriousness of the possible offense and not the quantum of evidence of which the lawyer is aware. A report should be made to the bar disciplinary agency unless some other agency, such as a peer review agency, is more appropriate in the circumstances. Similar considerations apply to the reporting of judicial misconduct.

[4] The duty to report professional misconduct does not apply to a lawyer retained to represent a lawyer whose professional conduct is in question. Such a situation is governed by the Rules applicable to the client-lawyer relationship.

[5] Information about a lawyer's or judge's misconduct or fitness may be received by a lawyer in the course of that lawyer's participation in an approved lawyers or judges assistance program. In that circumstance, providing for an exception to the reporting requirements of paragraphs (a) and (b) of this Rule encourages lawyers and judges to seek treatment through such a program. Conversely, without such an exception, lawyers and judges may hesitate to seek assistance from these programs, which may then result in additional harm to their professional careers and additional injury to the welfare of clients and the public. These Rules do not otherwise address the confidentiality of information received by a lawyer or judge participating in an approved lawyers assistance program; such an obligation, however, may be imposed by the rules of the program or other law.

Definitional Cross-References

"Knows" *See* Rule 1.0(f)
"Substantial" *See* Rule 1.0(l)

RULE 8.4: MISCONDUCT

It is professional misconduct for a lawyer to:

(a) violate or attempt to violate the Rules of Professional Conduct, knowingly assist or induce another to do so, or do so through the acts of another;

(b) commit a criminal act that reflects adversely on the lawyer's honesty, trustworthiness or fitness as a lawyer in other respects;

(c) engage in conduct involving dishonesty, fraud, deceit or misrepresentation;

(d) engage in conduct that is prejudicial to the administration of justice;

(e) state or imply an ability to influence improperly a government agency or official or to achieve results by means that violate the Rules of Professional Conduct or other law; or

(f) knowingly assist a judge or judicial officer in conduct that is a violation of applicable rules of judicial conduct or other law.

Comment

[1] Lawyers are subject to discipline when they violate or attempt to violate the Rules of Professional Conduct, knowingly assist or induce another to do so or do so through the acts of another, as when they request or instruct an agent to do so on the lawyer's behalf. Paragraph (a), however, does not prohibit a lawyer from advising a client concerning action the client is legally entitled to take.

[2] Many kinds of illegal conduct reflect adversely on fitness to practice law, such as offenses involving fraud and the offense of willful failure to file an income tax return. However, some kinds of offenses carry no such implication. Traditionally, the distinction was drawn in terms of offenses involving "moral turpitude." That concept can be construed to include offenses concerning some matters of personal morality, such as adultery and comparable offenses, that have no specific connection to fitness for the practice of law. Although a lawyer is personally answerable to the entire criminal law, a lawyer should be professionally answerable only for offenses that indicate lack of those characteristics relevant to law practice. Offenses involving violence, dishonesty, breach of trust, or serious interference with the administration of justice are in that category. A pattern of repeated offenses, even ones of minor significance when considered separately, can indicate indifference to legal obligation.

[3] A lawyer who, in the course of representing a client, knowingly

manifests by words or conduct, bias or prejudice based upon race, sex, religion, national origin, disability, age, sexual orientation or socioeconomic status, violates paragraph (d) when such actions are prejudicial to the administration of justice. Legitimate advocacy respecting the foregoing factors does not violate paragraph (d). A trial judge's finding that peremptory challenges were exercised on a discriminatory basis does not alone establish a violation of this rule.

[4] A lawyer may refuse to comply with an obligation imposed by law upon a good faith belief that no valid obligation exists. The provisions of Rule 1.2(d) concerning a good faith challenge to the validity, scope, meaning or application of the law apply to challenges of legal regulation of the practice of law.

[5] Lawyers holding public office assume legal responsibilities going beyond those of other citizens. A lawyer's abuse of public office can suggest an inability to fulfill the professional role of lawyers. The same is true of abuse of positions of private trust such as trustee, executor, administrator, guardian, agent and officer, director or manager of a corporation or other organization.

Definitional Cross-References

"Fraud" *See* Rule 1.0(d)
"Knowingly" *See* Rule 1.0(f)

RULE 8.5: DISCIPLINARY AUTHORITY; CHOICE OF LAW

(a) Disciplinary Authority. A lawyer admitted to practice in this jurisdiction is subject to the disciplinary authority of this jurisdiction, regardless of where the lawyer's conduct occurs. A lawyer not admitted in this jurisdiction is also subject to the disciplinary authority of this jurisdiction if the lawyer provides or offers to provide any legal services in this jurisdiction. A lawyer may be subject to the disciplinary authority of both this jurisdiction and another jurisdiction for the same conduct.

(b) Choice of Law. In any exercise of the disciplinary authority of this jurisdiction, the rules of professional conduct to be applied shall be as follows:

(1) for conduct in connection with a matter pending before a tribunal, the rules of the jurisdiction in which the tribunal sits, unless the rules of the tribunal provide otherwise; and

(2) for any other conduct, the rules of the jurisdiction in which the lawyer's conduct occurred, or, if the predominant effect of the conduct is in a different jurisdiction, the rules of that jurisdiction shall be applied to the conduct. A lawyer shall not be subject to discipline if the lawyer's conduct conforms to the rules of a jurisdiction in which the lawyer reasonably believes the predominant effect of the lawyer's conduct will occur.

Comment

Disciplinary Authority

[1] It is longstanding law that the conduct of a lawyer admitted to practice in this jurisdiction is subject to the disciplinary authority of this jurisdiction. Extension of the disciplinary authority of this jurisdiction to other lawyers who provide or offer to provide legal services in this jurisdiction is for the protection of the citizens of this jurisdiction. Reciprocal enforcement of a jurisdiction's disciplinary findings and sanctions will further advance the purposes of this Rule. See, Rules 6 and 22, ABA *Model Rules for Lawyer Disciplinary Enforcement*. A lawyer who is subject to the disciplinary authority of this jurisdiction under Rule 8.5(a) appoints an official to be designated by this court to receive service of process in this jurisdiction. The fact that the lawyer is subject to the disciplinary authority of this jurisdiction may be a factor in determining whether personal jurisdiction may be asserted over the lawyer for civil matters.

Choice of Law

[2] A lawyer may be potentially subject to more than one set of rules of professional conduct which impose different obligations. The lawyer may be licensed to practice in more than one jurisdiction with differing rules, or may be admitted to practice before a particular court with rules that differ from those of the jurisdiction or jurisdictions in which the lawyer is licensed to practice. Additionally, the lawyer's conduct may involve significant contacts with more than one jurisdiction.

[3] Paragraph (b) seeks to resolve such potential conflicts. Its premise is that minimizing conflicts between rules, as well as uncertainty about which rules are applicable, is in the best interest of both clients and the profession (as well as the bodies having authority to regulate the profession). Accordingly, it takes the approach of (i) providing that any particular conduct of a lawyer shall be subject to only one set of rules of professional conduct, (ii) making the determination of which set of rules applies

to particular conduct as straightforward as possible, consistent with recognition of appropriate regulatory interests of relevant jurisdictions, and
(iii) providing protection from discipline for lawyers who act reasonably
in the face of uncertainty.

[4] Paragraph (b)(1) provides that as to a lawyer's conduct relating to
a proceeding pending before a tribunal, the lawyer shall be subject only
to the rules of professional conduct of that tribunal. As to all other conduct, including conduct in anticipation of a proceeding not yet pending
before a tribunal, paragraph (b)(2) provides that a lawyer shall be subject
to the rules of the jurisdiction in which the lawyer's conduct occurred,
or, if the predominant effect of the conduct is in another jurisdiction, the
rules of that jurisdiction shall be applied to the conduct. In the case of
conduct in anticipation of a proceeding that is likely to be before a tribunal, the predominant effect of such conduct could be where the conduct
occurred, where the tribunal sits or in another jurisdiction.

[5] When a lawyer's conduct involves significant contacts with more
than one jurisdiction, it may not be clear whether the predominant effect of
the lawyer's conduct will occur in a jurisdiction other than the one in which
the conduct occurred. So long as the lawyer's conduct conforms to the rules
of a jurisdiction in which the lawyer reasonably believes the predominant
effect will occur, the lawyer shall not be subject to discipline under this Rule.
With respect to conflicts of interest, in determining a lawyer's reasonable
belief under paragraph (b)(2), a written agreement between the lawyer
and client that reasonably specifies a particular jurisdiction as within
the scope of that paragraph may be considered if the agreement was obtained with the client's informed consent confirmed in the agreement.

[6] If two admitting jurisdictions were to proceed against a lawyer
for the same conduct, they should, applying this rule, identify the same
governing ethics rules. They should take all appropriate steps to see that
they do apply the same rule to the same conduct, and in all events should
avoid proceeding against a lawyer on the basis of two inconsistent rules.

[7] The choice of law provision applies to lawyers engaged in trans-
national practice, unless international law, treaties or other agreements
between competent regulatory authorities in the affected jurisdictions
provide otherwise.

Definitional Cross-References

"Reasonably believes" See Rule 1.0(i)
"Tribunal" See Rule 1.0(m)

Appendix A

Subject Guide

A

Abuse of process,
  Rule 3.1 (Comment)

Accepting appointments,
  Rule 6.2

Accounting for funds,
  Rule 1.15

Acquiring interest in litigation,
  Rule 1.8(i)
  contingent fee,
  Rule 1.8(i)(2)

Adjudicative officers,
  negotiating for private
  employment,
  Rule 1.12(b)
  disqualification of former,
  Rule 1.12(a)

Administration of justice,
  conduct prejudicial to,
  Rule 8.4(d)
  interference with,
  Rule 8.4 (Comment)
  lawyer's duty to seek
  improvement in,
  Preamble

Administration of law,
  participation in,
  Rule 6.4

Administrative agencies
and tribunals,
  appearance before,
  Rule 3.9

Administrator,
  fee for representation of,
  Rule 1.5 (Comment)

Admiralty practice,
  communication of,
  Rule 7.4(c)

Admission to practice,
  Rule 8.1

Advance fee payments,
  propriety of,
  Rule 1.5 (Comment)
  deposit of,
  Rule 1.15(c)

Adversary system,
  duty of lawyer to,
  Preamble

Adverse legal authority,
  lawyer's duty to disclose,
  Rule 3.3(a)(2)

Advertising. (*See also* Solicitation,
Letterheads, Firm name.)
  class action members, to notify,
  Rule 7.2 (Comment)
  communications concerning a
  lawyer's services, generally,
  Rule 7.1
  comparisons with services
  of other lawyers,
  Rule 7.1 (Comment)
  fields of practice,
  Rule 7.4
  mail,
  Rule 7.3

Court order,
allowing communication
with represented person,
Rule 4.2
disclosure of client
confidences pursuant to,
Rule 1.6(b)(4)
Court rules, relation to Rules,
Scope
Creditors of client,
claim funds of client,
Rule 1.15 (Comment)
Crime,
client's use of lawyer's
services,
Rule 1.6,(b)(2)(3)
Criminal conduct,
by lawyer,
Rule 8.4(b)
counselling or assisting
client to engage in,
Rule 1.2(d), Rule 3.3(b),
Rule 4.1(b)
withdrawal when client
persists in,
Rule 1.2 (Comment),
Rule 1.6 (Comment),
Rule 1.13(c), Rule 1.16(b)(2),
Rule 3.3 (Comment),
Rule 4.1 (Comment)
Criminal representation,
aggregate plea bargain on
behalf of multiple defendants,
Rule 1.8(g)
codefendants,
representation of,
Rule 1.7 (Comment)
contingent fee for,
Rule 1.5(d)(2)

decision-making authority,
Rule 1.2(a)
frivolous defense,
Rule 3.1
perjury by client,
Rule 3.3(a)(3)
trial publicity,
Rule 3.6

D

Deceased lawyer,
avoiding neglect of matters of,
Rule 1.3 (Comment)
payments to estate of,
Rule 5.4(a)(2)
Deceit by lawyer,
Rule 8.4(c)
Declining representation,
causes,
Rule 1.16(a)
conflict of interest,
Rule 1.7 (Comment)
refusing to accept appointment,
Rule 6.2
when political contributions
have been made,
Rule 7.6
Decorum of tribunal,
Rule 3.5
Delay,
Rule 4.4(a)
Delivery of funds or property,
Rule 1.15(d)
Deposition,
disruption,
Rule 3.5 (Comment)
false statement,
Rule 3.3 (Comment)

APPENDIX A: SUBJECT GUIDE

obstructing access to,
    Rule 3.4(a)
offering false,
    Rule 3.3(a)(3)
Ex parte communications
with member of tribunal,
    Rule 3.5(b)
Ex parte proceedings,
    Rule 3.3(d)
Executor,
    lawyer's fee for
    representation of,
        Rule 1.5 (Comment)
Expediting litigation,
    Rule 3.2
Expenses of litigation,
    client's right to determine,
        Rule 1.2 (Comment)
    contingent fee,
        Rule 1.5(c)
    lawyer advancing to client,
        Rule 1.8(e)(1)
    indigent client, paying
    on behalf of,
        Rule 1.8(e)(2)
    reasonableness,
        Rule 1.5(a)
    termination of representation,
        Rule 1.16(d)
Expert witness. (*See* Witness.)
Expertise,
    competent representation,
        Rule 1.1 (Comment)

F

Failure to disclose adverse
legal authority,
    Rule 3.3(a)(2)

Fairness to opposing party
and counsel,
    Rule 3.4
False communications
concerning lawyer's services,
    Rule 7.1
False statement to tribunal,
    Rule 3.3(a)(1)
Falsification of evidence,
    Rule 3.3 (Comment),
    Rule 3.4(b)
Family of client with
diminished capacity,
    Rule 1.14 (Comment)
Family of lawyer,
    gift to,
        Rule 1.8(c)
    client of lawyer-relative,
        Rule 1.7 (Comment)
Fees,
    acquiring ownership interest
    in enterprise as,
        Rule 1.5 (Comment)
    advance fee payments,
        Rule 1.5 (Comment)
    advertising of,
        Rule 7.2 (Comment)
    arbitration of,
        Rule 1.5 (Comment)
    communication to client,
        Rule 1.5(b)
    contingent, prohibited
    representations,
        Rule 1.5(d)
    contingent, requirements of,
        Rule 1.5(c)
    determination of,
        Rule 1.5(a)

disclosure of confidential
information to collect,
  Rule 1.6(b)(3)
division with lawyer,
  Rule 1.5(e)
division with nonlawyer,
  Rule 5.4(a)
division with nonprofit
organization,
  Rule 5.4(a)(4)
former government lawyer,
  Rule 1.11(b)(1), Rule 1.11(c)
paid by one other than client,
  Rule 1.7 (Comment),
  Rule 1.8(f), Rule 5.4(c)
reasonableness,
  Rule 1.5(a)
termination of representation,
  Rule 1.16(d)
Fiduciary,
lawyer's obligation toward
beneficiary,
  Rule 1.2 (Comment)
standard for holding
property of others,
  Rule 1.15 (Comment)
Field of practice,
communication of,
  Rule 7.4
Fifth Amendment in bar
admission and disciplinary
matters,
  Rule 8.1 (Comment)
Financial assistance to client,
  Rule 1.8(c)
Firm. (*See* Law firm.)
Former client. (*See* Conflict
of interest.)

Former government lawyer,
"confidential government
information" defined,
  Rule 1.11(c)
conflict of interest,
  Rule 1.7 (Comment), Rule 1.11
"matter" defined,
  Rule 1.11(e)
Former judge. (*See* Judges.)
Fraud,
client's use of lawyer's services,
  Rule 1.6(b)(2)(3)
defined,
  Rule 1.0(d)
Fraudulent conduct,
counselling or assisting
client to engage in,
  Rule 1.2(d), Rule 4.1(b)
engaging in,
  Rule 8.4(c)
remediation,
  Rule 3.3 (Comment)
withdrawal when client
persists in,
  Rule 1.2 (Comment),
  Rule 1.6 (Comment),
  Rule 1.13(c), Rule 1.16(b)(2)
Frivolous claims and defenses,
  Rule 3.1
Frivolous discovery request,
  Rule 3.4(d)
Funds of client,
handling of,
  Rule 1.15
lawyer claims interest in,
  Rule 1.15(e)
responsibility of firm,
  Rule 5.1 (Comment)

G

Gift to lawyer by client,
Rule 1.8(c)

Government agency,

appearance before,
Rule 3.9

communication with,
Rule 4.2 (Comment)

conflict of interest,
Rule 1.11

constitutes firm,
Rule 1.0 (Comment),
Rule 5.1 (Comment)

improper influence on,
Rule 8.4(e)

representation of,
Rule 1.13 (Comment)

Government lawyer,

authority of,
Scope

communication with accused by,
Rule 4.2 (Comment)

conflict of interest,
Rule 1.11(d)

duties of,
Rule 1.13 (Comment)

representing multiple clients,
Scope

subject to Rules,
Rule 1.11 (Comment)

supervisory responsibilities,
Rule 5.1 (Comment)

Guardian of client with
diminished capacity,

acting adversely to ward,
Rule 1.14 (Comment)

appointment of,
Rule 1.14(b)

H

Harassment,
Preamble

Harm,
client's intent to commit
serious bodily,
Rule 1.6(b)(1)

Hearing officers.
(*See* Adjudicative officers.)

Homicide,
client's intent to commit,
Rule 1.6(b)(1)

Hotlines,
Rule 6.5 (Comment)

Hypotheticals,
Rule 1.6 (Comment)

I

Identity of client,

conflicts of interest,
Rule 1.0 (Comment)

explaining,
Rule 1.13(d)

government agency,
Rule 1.11 (Comment)

organization,
Rule 1.13 (Comment)

Impartiality and decorum
of tribunal,
Rule 3.5

Imperatives in rules,
Scope

Imputed disqualification,

firm of former judge or
other neutral,
Rule 1.12(c)

firm of political contributor,
Rule 7.6

Nonadjudicative proceedings,
  Rule 3.9

Nonlawyer assistants,
  conflict of interest,
    Rule 1.10 (Comment)
  responsibilities of lawyer,
    Rule 5.3

Nonlawyers,
  division of fees with,
    Rule 5.4(a)
  partnership,
    Rule 5.4(b)
  professional corporation,
    Rule 5.4(d)

Nonprofit legal services program,
  Rule 6.5

Nonprofit organization,
  division of fees with,
    Rule 5.4(a)(4)

Notice of receipt of funds
or other property,
    Rule 1.15(d)

O

Objectives of the representation,
  client's right to determine,
    Rule 1.2(a)

Obstruction of party's access
to evidence,
    Rule 3.3 (Comment),
    Rule 3.4(a)

Officer of legal system,
    Preamble

Opinions,
  evaluation for use by
  third persons,
    Rule 2.3

limit on malpractice liability,
    Rule 1.8 (Comment)

Opposing party,
  communication with
  represented party,
    Rule 4.2
  communication with
  unrepresented party,
    Rule 4.3
  duty of fairness to,
    Rule 3.4

Optional withdrawal,
    Rule 1.16(b)

Organization, representation of,
  board of directors, lawyer on,
    Rule 1.7 (Comment)
  communication with,
    Rule 1.4 (Comment)
  communication with
  constituents of,
    Rule 4.2 (Comment)
  conflict of interest,
    Rule 1.7 (Comment)
  intended conduct,
    Rule 1.6 (Comment)
  constituents, representing,
    Rule 1.13(g)
  identity of client,
    Rule 1.13(a), Rule 1.13(f)
  law department of,
    Rule 1.0 (Comment),
    Rule 1.10 (Comment),
    Rule 5.1 (Comment)
  misconduct, client
  engaged in,
    Rule 1.13(b)

Z

APPENDIX B

CORRELATION TABLES

TABLES A AND B: RELATED SECTIONS IN THE ABA MODEL CODE OF PROFESSIONAL RESPONSIBILITY

TABLE A*

ABA MODEL RULES	ABA MODEL CODE
Competence	
Rule 1.1	EC 1-1, EC 1-2, EC 6-1, EC 6-2, EC 6-3, EC 6-4, EC 6-5, DR 6-101(A)
Scope of Representation and Allocation of Authority between Client and Lawyer	
Rule 1.2(a)	EC 5-12, EC 7-7, EC 7-8, DR 7-101(A)(1)
Rule 1.2(b)	EC 7-17
Rule 1.2(c)	EC 7-8, EC 7-9, DR 7-101(B)(1)
Rule 1.2(d)	EC 7-1, EC 7-2, EC 7-5, EC 7-22, DR 7-102(A)(6), (7), & (8), DR 7-106
Diligence	
Rule 1.3	EC 2-31, EC 6-4, EC 7-1, EC 7-38, DR 6-101(A)(3), DR 7-101(A)(1) & (3)
Communication	
Rule 1.4(a)	EC 7-8, EC 9-2, DR 2-110(C)(1)(c), DR 6-101(A)(3), DR 9-102(B)(1)
Rule 1.4(b)	EC 7-8
Fees	
Rule 1.5(a)	EC 2-16, EC 2-17, EC 2-18, DR 2-106(A) & (B)
Rule 1.5(b)	EC 2-19
Rule 1.5(c)	EC 2-20, EC 5-7
Rule 1.5(d)	EC 2-20, DR 2-106(C)
Rule 1.5(e)	EC 2-22, DR 2-107(A)

---

* Table A provides cross-references to related provisions, but only in the sense that the provisions consider substantially similar subject matter or reflect similar concerns. A cross-reference does not indicate that a provision of the ABA Model Code of Professional Responsibility has been incorporated by the provision of a Model Rule. The Canons of the Code are not cross-referenced.

ABA MODEL RULES	ABA MODEL CODE

Confidentiality of Information

Rule 1.6(a)	EC 4-1, EC 4-2, EC 4-3, EC 4-4, DR 4-101(A), (B), & (C)
Rule 1.6(b)(1)	EC 4-2, DR 4-101(C)(3), DR 7-102(B)
Rule 1.6(b)(2)	DR 4-101(C)(3)
Rule 1.6(b)(3)	None
Rule 1.6(b)(4)	None
Rule 1.6(b)(5)	DR 4-101(C)(4)
Rule 1.6(b)(6)	DR 4-101(C)(2)
Rule 1.6(b)(7)	None
Rule 1.6(c)	None

Conflict of Interest: Current Clients

Rule 1.7(a)	EC 2-21, EC 5-1, EC 5-2, EC 5-3, EC 5-9, EC 5-11, EC 5-13, EC 5-14, EC 5-15, EC 5-17, EC 5-21, EC 5-22, EC 5-23, DR 5-101(A) & (B), DR 5-102, DR 5-104(A), DR 5-105(A) & (B), DR 5-107(A) & (B)
Rule 1.7(b)	EC 2-21, EC 5-15, EC 5-16, EC 5-17, EC 5-19, EC 5-23, DR 5-101(A) & (B), DR 5-102, DR 5-104(A), DR 5-105(C), DR 5-107(A)

Conflict of Interest: Current Clients: Specific Rules

Rule 1.8(a)	EC 5-3, EC 5-5, DR 5-104(A)
Rule 1.8(b)	EC 4-5, DR 4-101(B)
Rule 1.8(c)	EC 5-1, EC 5-2, EC 5-5, EC 5-6
Rule 1.8(d)	EC 5-1, EC 5-3, EC 5-4, DR 5-104(B)
Rule 1.8(e)	EC 5-1, EC 5-3, EC 5-7, EC 5-8, DR 5-103(B)
Rule 1.8(f)	EC 2-21, EC 5-1, EC 5-22, EC 5-23, DR 5-107(A) & (B)
Rule 1.8(g)	EC 5-1, DR 5-106(A)
Rule 1.8(h)	EC 6-6, DR 6-102(A)
Rule 1.8(i)	EC 5-1, EC 5-7, DR 5-101(A), DR 5-103(A)
Rule 1.8(j)	None
Rule 1.8(k)	None

Duties to Former Clients

Rule 1.9(a)	DR 5-105(C)
Rule 1.9(b)	EC 4-5, EC 4-6
Rule 1.9(c)	None

Imputation of Conflicts of Interest: General Rule

Rule 1.10(a)	EC 4-5, DR 5-105(D)
Rule 1.10(b)	EC 4-5, DR 5-105(D)

ABA MODEL RULES	ABA MODEL CODE
Rule 1.10(c)	DR 5-105(A)
Rule 1.10(d)	None

*Special Conflicts of Interest for Former and
Current Government Officers and Employees*

Rule 1.11(a)	EC 9-3, DR 9-101(B)
Rule 1.11(b)	None
Rule 1.11(c)	None
Rule 1.11(d)	EC 8-8
Rule 1.11(e)	None

Former Judge, Arbitrator, Mediator or Other Third-Party Neutral

Rule 1.12(a)&(b)	EC 5-20, EC 9-3, DR 9-101(A) & (B)
Rule 1.12(c)	DR 5-105(D)
Rule 1.12(d)	None

Organization as Client

Rule 1.13(a)	EC 5-18, EC 5-24
Rule 1.13(b)	EC 5-18, EC 5-24, DR 5-107(B)
Rule 1.13(c)	EC 5-18, EC 5-24, DR 5-105(D), DR 5-107(B)
Rule 1.13(d)	None
Rule 1.13(e)	None
Rule 1.13(f)	EC 5-16
Rule 1.13(g)	EC 4-4, EC 5-16, DR 5-105(B) & (C)

Client with Diminished Capacity

Rule 1.14(a)	EC 7-11, EC 7-12
Rule 1.14(b)	EC 7-12
Rule 1.14(c)	None

Safekeeping Property

Rule 1.15	EC 5-7, EC 9-5, EC 9-7, DR 5-103(A)(1), DR 9-102

Declining or Terminating Representation

Rule 1.16(a)(1)	EC 2-30, EC 2-31, EC 2-32, DR 2-103(E), DR 2-104(A), DR 2-109(A), DR 2-110(B)(1) & (2)
Rule 1.16(a)(2)	EC 1-6, EC 2-30, EC 2-31, EC 2-32, DR 2-110(B)(3), DR 2-110(C)(4)
Rule 1.16(a)(3)	EC 2-31, EC 2-32, DR 2-110(B)(4)
Rule 1.16(b)(1)	EC 2-32, DR 2-110(A)(2), DR 2-110(C)(5)
Rule 1.16(b)(2)	EC 2-31, EC 2-32, DR 2-110(C)(1)(b) & (c), DR 2-110(C)(2)

ABA MODEL RULES	ABA MODEL CODE
Rule 1.16(b)(3)	EC 2-31, EC 2-32, DR 2-110(C)(2)
Rule 1.16(b)(4)	EC 2-30, EC 2-31, EC 2-32, DR 2-110(C)(1)(d)
Rule 1.16(b)(5)	EC 2-31, EC 2-32, DR 2-110(C)(1)(f)(i)(j)
Rule 1.16(b)(6)	EC 2-32, DR 2-110(C)(1)(d) & (e)
Rule 1.16(b)(7)	EC 2-32, DR 2-110(C)(6)
Rule 1.16(c)	EC 2-32, DR 2-110(A)(1)
Rule 1.16(d)	EC 2-32, DR 2-110(A)(2) & (3)

Sale of Law Practice

Rule 1.17	None

Duties to Prospective Client

Rule 1.18	EC 4-1

Advisor

Rule 2.1	EC 5-11, EC 7-3, EC 7-8, DR 5-107(B)

Evaluation for Use by Third Persons

Rule 2.3	None

Lawyer Serving as Third-Party Neutral

Rule 2.4	EC 5-20

Meritorious Claims and Contentions

Rule 3.1	EC 7-1, EC 7-4, EC 7-5, EC 7-14, EC 7-25, DR 5-102(A)(5), DR 2-109(A)(B)(1), DR 7-102(A)(1) & (2)

Expediting Litigation

Rule 3.2	EC 7-20, DR 1-102(A)(5), DR 7-101(A)(1) & (2)

Candor toward the Tribunal

Rule 3.3(a)(1)	EC 7-4, EC 7-26, EC 7-32, EC 8-5, DR 1-102(A)(4) & (5), DR 7-102(A)(4) & (5)
Rule 3.3(a)(2)	EC 7-23, DR 1-102(A)(5), DR 7-106(B)(1)
Rule 3.3(a)(3)	EC 7-5, EC 7-6, EC 7-26, EC 8-5, DR 1-102(A)(4) & (5), DR 7-102(A)(4), (6), & (7), DR 7-102(B)(1) & (2)
Rule 3.3(b)	EC 7-5, EC 7-26, EC 7-27, EC 7-32, EC 8-5, DR 1-102(A)(4) & (5), DR 7-102(A)(4), (6), & (7), DR 7-102(B)(1) & (2), DR 7-108(G), DR 7-109(A) & (B)
Rule 3.3(c)	EC 8-5, DR 7-102(B)
Rule 3.3(d)	EC 7-24, EC 7-27

ABA MODEL RULES	ABA MODEL CODE

Fairness to Opposing Party and Counsel

Rule 3.4(a)	EC 7-6, EC 7-27, DR 1-102(A)(4) & (5), DR 7-106(C)(7), DR 7-109(A) & (B)
Rule 3.4(b)	EC 7-6, EC 7-28, DR 1-102(A)(4), (5), & (6), DR 7-102(A)(6), DR 7-109(C)
Rule 3.4(c)	EC 7-22, EC 7-25, EC 7-38, DR 1-102(A)(5), DR 7-106(A), DR 7-106(C)(5) & (7)
Rule 3.4(d)	DR 1-102(A)(5), DR 7-106(A), DR 7-106(C)(7)
Rule 3.4(e)	EC 7-24, EC 7-25, DR 1-102(A)(5), DR 7-106(C)(1), (2), (3), & (4)
Rule 3.4(f)	EC 7-27, DR 1-102(A)(5), DR 7-104(A)(2), DR 7-109(B)

Impartiality and Decorum of the Tribunal

Rule 3.5(a)	EC 7-20, EC 7-29, EC 7-31, EC 7-32, EC 7-34, DR 7-106, DR 7-108, DR 7-109, DR 7-110, DR 8-101(A)
Rule 3.5(b)	EC 7-35, DR 7-108, DR 7-110(A) & (B)
Rule 3.5(c)	EC 7-29, EC 7-30, EC 7-31, EC 7-32, DR 7-108
Rule 3.5(d)	EC 7-20, EC 7-25, EC 7-36, EC 7-37, DR 7-101(A)(1), DR 7-106(C)(6)

Trial Publicity

Rule 3.6	EC 7-25, EC 7-33, DR 7-107

Lawyer as Witness

Rule 3.7(a)	EC 5-9, EC 5-10, DR 5-101(B)(1) & (2), DR 5-102
Rule 3.7(b)	EC 5-9, DR 5-101(B), DR 5-102

Special Responsibilities of a Prosecutor

Rule 3.8(a)	EC 7-11, EC 7-13, EC 7-14, DR 7-103(A)
Rule 3.8(b)	EC 7-11, EC 7-13
Rule 3.8(c)	EC 7-11, EC 7-13, EC 7-18
Rule 3.8(d)	EC 7-11, EC 7-13, DR 7-103(B)
Rule 3.8(e)	None
Rule 3.8(f)	EC 7-14

Advocate in Nonadjudicative Proceedings

Rule 3.9	EC 7-11, EC 7-15, EC 7-16, EC 8-4, EC 8-5, DR 7-106(B)(2), DR 9-101(C)

Truthfulness in Statements to Others

Rule 4.1	EC 7-5, DR 7-102(A)(3), (4), (5), & (7), DR 7-102(B)

ABA MODEL RULES	ABA MODEL CODE

Communication with Person Represented by Counsel

Rule 4.2   EC 2-30, EC 7-18, DR 7-104(A)(1)

Dealing with Unrepresented Person

Rule 4.3   EC 2-3, EC 7-18, DR 7-104(A)(2)

Respect for Rights of Third Persons

Rule 4.4(a)   EC 7-10, EC 7-14, EC 7-21, EC 7-25, EC 7-29,
EC 7-30, EC 7-37, DR 2-110(B)(1), DR 7-101(A)(1),
DR 7-102(A)(1), DR 7-106(C)(2), DR 7-107(D), (E),
& (F), DR 7-108(D), (E), & (F)

Rule 4.4(b)   None

Responsibilities of Partners, Managers, and Supervisory Lawyers

Rule 5.1(a)&(b)   EC 4-5, DR 4-101(D), DR 7-107(J)

Rule 5.1(c)   DR 1-102(A)(2), DR 1-103(A), DR 7-108(E)

Responsibilities of a Subordinate Lawyer

Rule 5.2   None

Responsibilities regarding Nonlawyer Assistance

Rule 5.3(a)   EC 3-6, EC 4-2, EC 4-5, EC 7-28, DR 4-101(D),
DR 7-107(J)

Rule 5.3(b)   DR 1-102(A)(2), DR 7-107(J), DR 7-108(B),
DR 7-108(E)

Rule 5.3(c)   None

Professional Independence of a Lawyer

Rule 5.4(a)   EC 2-33, EC 3-8, EC 5-24, DR 2-103(D)(1),
DR 2-103(D)(2), DR 2-103(D)(4)(a), (d), (e),
& (f), DR 3-102(A), DR 5-107(C)(3)

Rule 5.4(b)   EC 2-33, EC 3-8, DR 3-103(A)

Rule 5.4(c)   EC 2-33, EC 5-22, EC 5-23, DR 2-103(C),
DR 5-107(B)

Rule 5.4(d)   EC 2-33, EC 3-8, DR 5-107(C)

Unauthorized Practice of Law; Multijurisdictional Practice of Law

Rule 5.5(a)   DR 3-101(A) & (B)

Rule 5.5(b)   None

Rule 5.5(c)   None

Rule 5.5(d)   None

Rule 5.5(e)   None

APPENDIX B: CORRELATION TABLES

ABA MODEL RULES	ABA MODEL CODE

Restrictions on Right to Practice
Rule 5.6   DR 2-108

Responsibilities regarding Law-Related Services
Rule 5.7   None

Voluntary Pro Bono Publico Service
Rule 6.1   EC 1-2, EC 1-4, EC 2-1, EC 2-2, EC 2-16, EC 2-24, EC 2-25, EC 6-2, EC 8-1, EC 8-2, EC 8-3, EC 8-7, EC 8-9

Accepting Appointments
Rule 6.2 (a)   EC 2-1, EC 2-25, EC 2-27, EC 2-28, EC 2-29, EC 8-3
Rule 6.2(b)   EC 2-16, EC 2-25, EC 2-29, EC 2-30
Rule 6.2(c)   EC 2-25, EC 2-27, EC 2-29, EC 2-30

Membership in Legal Services Organization
Rule 6.3   EC 2-33, DR 5-101(A)

Law Reform Activities Affecting Client Interests
Rule 6.4   EC 2-33, DR 5-101(A), DR 8-101

Nonprofit and Court-Annexed Limited Legal Services Programs
Rule 6.5   None

Communications Concerning a Lawyer's Services
Rule 7.1   EC 2-8, EC 2-9, EC 2-10, DR 2-101(A), (B), (C), (E), (F), & (G), DR 2-102(E)

Advertising
Rule 7.2(a)   EC 2-1, EC 2-2, EC 2-6, EC 2-7, EC 2-8, EC 2-15, DR 2-101(B) & (H), DR 2-102(A) & (B), DR 2-103(B), DR 2-104(A)(4) & (5)
Rule 7.2(b)   EC 2-8, EC 2-15, DR 2-101(I), DR 2-103(B), (C), & (D)
Rule 7.2(c)   None

Solicitation of Clients
Rule 7.3   EC 2-3, EC 2-4, EC 5-6, DR 2-103(A), DR 2-103(C)(1), DR 2-103(D)(4)(b) & (c), DR 2-104(A)(1), (2), (3), & (5)

ABA MODEL RULES	ABA MODEL CODE

Communication of Fields of Practice and Specialization

Rule 7.4(a)	EC 2-1, EC 2-7, EC 2-8, EC 2-14, DR 2-101(B)(2), DR 2-102(A)(3), DR 2-102(E), DR 2-105(A)
Rule 7.4(b)	DR 2-105(A)(1)
Rule 7.4(c)	EC 2-14
Rule 7.4(d)	EC 2-8, EC 2-14, DR 2-105(A)(2) & (3)

Firm Names and Letterheads

Rule 7.5(a)	EC 2-11, EC 2-13, DR 2-102(A)(4), DR 2-102(B), (D), & (E), DR 2-105
Rule 7.5(b)	EC 2-11, DR 2-102(D)
Rule 7.5(c)	EC 2-11, EC 2-12, DR 2-102(B)
Rule 7.5(d)	EC 2-11, EC 2-13, DR 2-102(C)

Political Contributions to Obtain Government
Legal Engagements or Appointments by Judges

Rule 7.6	None

Bar Admission and Disciplinary Matters

Rule 8.1(a)	EC 1-1, EC 1-2, EC 1-3, DR 1-101(A) & (B)
Rule 8.1(b)	DR 1-102(A)(5), DR 1-103(B)

Judicial and Legal Officials

Rule 8.2(a)	EC 8-6, DR 8-102
Rule 8.2(b)	DR 8-103

Reporting Professional Misconduct

Rule 8.3	EC 1-3, DR 1-103(A)

Misconduct

Rule 8.4(a)	EC 1-5, EC 1-6, EC 9-6, DR 1-102(A)(1) & (2), DR 2-103(E), DR 7-102(A) & (B)
Rule 8.4(b)	EC 1-5, DR 1-102(A)(3) & (6), DR 7-102(A)(8), DR 8-101(A)(3)
Rule 8.4(c)	EC 1-5, EC 9-4, DR 1-102(A)(4), DR 8-101(A)(3)
Rule 8.4(d)	EC 3-9, EC 8-3, DR 1-102(A)(5), DR 3-101(B)
Rule 8.4(e)	EC 1-5, EC 9-2, EC 9-4, EC 9-6, DR 9-101(C)
Rule 8.4(f)	EC 1-5, EC 7-34, EC 9-1, DR 1-102(A)(3), (4), (5), & (6), DR 7-110(A), DR 8-101(A)(2)

Disciplinary Authority; Choice of Law

Rule 8.5	None

TABLE B*

ABA MODEL CODE	ABA MODEL RULES

Canon 1: Integrity of Profession

EC 1-1	Rules 1.1, 8.1(a)
EC 1-2	Rules 1.1, 6.1, 8.1(a)
EC 1-3	Rules 8.1(a), 8.3
EC 1-4	Rule 6.1
EC 1-5	Rule 8.4(a), (b), (c), (e), & (f)
EC 1-6	Rules 1.16(a)(2), 8.4(a)
DR 1-101	Rule 8.1(a)
DR 1-102(A)(1)	Rule 8.4(a)
DR 1-102(A)(2)	Rules 5.1(c), 5.3(b), 8.4(a)
DR 1-102(A)(3)	Rule 8.4(b) & (f)
DR 1-102(A)(4)	Rules 3.3(a)(1), (3), & (b), 3.4(a) & (b), 8.4(c) & (f)
DR 1-102(A)(5)	Rules 3.1, 3.2, 3.3(a) & (b), 3.4, 8.4(d) & (f)
DR 1-102(A)(6)	Rules 3.4(b), 8.4(b) & (f)
DR 1-103(A)	Rules 5.1(c), 8.3
DR 1-103(B)	Rule 8.1(b)

Canon 2: Making Counsel Available

EC 2-1	Rules 6.1, 6.2(a), 7.2(a), 7.4
EC 2-2	Rules 6.1, 7.2(a)
EC 2-3	Rules 4.3, 7.3
EC 2-4	Rule 7.3
EC 2-5	None
EC 2-6	Rule 7.2(a)
EC 2-7	Rules 7.2(a), 7.4
EC 2-8	Rules 7.1, 7.2(a) & (b), 7.4
EC 2-9	Rule 7.1
EC 2-10	Rule 7.1
EC 2-11	Rule 7.5
EC 2-12	Rule 7.5(c)
EC 2-13	Rule 7.5(a) & (d)
EC 2-14	Rule 7.4
EC 2-15	Rule 7.2(a) & (b)
EC 2-16	Rules 1.5(a), 6.1, 6.2(b)

** Table B provides cross-references to related provisions, but only in the sense that the provisions consider substantially similar subject matter or reflect similar concerns. A cross-reference does not indicate that a provision of the ABA Model Code of Professional Responsibility has been incorporated by the provision of a Model Rule. The Canons of the Code are not cross-referenced.

ABA MODEL CODE	ABA MODEL RULES
EC 2-17	Rule 1.5(a)
EC 2-18	Rule 1.5(a)
EC 2-19	Rule 1.5(b)
EC 2-20	Rule 1.5(c) & (d)
EC 2-21	Rules 1.7(a), 1.8(f)
EC 2-22	Rule 1.5(e)
EC 2-23	None
EC 2-24	Rule 6.1
EC 2-25	Rules 6.1, 6.2
EC 2-26	None
EC 2-27	Rule 6.2(a) & (c)
EC 2-28	Rule 6.2(a)
EC 2-29	Rule 6.2
EC 2-30	Rules 1.16(a)(1) & (2), 1.16(b)(4), 4.2, 6.2(b) & (c)
EC 2-31	Rules 1.3, 1.16(a) & (b)
EC 2-32	Rule 1.16
EC 2-33	Rules 5.4, 6.3, 6.4
DR 2-101(A)	Rule 7.1
DR 2-101(B)	Rules 7.1, 7.2(a)
DR 2-101(C)	Rule 7.1
DR 2-101(D)	None
DR 2-101(E)	Rule 7.1
DR 2-101(F)	Rule 7.1
DR 2-101(G)	Rule 7.1
DR 2-101(H)	Rule 7.2
DR 2-101(I)	Rule 7.2(b)
DR 2-102(A)	Rules 7.2(a), 7.4
DR 2-102(B)	Rules 7.2(a), 7.5(a) & (c)
DR 2-102(C)	Rule 7.5(d)
DR 2-102(D)	Rule 7.5(a) & (b)
DR 2-102(E)	Rules 7.1, 7.4, 7.5(a)
DR 2-103(A)	Rule 7.3
DR 2-103(B)	Rule 7.2(a) & (b)
DR 2-103(C)	Rules 5.4(a), 7.2(b), 7.3
DR 2-103(D)	Rules 1.16(a)(1), 5.4(a), 7.2(b), 7.3
DR 2-103(E)	Rules 1.16(a), 7.2(a), 7.3
DR 2-104	Rules 1.16(a), 7.3
DR 2-105	Rule 7.4
DR 2-106(A)	Rule 1.5(a)

APPENDIX B: CORRELATION TABLES

ABA MODEL CODE	ABA MODEL RULES
DR 2-106(B)	Rule 1.5(a)
DR 2-106(C)	Rule 1.5(d)
DR 2-107(A)	Rule 1.5(e)
DR 2-107(B)	Rule 5.4(a)(1)
DR 2-108(A)	Rule 5.6
DR 2-108(B)	Rule 5.6
DR 2-109(A)	Rules 1.16(a)(1), 3.1
DR 2-110(A)	Rule 1.16(b)(1), (c), & (d)
DR 2-110(B)	Rules 1.16(a), 3.1, 4.4(a)
DR 2-110(C)	Rules 1.4(a)(5), 1.16(a) & (b)

Canon 3: Unauthorized Practice

EC 3-1	None
EC 3-2	None
EC 3-3	Rule 8.4(e)
EC 3-4	None
EC 3-5	None
EC 3-6	Rule 5.3(a)
EC 3-7	None
EC 3-8	Rule 5.4(a), (b), & (d)
EC 3-9	Rule 8.4(d)
DR 3-101(A)	Rule 5.5(a)
DR 3-101(B)	Rules 5.5(a), 8.4(d)
DR 3-102	Rule 5.4(a)
DR 3-103	Rule 5.4(b)

Canon 4: Confidences and Secrets

EC 4-1	Rules 1.6(a), 1.18
EC 4-2	Rules 1.6(a) & (b)(1), 5.3(a)
EC 4-3	Rule 1.6(a)
EC 4-4	Rules 1.6(a), 1.13(g)
EC 4-5	Rules 1.8(b), 1.9(b), 1.10(a) & (b), 5.1(a) & (c), 5.3(a)
EC 4-6	Rule 1.9(b)
DR 4-101(A)	Rule 1.6(a)
DR 4-101(B)	Rules 1.6(a), 1.8(b), 1.9(b)
DR 4-101(C)	Rule 1.6(a) & (b)
DR 4-101(D)	Rules 5.1(a) & (b), 5.3(a) & (b)

ABA MODEL CODE	ABA MODEL RULES
Canon 5: Independent Judgment	
EC 5-1	Rules 1.7(a), 1.8(c), (d), (e), (f), (g), & (i)
EC 5-2	Rules 1.7(a), 1.8(c)
EC 5-3	Rules 1.7, 1.8(a), (d), & (e)
EC 5-4	Rule 1.8(d)
EC 5-5	Rule 1.8(a) & (c)
EC 5-6	Rules 1.8(c), 7.3
EC 5-7	Rules 1.5(c), 1.8(e) & (i), 1.15
EC 5-8	Rule 1.8(e)
EC 5-9	Rules 1.7(a), 3.7
EC 5-10	Rule 3.7(a)
EC 5-11	Rules 1.7(a), 2.1
EC 5-12	Rule 1.2(a)
EC 5-13	Rule 1.7(a)
EC 5-14	Rule 1.7(a)
EC 5-15	Rule 1.7
EC 5-16	Rules 1.7(b), 1.13(f) & (g)
EC 5-17	Rule 1.7
EC 5-18	Rule 1.13(a), (b), & (c)
EC 5-19	Rule 1.7(b)
EC 5-20	Rules 1.12(a) & (b), 2.4
EC 5-21	Rule 1.7
EC 5-22	Rule 1.7
EC 5-23	Rules 1.7(a), 1.8(f), 5.4(c)
EC 5-24	Rules 1.13(a), (b), & (c), 5.4(a)
DR 5-101(A)	Rules 1.7, 1.8(i), 6.3, 6.4
DR 5-101(B)	Rules 1.7, 3.7
DR 5-102(A)	Rules 1.7, 3.7
DR 5-102(B)	Rules 1.7(b), 3.7
DR 5-103(A)	Rules 1.8(i), 1.15
DR 5-103(B)	Rule 1.8(e)
DR 5-104(A)	Rules 1.7, 1.8(a)
DR 5-104(B)	Rule 1.8(d)
DR 5-105(A)	Rules 1.7, 1.10(c)
DR 5-105(B)	Rules 1.7, 1.13(g)
DR 5-105(C)	Rules 1.7(b), 1.13(g), 1.9(a)
DR 5-105(D)	Rules 1.10(a), 1.12(c), 1.13(c)
DR 5-106	Rule 1.8(g)
DR 5-107(A)	Rules 1.7(b), 1.8(f)

ABA **MODEL CODE**	**ABA** **MODEL RULES**
DR 5-107(B)	Rules 1.7(a), 1.8(f), 1.13(b) & (c), 2.1, 5.4(c)
DR 5-107(C)	Rule 5.4(a) & (d)

Canon 6: Competence

EC 6-1	Rule 1.1
EC 6-2	Rules 1.1, 5.1(a) & (b), 6.1
EC 6-3	Rule 1.1
EC 6-4	Rules 1.1, 1.3
EC 6-5	Rule 1.1
EC 6-6	Rule 1.8(h)
DR 6-101	Rules 1.1, 1.3, 1.4(a)
DR 6-102	Rule 1.8(h)

Canon 7: Zeal Within the Law

EC 7-1	Rules 1.2(d), 1.3, 3.1
EC 7-2	Rule 1.2(d)
EC 7-3	Rule 2.1
EC 7-4	Rules 3.1, 3.3(a)(1)
EC 7-5	Rules 1.2(d), 3.1, 3.3(a)(3) & (b), 4.1
EC 7-6	Rule 3.4(a) & (b)
EC 7-7	Rule 1.2(a)
EC 7-8	Rules 1.2(a) & (c), 1.4, 2.1
EC 7-9	Rule 1.2(c)
EC 7-10	Rule 4.4(a)
EC 7-11	Rules 1.14(a), 3.8(a), (b), (c), & (d), 3.9
EC 7-12	Rule 1.14
EC 7-13	Rule 3.8
EC 7-14	Rules 3.1, 3.8(a) & (f), 4.4(a)
EC 7-15	Rule 3.9
EC 7-16	Rule 3.9
EC 7-17	Rule 1.2(b)
EC 7-18	Rules 3.8(c), 4.2, 4.3
EC 7-19	None
EC 7-20	Rules 3.2, 3.5(a) & (d)
EC 7-21	Rule 4.4(a)
EC 7-22	Rules 1.2(d), 3.4(c)
EC 7-23	Rule 3.3(a)(2)
EC 7-24	Rules 3.3(d), 3.4(e)
EC 7-25	Rules 3.1, 3.4(c) & (e), 3.5(d), 3.6, 4.4(a)
EC 7-26	Rule 3.3(a)(3) & (b)

ABA MODEL CODE	ABA MODEL RULES
EC 7-27	Rules 3.3(b) & (d), 3.4(a) & (f)
EC 7-28	Rules 3.4(b), 5.3(a)
EC 7-29	Rules 3.5(a) & (c), 4.4(a)
EC 7-30	Rules 3.5(c), 4.4(a)
EC 7-31	Rule 3.5(a) & (c)
EC 7-32	Rules 3.3(a)(1) & (b), 3.5(a) & (c)
EC 7-33	Rule 3.6
EC 7-34	Rules 3.5(a), 8.4(f)
EC 7-35	Rule 3.5(b)
EC 7-36	Rule 3.5(d)
EC 7-37	Rules 3.5(d), 4.4(a)
EC 7-38	Rules 1.3, 3.4(c)
EC 7-39	None
DR 7-101(A)	Rules 1.2(a), 1.3, 3.2, 3.5(d), 4.4(a)
DR 7-101(B)	Rules 1.2(b), 1.16(b)
DR 7-102(A)(1)	Rules 3.1, 4.4(a)
DR 7-102(A)(2)	Rule 3.1
DR 7-102(A)(3)	Rules 3.3(a)(1), (a)(3), & (b), 4.1
DR 7-102(A)(4)	Rules 3.3(a) & (b), 4.1
DR 7-102(A)(5)	Rules 3.3(a)(1), 4.1
DR 7-102(A)(6)	Rules 1.2(d), 3.3(b), 3.4(b)
DR 7-102(A)(7)	Rules 1.2(d), 3.3(a)(3) & (b), 4.1
DR 7-102(A)(8)	Rules 1.2(d), 8.4(a) & (b)
DR 7-102(B)	Rules 1.6(b)(1), 3.3(b) & (c), 4.1
DR 7-103(A)	Rule 3.8(a)
DR 7-103(B)	Rule 3.8(d)
DR 7-104	Rules 3.4(f), 4.2, 4.3
DR 7-105	None
DR 7-106(A)	Rules 1.2(d), 3.4(c) & (d), 3.5(a)
DR 7-106(B)	Rules 3.3(a)(2), 3.9
DR 7-106(C)	Rules 3.4(a), (c), (d), & (e), 3.5(d), 4.4(a)
DR 7-107(A)–(I)	Rule 3.6
DR 7-107(D)–(F)	Rule 4.4(a)
DR 7-107(J)	Rules 5.1(a) & (b), 5.3(a) & (b)
DR 7-108(A)	Rule 3.5(a), (b), & (c)
DR 7-108(B)	Rules 3.5(a), (b), & (c), 5.3(b)
DR 7-108(C)	Rule 3.5(a), (b), & (c)
DR 7-108(D)	Rules 3.5(c)(3), 4.4(a)
DR 7-108(E)	Rules 3.5(a), (b), & (c), 4.4(a), 5.1(c), 5.3(b)

ABA MODEL CODE	ABA MODEL RULES
DR 7-108(F)	Rules 3.5(a), (b), & (c), 4.4(a)
DR 7-108(G)	Rules 3.3(b), 3.5(c)
DR 7-109(A)	Rules 3.3(a)(1), (a)(3), & (b), 3.4(a)
DR 7-109(B)	Rules 3.3(b), 3.4(a) & (f)
DR 7-109(C)	Rule 3.4(b)
DR 7-110(A)	Rules 3.5(a), 8.4(f)
DR 7-110(B)	Rule 3.5(a) & (b)

Canon 8: Improving Legal System

EC 8-1	Rule 6.1
EC 8-2	Rule 6.1
EC 8-3	Rules 6.1, 6.2(a), 8.4(d)
EC 8-4	Rule 3.9
EC 8-5	Rules 3.3(a)(1), (a)(3), & (b), 3.9
EC 8-6	Rule 8.2(a)
EC 8-7	Rule 6.1
EC 8-8	Rule 1.11(d)
EC 8-9	Rule 6.1
DR 8-101	Rules 3.5, 8.4(b), (c), & (f)
DR 8-102	Rule 8.2(a)
DR 8-103	Rule 8.2(b)

Canon 9: Appearance of Impropriety

EC 9-1	Rule 8.4(f)
EC 9-2	Rules 1.4(a), 8.4(e)
EC 9-3	Rules 1.11(a), 1.12(a) & (b)
EC 9-4	Rule 8.4(c) & (e)
EC 9-5	Rule 1.15
EC 9-6	Preamble, Rule 8.4(e)
EC 9-7	Rule 1.15
DR 9-101(A)	Rule 1.12(a) & (b)
DR 9-101(B)	Rules 1.11(a), 1.12(a) & (b)
DR 9-101(C)	Rules 1.4(a)(5), 3.9, 8.4(e)
DR 9-102	Rules 1.4(a), 1.15

ABA STANDING COMMITTEE ON ETHICS AND PROFESSIONAL RESPONSIBILITY

COMPOSITION AND JURISDICTION

The Standing Committee on Ethics and Professional Responsibility, which consists of ten members, may:

(1) by the concurrence of a majority of its members, express its opinion on proper professional or judicial conduct, either on its own initiative or when requested to do so by a member of the bar or the judiciary;

(2) periodically publish its issued opinions to the profession in summary or complete form and, on request, provide copies of opinions to members of the bar, the judiciary and the public;

(3) provide under its supervision informal responses to ethics inquiries the answers to which are substantially governed by applicable ethical codes and existing written opinions;

(4) on request, advise or otherwise assist professional organizations and courts in their activities relating to the development, modification and interpretation of statements of the ethical standards of the profession such as the Model Rules of Professional Conduct, the predecessor Model Code of Professional Responsibility and the Model Code of Judicial Conduct;

(5) recommend amendments to or clarifications of the Model Rules of Professional Conduct or the Model Code of Judicial Conduct; and

(6) adopt rules relating to the procedures to be used in issuing opinions, effective when approved by the Board of Governors.

[The above Composition and Jurisdiction statement is found at §31.7 of the Bylaws of the Association. The Rules of Procedure are not incorporated into the Bylaws.]

RULES OF PROCEDURE

1. The Committee may express its opinion on questions of proper professional and judicial conduct. The Model Rules of Professional Conduct and the Model Code of Judicial Conduct, as they may be amended or superseded, contain the standards to be applied. For as long as a significant number of jurisdictions continue to base their professional standards on the predecessor Model Code of Professional Responsibility, the Committee will continue to refer also to the Model Code in its opinions.

2. The Committee may issue an opinion on its own initiative or upon a request from a member of the bar or the judiciary or from a professional organization or a court.

3. The Committee may issue opinions of two kinds: Formal Opinions and Informal Opinions. Formal Opinions are those upon subjects the Committee determines to be of widespread interest or unusual importance. Other opinions are Informal Opinions. The Committee will assign to each opinion a non-duplicative identifying number, with distinction between Formal Opinions and Informal Opinions.

4. The Committee will not usually issue an opinion on a question that is known to be pending before a court in a proceeding in which the requestor is involved. The Committee's published opinions will not identify the person who was the requestor or whose conduct is the subject of the opinion. The Committee will not issue an opinion on a question of law.

5. The Committee may invite or accept written information relevant to a particular opinion from a person or persons interested in such an opinion before the Committee begins its work on an opinion. Ordinarily, the Committee will not invite anyone to make an oral presentation or argument in support of that position.

6. When a Committee or staff member receives an inquiry about the status of a draft opinion from anyone outside the Committee, the member may inform the inquirer that the Committee is considering the question. Draft opinions may, in appropriate circumstances, be shown to other interested ABA Committees and entities. Committee and staff members shall not, absent unusual circumstances, discuss the substance of pending opinions with the public, but may mention topics related to pending opinions in a general fashion.

7. Before issuing an opinion with respect to judicial conduct the Committee will submit the proposed opinion to the Judges' Advisory Committee and consider any objection or comment from the Judges' Advisory

Committee and any member of it. The Committee may assume that the Judges' Advisory Committee and its members have no objection or comment if none is received by the Committee within 30 days after the submission.

8. If the Committee decides not to issue a requested opinion the requestor will be promptly notified.

9. The Committee will issue an opinion only with the concurrence of six members in a vote taken at a meeting or in a telephone conference call. When a Committee member votes against a position declaring a Committee policy, that vote may be recorded in the minutes, which may include the name of the dissenting Committee member. The minutes shall not reflect the names of Committee members voting for or against any non-Committee policy question except that a member's vote shall be recorded and identified at the member's request. When drafting an opinion, policy statement or other document to be publicly disseminated, the Committee shall make every effort to reach a consensus. When, after a full examination of the issue and an exchange of views, the Committee cannot reach a consensus, a dissenting opinion may be appropriate to express the views of a Committee member or members. A member may place a statement of dissent in the Committee file or request that the dissent be published with the opinion.

10. The Chair may assign to one or more members the responsibility of preparing a proposed opinion for consideration by the Committee. The Committee will issue a requested opinion as promptly as feasible.

11. A Formal Opinion overrules an earlier Formal Opinion or Informal Opinion to the extent of conflict. An Informal Opinion overrules an earlier Informal Opinion to the extent of conflict but does not overrule an earlier Formal Opinion.

12. Opinions of the Committee issued before the effective dates of the Model Rules of Professional Conduct, the predecessor Model Code of Professional Responsibility and the Model Code of Judicial Conduct continue in effect to the extent not inconsistent with those standards and not overruled or limited by later opinions.

13. The Committee will make opinions and/or summaries of opinions available for publication in the American Bar Association journal. The Committee will cause Formal Opinions and Informal Opinions to be published in looseleaf form.

14. The Committee may through its staff arrange to provide informal responses to ethics inquiries the answers to which are substantially gov-

erned by applicable ethical codes and opinions of this Committee or other ethics committees. The staff will maintain a log of such inquiries that will periodically be reviewed by the Committee.

15. Information contained in Committee files relating to requests for opinions that would disclose the identity of the inquirer or the person whose conduct is the subject of the opinion will not voluntarily be disclosed by the Association without the consent of the affected persons.

ABA SPECIAL COMMITTEE ON IMPLEMENTATION OF THE MODEL RULES OF PROFESSIONAL CONDUCT (1983–1987)

MICHAEL FRANCK, *Chair*
Lansing, Michigan

EDWARD L. BENOIT
Twin Falls, Idaho

W. STELL HUIE
Atlanta, Georgia

ROGER BROSNAHAN
Minneapolis, Minnesota

JAMES T. JENNINGS
Roswell, New Mexico

WAYNE A. BUDD
Boston, Massachusetts

CAROLYN B. LAMM
Washington, D.C.

RICHARD M. COLEMAN
Los Angeles, California

LLOYD LOCHRIDGE
Austin, Texas

JOHN C. ELAM
Columbus, Ohio

LEON SILVERMAN
New York, New York

JOSEPH E. GALLAGHER
Scranton, Pennsylvania

E.C. WARD
Natchez, Mississippi

ROBERT O. HETLAGE
St. Louis, Missouri

BEN J. WEAVER
Indianapolis, Indiana

AMERICAN BAR ASSOCIATION
COMMISSION ON MULTIJURISDICTIONAL PRACTICE
(2000–2002)

CHAIR
WAYNE J. POSITAN
Roseland, New Jersey

MEMBERS

ALAN T. DIMOND
Miami, Florida

PETER D. EHRENHAFT
Washington, D.C.

JOANNE M. GARVEY
San Francisco, California

STEPHEN GILLERS
New York, New York

W. ANTHONY JENKINS
Detroit, Michigan

CHARLES E. MCCALLUM
Grand Rapids, Michigan

CHERYL I. NIRO
Chicago, Illinois

HON. LARRY RAMIREZ
Las Cruces, New Mexico

HON. RANDALL
T. SHEPARD
Indianapolis, Indiana

MARNA S. TUCKER
Washington, D.C.

DIANE C. YU
New York, New York

REPORTER
BRUCE A. GREEN
New York, New York

LIAISONS

ANTHONY E. DAVIS
Denver, Colorado
*Association of Professional
Responsibility Lawyers*

THOMAS A. DECKER
Philadelphia, Pennsylvania
*Standing Committee on
Professional Discipline*

SUSAN HACKETT
Washington, D.C.
*American Corporate
Counsel Association*

JOHN L. MCDONNELL, JR.
Oakland, California
Board of Governors

ERICA MOESER
Madison, Wisconsin
*National Conference
of Bar Examiners*

M. PETER MOSER
Baltimore, Maryland
*Standing Committee on Ethics
and Professional Responsibility*

LUCIAN T. PERA
Memphis, Tennessee
*Commission on Evaluation of the
Rules of Professional Conduct*

BURNELE V. POWELL
Kansas City, Missouri
*Coordinating Council of
the Center for Professional
Responsibility*

WILLIAM P. SMITH, III
Atlanta, Georgia
*National Organization
of Bar Counsel*

JAMES E. TOWERY
San Jose, California
*Standing Committee on
Client Protection*

AMERICAN BAR ASSOCIATION
CENTER FOR PROFESSIONAL RESPONSIBILITY
JEANNE P. GRAY
Director

JOHN A. HOLTAWAY
Commission Counsel

CHARLOTTE K. STRETCH
Special Counsel

Appendix F

Amendments to the Model Rules of Professional Conduct (By Rule) (1983–2013)

Preamble
Amended 2002 per Midyear Meeting Report 401.

Scope
Amended 2002 per Midyear Meeting Report 401.

Rule 1.0
Amended 2002 per Midyear Meeting Report 401.
Amended 2009 per Midyear Meeting Report 109.
Amended 2012 per Annual Meeting Report 105A.

Rule 1.1
Amended 2002 per Midyear Meeting Report 401.
Amended 2012 per Annual Meeting Reports 105A and C.

Rule 1.2
Amended 2002 per Midyear Meeting Report 401.

Rule 1.3
Amended 2002 per Midyear Meeting Report 401.

Rule 1.4
Amended 2002 per Midyear Meeting Report 401.
Amended 2012 per Annual Meeting Report 105A.

Rule 1.5
Amended 2002 per Midyear Meeting Report 401.

Rule 1.6
Amended 2002 per Midyear Meeting Report 401.
Amended 2003 per Annual Meeting Report 119A.
Amended 2012 per Annual Meeting Reports 105A and F.

Rule 1.7
Amended 1987 per Midyear Meeting Report 121.
Amended 2002 per Midyear Meeting Report 401.

Rule 1.8
Amended 1987 per Midyear Meeting Report 121.
Amended 2002 per Midyear Meeting Report 401.

Rule 1.9
Amended 1987 per Midyear Meeting Report 121.
Amended 1989 per Midyear Meeting Report 120A.
Amended 2002 per Midyear Meeting Report 401.

Rule 1.10
Amended 1989 per Midyear Meeting Report 120A.
Amended 2002 per Midyear Meeting Report 401.
Amended 2009 per Midyear Meeting Report 109.
Amended 2009 per Annual Meeting Report 109.

Rule 1.11
Amended 1987 per Midyear Meeting Report 121.
Amended 2002 per Midyear Meeting Report 401.

Rule 1.12
Amended 1987 per Midyear Meeting Report 121.
Amended 2002 per Midyear Meeting Report 401.

Rule 1.13
Amended 2002 per Midyear Meeting Report 401.
Amended 2003 per Annual Meeting Report 119B.

Rule 1.14
Amended 1997 per Midyear Meeting Report 113.
Amended 2002 per Midyear Meeting Report 401.

Rule 1.15
Amended 2002 per Midyear Meeting Report 401.

Rule 1.16
Amended 2002 per Midyear Meeting Report 401.

Rule 1.17
Added 1990 per Midyear Meeting Report 8A.
Amended 2002 per Midyear Meeting Report 401.
Amended 2012 per Annual Meeting Report 105F.

Rule 1.18
Added 2002 per Midyear Meeting Report 401.
Amended 2012 per Annual Meeting Report 105B.

APPENDIX F: AMENDMENTS TO THE MODEL RULES

Rule 2.1
Amended 2002 per Midyear Meeting Report 401.

Rule 2.2
Deleted 2002 per Midyear Meeting Report 401.

Rule 2.3
Amended 2002 per Midyear Meeting Report 401.

Rule 2.4
Added 2002 per Midyear Meeting Report 401.

Rule 3.1
Amended 2002 per Midyear Meeting Report 401.

Rule 3.2
Amended 2002 per Midyear Meeting Report 401.

Rule 3.3
Amended 2002 per Midyear Meeting Report 401.

Rule 3.4
Amended 2002 per Midyear Meeting Report 401.

Rule 3.5
Amended 2002 per Midyear Meeting Report 401.

Rule 3.6
Amended 1994 per Annual Meeting Report 100.
Amended 2002 per Midyear Meeting Report 401.

Rule 3.7
Amended 2002 per Midyear Meeting Report 401.

Rule 3.8
Amended 1990 per Midyear Meeting Report 118.
Amended 1994 per Annual Meeting Report 100.
Amended 1995 per Annual Meeting Report 101.
Amended 2002 per Midyear Meeting Report 401.
Amended 2008 per Midyear Meeting Report 105B.

Rule 3.9
Amended 2002 per Midyear Meeting Report 401.

Rule 4.1
Amended 2002 per Midyear Meeting Report 401.

Rule 4.2
Amended 1995 per Annual Meeting Report 100.
Amended 2002 per Midyear Meeting Report 401.

Rule 4.3
Amended 2002 per Midyear Meeting Report 401.

Rule 4.4
Amended 2002 per Midyear Meeting Report 401.
Amended 2012 per Annual Meeting Report 105A.

Rule 5.1
Amended 2002 per Midyear Meeting Report 401.

Rule 5.3
Amended 2002 per Midyear Meeting Report 401.
Amended 2012 per Annual Meeting Report 105C.

Rule 5.4
Amended 1990 per Midyear Meeting Report 8A.
Amended 2002 per Midyear Meeting Report 401.

Rule 5.5
Amended 2002 per Annual Meeting Report 201B.
Amended 2007 per Midyear Meeting Report 104.
Amended 2012 per Annual Meeting Reports 105 B and C.
Amended 2013 per Midyear Meeting Report 107A.

Rule 5.6
Amended 1990 per Midyear Meeting Report 8A.
Amended 2002 per Midyear Meeting Report 401.

Rule 5.7
Added 1994 per Midyear Meeting Report 113.
Amended 2002 per Midyear Meeting Report 401.

Rule 6.1
Amended 1993 per Midyear Meeting Report 8A.
Amended 2002 per Midyear Meeting Report 401.

Rule 6.3
Amended 1987 per Midyear Meeting Report 121.

Rule 6.5
Added 2002 per Midyear Meeting Report 401.

APPENDIX F: AMENDMENTS TO THE MODEL RULES

Rule 7.1
Amended 2002 per Midyear Meeting Report 401.
Amended 2012 per Annual Meeting Report 105B.

Rule 7.2
Amended 1989 per Midyear Meeting Report 120B.
Amended 1990 per Midyear Meeting Report 8A.
Amended 2002 per Midyear Meeting Report 401.
Amended 2002 per Annual Meeting Report 114.
Amended 2012 per Annual Meeting Report 105B.

Rule 7.3
Amended 1989 per Midyear Meeting Reports 115 and 120B.
Amended 2002 per Midyear Meeting Report 401.
Amended 2012 per Annual Meeting Report 105B.

Rule 7.4
Amended 1989 per Midyear Meeting Report 121.
Amended 1992 per Annual Meeting Revised Report 128.
Amended 1994 per Annual Meeting Report 121.
Amended 2002 per Midyear Meeting Report 401.

Rule 7.5
Amended 2002 per Midyear Meeting Report 401.
Amended 2002 per Annual Meeting Report 114.

Rule 7.6
Added 2000 per Midyear Meeting Report 110.

Rule 8.1
Amended 2002 per Midyear Meeting Report 401.

Rule 8.3
Amended 1991 per Midyear Meeting Report 108C.
Amended 2002 per Midyear Meeting Report 401.

Rule 8.4
Amended 1998 per Annual Meeting Report 117.
Amended 2002 per Midyear Meeting Report 401.

Rule 8.5
Amended 1993 per Annual Meeting Report 114.
Amended 2002 per Annual Meeting Report 201C.
Amended 2013 per Midyear Meeting Report 107D.

AMENDMENTS TO THE MODEL RULES OF PROFESSIONAL CONDUCT (BY DATE) (1983–2013)

1987 Midyear Meeting
Rules 1.7, 1.8, 1.9, 1.11, 1.12 and 6.3

1989 Midyear Meeting
Rules 1.9, 1.10, 7.2, 7.3 and 7.4

1990 Midyear Meeting
Rules 1.17, 3.8, 5.4, 5.6 and 7.2

1991 Midyear Meeting
Rule 8.3

1992 Annual Meeting
Rule 7.4

1993 Midyear Meeting
Rule 6.1

1993 Annual Meeting
Rule 8.5

1994 Midyear Meeting
Rule 5.7

1994 Annual Meeting
Rules 3.6, 3.8 and 7.4

1995 Annual Meeting
Rules 3.8 and 4.2

1997 Midyear Meeting
Rule 1.14

1998 Annual Meeting
Rule 8.4

2000 Midyear Meeting
Rule 7.6

2002 Midyear Meeting
Preamble, Scope, Rules 1.0, 1.1, 1.2, 1.3, 1.4, 1.5, 1.6, 1.7, 1.8, 1.9, 1.10, 1.11, 1.12, 1.13, 1.14, 1.15, 1.16, 1.17, 1.18, 2.1, 2.2, 2.3, 2.4, 3.1, 3.2, 3.3, 3.4, 3.5, 3.6, 3.7, 3.8, 3.9, 4.1, 4.2, 4.3, 4.4, 5.1, 5.3. 5.4, 5.6, 5.7, 6.1, 6.5, 7.1, 7.2, 7.3, 7.4, 7.5, 8.1, 8.3 and 8.4

2002 Annual Meeting
Rules 5.5, 7.2, 7.5 and 8.5

2003 Annual Meeting
Rules 1.6 and 1.13

2007 Midyear Meeting
Rule 5.5

2008 Midyear Meeting
Rule 3.8

2009 Midyear Meeting
Rules 1.0 and 1.10

2009 Annual Meeting
Rule 1.10

2012 Annual Meeting
Rules 1.0, 1.1, 1.4, 1.6, 1.17, 1.18, 4.4, 5.3, 5.5, 7.1, 7.2 and 7.3

2013 Midyear Meeting
Rules 5.5 and 8.5

FORMAL ETHICS OPINION

AMERICAN BAR ASSOCIATION
STANDING COMMITTEE ON ETHICS AND PROFESSIONAL RESPONSIBILITY

Formal Opinion 466   **April 24, 2014**

Lawyer Reviewing Jurors' Internet Presence

Unless limited by law or court order, a lawyer may review a juror's or potential juror's Internet presence, which may include postings by the juror or potential juror in advance of and during a trial, but a lawyer may not communicate directly or through another with a juror or potential juror.

A lawyer may not, either personally or through another, send an access request to a juror's electronic social media. An access request is a communication to a juror asking the juror for information that the juror has not made public and that would be the type of ex parte communication prohibited by Model Rule 3.5(b).

The fact that a juror or a potential juror may become aware that a lawyer is reviewing his Internet presence when a network setting notifies the juror of such does not constitute a communication from the lawyer in violation of Rule 3.5(b).

In the course of reviewing a juror's or potential juror's Internet presence, if a lawyer discovers evidence of juror or potential juror misconduct that is criminal or fraudulent, the lawyer must take reasonable remedial measures including, if necessary, disclosure to the tribunal.

The Committee has been asked whether a lawyer who represents a client in a matter that will be tried to a jury may review the jurors' or potential jurors'[1] presence on the Internet leading up to and during trial, and, if so, what ethical obligations the lawyer might have regarding information discovered during the review.

Juror Internet Presence

Jurors may and often will have an Internet presence through electronic social media or websites. General public access to such will vary. For example, many blogs, websites, and other electronic media are readily accessible by anyone who chooses to access them through the Internet. We will refer to these publicly accessible Internet media as "websites."

---

1. Unless there is reason to make a distinction, we will refer throughout this opinion to jurors as including both potential and prospective jurors and jurors who have been empaneled as members of a jury.

For the purposes of this opinion, Internet-based social media sites that readily allow account-owner restrictions on access will be referred to as "electronic social media" or "ESM." Examples of commonly used ESM at the time of this opinion include Facebook, MySpace, LinkedIn, and Twitter. Reference to a request to obtain access to another's ESM will be denoted as an "access request," and a person who creates and maintains ESM will be denoted as a "subscriber."

Depending on the privacy settings chosen by the ESM subscriber, some information posted on ESM sites might be available to the general public, making it similar to a website, while other information is available only to a fellow subscriber of a shared ESM service, or in some cases only to those whom the subscriber has granted access. Privacy settings allow the ESM subscriber to establish different degrees of protection for different categories of information, each of which can require specific permission to access. In general, a person who wishes to obtain access to these protected pages must send a request to the ESM subscriber asking for permission to do so. Access depends on the willingness of the subscriber to grant permission.[2]

This opinion addresses three levels of lawyer review of juror Internet presence:

1. passive lawyer review of a juror's website or ESM that is available without making an access request where the juror is unaware that a website or ESM has been reviewed;
2. active lawyer review where the lawyer requests access to the juror's ESM; and
3. passive lawyer review where the juror becomes aware through a website or ESM feature of the identity of the viewer;

Trial Management and Jury Instructions

There is a strong public interest in identifying jurors who might be tainted by improper bias or prejudice. There is a related and equally strong public policy in preventing jurors from being approached ex parte by the parties to the case or their agents. Lawyers need to know where the line should be drawn between properly investigating jurors and improperly communi-

---

2. The capabilities of ESM change frequently. The committee notes that this opinion does not address particular ESM capabilities that exist now or will exist in the future. For purposes of this opinion, key elements like the ability of a subscriber to control access to ESM or to identify third parties who review a subscriber's ESM are considered generically.

cating with them.[3] In today's Internet-saturated world, the line is increasingly blurred.

For this reason, we strongly encourage judges and lawyers to discuss the court's expectations concerning lawyers reviewing juror presence on the Internet. A court order, whether in the form of a local rule, a standing order, or a case management order in a particular matter, will, in addition to the applicable Rules of Professional Conduct, govern the conduct of counsel.

Equally important, judges should consider advising jurors during the orientation process that their backgrounds will be of interest to the litigants and that the lawyers in the case may investigate their backgrounds, including review of their ESM and websites.[4] If a judge believes it to be necessary, under the circumstances of a particular matter, to limit lawyers' review of juror websites and ESM, including on ESM networks where it is possible or likely that the jurors will be notified that their ESM is being viewed, the judge should formally instruct the lawyers in the case concerning the court's expectations.

Reviewing Juror Internet Presence

If there is no court order governing lawyers reviewing juror Internet presence, we look to the ABA Model Rules of Professional Conduct for relevant strictures and prohibitions. Model Rule 3.5 addresses communications with jurors before, during, and after trial, stating:

A lawyer shall not:

(a) seek to influence a judge, juror, prospective juror or other official by means prohibited by law;

---

3. While this Committee does not take a position on whether the standard of care for competent lawyer performance requires using Internet research to locate information about jurors that is relevant to the jury selection process, we are also mindful of the recent addition of Comment [8] to Model Rule 1.1. This comment explains that a lawyer "should keep abreast of changes in the law and its practice, including the benefits and risks associated with relevant technology." *See also* Johnson v. McCullough, 306 S.W.3d 551 (Mo. 2010) (lawyer must use "reasonable efforts" to find potential juror's litigation history in Case.net, Missouri's automated case management system); N. H. Bar Ass'n, Op. 2012-13/05 (lawyers "have a general duty to be aware of social media as a source of potentially useful information in litigation, to be competent to obtain that information directly or through an agent, and to know how to make effective use of that information in litigation"); Ass'n of the Bar of the City of N. Y. Comm. on Prof'l Ethics, Formal Op. 2012-2 ("Indeed, the standards of competence and diligence may require doing everything reasonably possible to learn about jurors who will sit in judgment on a case.").

4. Judges also may choose to work with local jury commissioners to ensure that jurors are advised during jury orientation that they may properly be investigated by lawyers in the case to which they are assigned. This investigation may include review of the potential juror's Internet presence.

(b) communicate ex parte with such a person during the proceeding unless authorized to do so by law or court order;
(c) communicate with a juror or prospective juror after discharge of the jury if:
   (1) the communication is prohibited by law or court order;
   (2) the juror has made known to the lawyer a desire not to communicate; or
   (3) the communication involves misrepresentation, coercion, duress or harassment . . .

Under Model Rule 3.5(b), a lawyer may not communicate with a potential juror leading up to trial or any juror during trial unless authorized by law or court order. *See, e.g., In re Holman*, 286 S.E.2d 148 (S.C. 1982) (communicating with member of jury selected for trial of lawyer's client was "serious crime" warranting disbarment).

A lawyer may not do through the acts of another what the lawyer is prohibited from doing directly. Model Rule 8.4(a). *See also In re Myers*, 584 S.E.2d 357 (S.C. 2003) (improper for prosecutor to have a lay member of his "jury selection team" phone venire member's home); *cf.* S.C. Ethics Op. 93-27 (1993) (lawyer "cannot avoid the proscription of the rule by using agents to communicate improperly" with prospective jurors).

Passive review of a juror's website or ESM, that is available without making an access request, and of which the juror is unaware, does not violate Rule 3.5(b). In the world outside of the Internet, a lawyer or another, acting on the lawyer's behalf, would not be engaging in an improper ex parte contact with a prospective juror by driving down the street where the prospective juror lives to observe the environs in order to glean publicly available information that could inform the lawyer's jury-selection decisions. The mere act of observing that which is open to the public would not constitute a communicative act that violates Rule 3.5(b).[5]

---

5. Or. State Bar Ass'n, Formal Op. 2013-189 ("Lawyer may access publicly available information [about juror, witness, and opposing party] on social networking website"); N.Y. Cnty. Lawyers Ass'n, Formal Op. 743 (2011) (lawyer may search juror's "publicly available" webpages and ESM); Ass'n of the Bar of the City of N.Y. Comm. on Prof'l Ethics, *supra* note 3 (lawyer may use social media websites to research jurors); Ky. Bar Ass'n, Op. E-434 (2012) ("If the site is 'public,' and accessible to all, then there does not appear to be any ethics issue."). *See also* N.Y. State Bar Ass'n, Advisory Op. 843 (2010) ("A lawyer representing a client in pending litigation may access the public pages of another party's social networking website (such as Facebook or MySpace) for the purpose of obtaining possible impeachment material for use in the litigation"); Or. State Bar Ass'n, Formal Op. 2005-164 ("Accessing an adversary's public Web [sic] site is no different from reading a magazine or purchasing a book written by that adversary"); N.H. Bar Ass'n, *supra* note 3 (viewing a Facebook user's page or following on Twitter is not communication if pages are open to all members of that social media site); San Diego Cnty. Bar Legal Ethics Op. 2011-2 (opposing party's public Facebook page may be viewed by lawyer).

It is the view of the Committee that a lawyer may not personally, or through another, send an access request to a juror. An access request is an active review of the juror's electronic social media by the lawyer and is a communication to a juror asking the juror for information that the juror has not made public. This would be the type of ex parte communication prohibited by Model Rule 3.5(b).[6] This would be akin to driving down the juror's street, stopping the car, getting out, and asking the juror for permission to look inside the juror's house because the lawyer cannot see enough when just driving past.

Some ESM networks have a feature that allows the juror to identify fellow members of the same ESM network who have passively viewed the juror's ESM. The details of how this is accomplished will vary from network to network, but the key feature that is relevant to this opinion is that the juror-subscriber is able to determine not only that his ESM is being viewed, but also the identity of the viewer. This capability may be beyond the control of the reviewer because the notice to the subscriber is generated by the ESM network and is based on the identity profile of the subscriber who is a fellow member of the same ESM network.

Two recent ethics opinions have addressed this issue. The Association of the Bar of the City of New York Committee on Professional Ethics, in Formal Opinion 2012-2[7], concluded that a network-generated notice to the juror that the lawyer has reviewed the juror's social media was a communication from the lawyer to a juror, albeit an indirect one generated by the ESM network. Citing the definition of "communication" from Black's Law Dictionary (9th ed.) and other authority, the opinion concluded that the message identifying the ESM viewer was a communication because it entailed "the process of bringing an idea, information or knowledge to another's perception—including the fact that they have been researched." While the ABCNY Committee

---

6. *See* Or. State Bar Ass'n, *supra* note 5, fn. 2, (a "lawyer may not send a request to a juror to access non-public personal information on a social networking website, nor may a lawyer ask an agent to do so"); N.Y. Cnty. Lawyers Ass'n, *supra* note 5 ("Significant ethical concerns would be raised by sending a 'friend request,' attempting to connect via LinkedIn.com, signing up for an RSS feed for a juror's blog, or 'following' a juror's Twitter account"); Ass'n of the Bar of the City of N.Y. Comm. on Prof'l Ethics, *supra* note 3 (lawyer may not chat, message or send a "friend request" to a juror); Conn. Bar Ass'n, Informal Op. 2011-4 (friend request is a communication); Mo. Bar Ass'n, Informal Op. 2009-0003 (friend request is a communication pursuant to Rule 4.2). *But see* N.H. Bar Ass'n, *supra* note 3 (lawyer may request access to witness's private ESM, but request must "correctly identify the lawyer . . . [and] . . . inform the witness of the lawyer's involvement" in the matter); Phila. Bar Ass'n, Advisory Op. 2009-02 (lawyer may not use deception to secure access to witness's private ESM, but may ask the witness "forthrightly" for access).

7. Ass'n of the Bar of the City of N.Y. Comm. on Prof'l Ethics, *supra*, note 3.

found that the communication would "constitute a prohibited communication if the attorney was aware that her actions" would send such a notice, the Committee took "no position on whether an inadvertent communication would be a violation of the Rules." The New York County Lawyers' Association Committee on Professional Ethics in Formal Opinion 743 agreed with ABCNY's opinion and went further explaining, "If a juror becomes aware of an attorney's efforts to see the juror's profiles on websites, the contact may well consist of an impermissible communication, as it might tend to influence the juror's conduct with respect to the trial."[8]

This Committee concludes that a lawyer who uses a shared ESM platform to passively view juror ESM under these circumstances does not communicate with the juror. The lawyer is not communicating with the juror; the ESM service is communicating with the juror based on a technical feature of the ESM. This is akin to a neighbor's recognizing a lawyer's car driving down the juror's street and telling the juror that the lawyer had been seen driving down the street.

Discussion by the trial judge of the likely practice of trial lawyers reviewing juror ESM during the jury orientation process will dispel any juror misperception that a lawyer is acting improperly merely by viewing what the juror has revealed to all others on the same network.

While this Committee concludes that ESM-generated notice to a juror that a lawyer has reviewed the juror's information is not communication from the lawyer to the juror, the Committee does make two additional recommendations to lawyers who decide to review juror social media. First, the Committee suggests that lawyers be aware of these automatic, subscriber-notification features. By accepting the terms of use, the subscriber-notification feature is not secret. As indicated by Rule 1.1, Comment 8, it is important for a lawyer to be current with technology. While many people simply click their agreement to the terms and conditions for use of an ESM network, a lawyer who uses an ESM network in his practice should review the terms and conditions, including privacy features—which change frequently—prior to using such a network. And, as noted above, jurisdictions differ on issues that arise when a lawyer uses social media in his practice.

Second, Rule 4.4(a) prohibits lawyers from actions "that have no substantial purpose other than to embarrass, delay, or burden a third person . . ." Lawyers who review juror social media should ensure that their review is purposeful and not crafted to embarrass, delay, or burden the juror or the proceeding.

---

8. N.Y. Cnty. Lawyers' Ass'n, *supra* note 5.

Discovery of Juror Misconduct

Increasingly, courts are instructing jurors in very explicit terms about the prohibition against using ESM to communicate about their jury service or the pending case and the prohibition against conducting personal research about the matter, including research on the Internet. These warnings come because jurors have discussed trial issues on ESM, solicited access to witnesses and litigants on ESM, not revealed relevant ESM connections during jury selection, and conducted personal research on the trial issues using the Internet.[9]

In 2009, the Court Administration and Case Management Committee of the Judicial Conference of the United States recommended a model jury instruction that is very specific about juror use of social media, mentioning many of the popular social media by name.[10] The recommended instruction states in part:

> I know that many of you use cell phones, Blackberries, the internet and other tools of technology. You also must not talk to anyone at any time about this case or use these tools to communicate electronically with anyone about the case . . . You may not communicate with anyone about the case on your cell phone, through e- mail, Blackberry, iPhone, text messaging, or on Twitter, through any blog or website, including Facebook, Google+, My Space, LinkedIn, or YouTube. . . . I expect you will inform me as soon as you become aware of another juror's violation of these instructions.

These same jury instructions were provided by both a federal district court and state criminal court judge during a three-year study on juries and social media. Their research found that "jury instructions are the most effective tool to mitigate the risk of juror misconduct through social media."[11] As a result, the authors recommend jury instruction on social media "early and often" and daily in lengthy trials.[12]

---

9. For a review of recent cases in which a juror used ESM to discuss trial proceedings and/or used the Internet to conduct private research, read Hon. Amy J. St. Eve et al., *More from the #Jury Box: The Latest on Juries and Social Media*, 12 Duke Law & Technology Review no. 1, 69-78 (2014), *available at* http://scholarship.law.duke.edu/cgi/viewcontent.cgi?article=1247&context=dltr.

10. Judicial Conference Committee on Court Administration and Case Management, *Proposed Model Jury Instructions: The Use of Electronic Technology to Conduct Research on or Communicate about a Case*, USCourts.gov (June 2012), http://www.uscourts.gov/uscourts/News/2012/jury-instructions.pdf.

11. *Id.* at 66.

12. *Id.* at 87.

Analyzing the approximately 8% of the jurors who admitted to being "tempted" to communicate about the case using social media, the judges found that the jurors chose not to talk or write about the case because of the specific jury instruction not to do so.

While juror misconduct via social media itself is not the subject of this Opinion, lawyers reviewing juror websites and ESM may become aware of misconduct. Model Rule 3.3 and its legislative history make it clear that a lawyer has an obligation to take remedial measures including, if necessary, informing the tribunal when the lawyer discovers that a juror has engaged in criminal or fraudulent conduct related to the proceeding. But the history is muddled concerning whether a lawyer has an affirmative obligation to act upon learning that a juror has engaged in improper conduct that falls short of being criminal or fraudulent.

Rule 3.3 was amended in 2002, pursuant to the ABA Ethics 2000 Commission's proposal, to expand on a lawyer's previous obligation to protect a tribunal from criminal or fraudulent conduct by the lawyer's client to also include such conduct by any person.[13]

Model Rule 3.3(b) reads:

(b) A lawyer who represents a client in an adjudicative proceeding and who knows that a person intends to engage, is engaging or has engaged in criminal or fraudulent conduct related to the proceeding shall take reasonable remedial measures including, if necessary, disclosure to the tribunal.

Comment [12] to Rule 3.3 provides:

Lawyers have a special obligation to protect a tribunal against criminal or fraudulent conduct that undermines the integrity of the adjudicative process, such as bribing, intimidating or otherwise unlawfully communicating with a witness, juror, court official or other participant in the proceeding, unlawfully destroying or concealing documents or other evidence or failing to disclose information to the tribunal when required by law to do so. Thus, paragraph (b)

13. Ethics 2000 Commission, *Model Rule 3.3: Candor Toward the Tribunal*, AMERICAN BAR ASSOCIATION, http://www.americanbar.org/groups/professional_responsibility/policy/ethics_2000_commission/e2k_rule33.html (last visited Apr. 18, 2014).

requires a lawyer to take reasonable remedial measures, including disclosure if necessary, whenever the lawyer knows that a person, including the lawyer's client, intends to engage, is engaging or has engaged in criminal or fraudulent conduct related to the proceeding.

Part of Ethics 2000's stated intent when it amended Model Rule 3.3 was to incorporate provisions from Canon 7 of the ABA Model Code of Professional Responsibility (Model Code) that had placed an affirmative duty upon a lawyer to notify the court upon learning of juror misconduct:

> This new provision incorporates the substance of current paragraph (a)(2), as well as ABA Model Code of Professional Responsibility DR 7-102(B)(2) ("A lawyer who receives information clearly establishing that a person other than the client has perpetrated a fraud upon a tribunal shall promptly reveal the fraud to the tribunal") and DR 7-108(G) ("A lawyer shall reveal promptly to the court improper conduct by a venireperson or juror, or by another toward a venireperson or juror or a member of the venireperson's or juror's family, of which the lawyer has knowledge"). *Reporter's Explanation of Changes, Model Rule 3.3.*[14]

However, the intent of the Ethics 2000 Commission expressed above to incorporate the substance of DR 7-108(G) in its new subsection (b) of Model Rule 3.3 was never carried out. Under the Model Code's DR 7-108(G), a lawyer knowing of "improper conduct" by a juror or venireperson was required to report the matter to the tribunal. Under Rule 3.3(b), the lawyer's obligation to act arises only when the juror or venireperson engages in conduct that is *fraudulent or criminal.*[15] While improper conduct was not defined in the Model Code, it clearly imposes a broader duty to take remedial action than exists under the Model Rules. The Committee is constrained to provide guidance based upon the language of Rule 3.3(b) rather than any expressions of intent in the legislative history of that rule.

---

14. Ethics 2000 Commission, *Model Rule 3.3 Reporter's Explanation of Changes*, AMERICAN BAR ASSOCIATION, http://www.americanbar.org/groups/professional_responsibility/policy/ethics_2000_commission/e2k_rule33rem.html (last visited Apr. 18, 2014).

15. Compare MODEL RULES OF PROF'L CONDUCT R. 3.3(b) (2002) to N.Y. RULES OF PROF'L CONDUCT R. 3.5(d) (2013) ("a lawyer shall reveal promptly to the court improper conduct by a member of the venire or a juror....").

By passively viewing juror Internet presence, a lawyer may become aware of a juror's conduct that is criminal or fraudulent, in which case, Model Rule 3.3(b) requires the lawyer to take remedial measures including, if necessary, reporting the matter to the court. But the lawyer may also become aware of juror conduct that violates court instructions to the jury but does not rise to the level of criminal or fraudulent conduct, and Rule 3.3(b) does not prescribe what the lawyer must do in that situation. While considerations of questions of law are outside the scope of the Committee's authority, applicable law might treat such juror activity as conduct that triggers a lawyer's duty to take remedial action including, if necessary, reporting the juror's conduct to the court under current Model Rule 3.3(b).[16]

While any Internet postings about the case by a juror during trial may violate court instructions, the obligation of a lawyer to take action will depend on the lawyer's assessment of those postings in light of court instructions and the elements of the crime of contempt or other applicable criminal statutes. For example, innocuous postings about jury service, such as the quality of the food served at lunch, may be contrary to judicial instructions, but fall short of conduct that would warrant the extreme response of finding a juror in criminal contempt. A lawyer's affirmative duty to act is triggered only when the juror's known conduct is criminal or fraudulent, including conduct that is criminally contemptuous of court instructions. The materiality of juror Internet communications to the integrity of the trial will likely be a consideration in determining whether the juror has acted criminally or fraudulently. The remedial duty flowing from known criminal or fraudulent juror conduct is triggered by knowledge of the conduct and is not preempted by a lawyer's belief that the court will not choose to address the conduct as a crime or fraud.

Conclusion

In sum, a lawyer may passively review a juror's public presence on the Internet, but may not communicate with a juror. Requesting access to a private area on a juror's ESM is communication within this framework.

---

16. *See, e.g.*, U.S. v. Juror Number One, 866 F.Supp.2d 442 (E.D. Pa. 2011) (failure to follow jury instructions and emailing other jurors about case results in criminal contempt). The use of criminal contempt remedies for disregarding jury instructions is not confined to improper juror use of ESM. U.S. v. Rowe, 906 F.2d 654 (11th Cir. 1990) (juror held in contempt, fined, and dismissed from jury for violating court order to refrain from discussing the case with other jurors until after jury instructions delivered).

The fact that a juror or a potential juror may become aware that the lawyer is reviewing his Internet presence when an ESM network setting notifies the juror of such review does not constitute a communication from the lawyer in violation of Rule 3.5(b).

If a lawyer discovers criminal or fraudulent conduct by a juror related to the proceeding, the lawyer must take reasonable remedial measures including, if necessary, disclosure to the tribunal.

AMERICAN BAR ASSOCIATION
STANDING COMMITTEE ON ETHICS AND PROFESSIONAL RESPONSIBILITY
321 N. Clark Street, Chicago, Illinois 60654-4714 Telephone (312) 988-5310
CHAIR: Paula J. Frederick, Atlanta, GA ■ T. Maxfield Bahner, Chattanooga, TN
Barbara S. Gillers, New York, NY ■ Amanda Jones, Chicago, IL
Donald R. Lundberg, Indianapolis, IN ■ Myles V. Lynk, Tempe, AZ
J. Charles Mokriski, Boston, MA ■ Ellen A. Pansky, South Pasadena, CA
Jennifer A. Paradise, New York, NY ■ Richard H. Underwood, Lexington, KY

CENTER FOR PROFESSIONAL RESPONSIBILITY:
Dennis A. Rendleman, Ethics Counsel ■ Mary McDermott, Associate Ethics Counsel

AMERICAN BAR ASSOCIATION
STANDING COMMITTEE ON ETHICS AND PROFESSIONAL RESPONSIBILITY

Formal Opinion 467   **September 8, 2014**

Managerial and Supervisory Obligations of Prosecutors Under Rules 5.1 and 5.3

Model Rules 5.1 and 5.3 require lawyers with managerial authority and supervisory lawyers, including prosecutors, to make "reasonable efforts to ensure" that all lawyers and nonlawyers in their offices conform to the Model Rules. Prosecutors with managerial authority must adopt reasonable policies and procedures to achieve these goals. Prosecutors with direct supervisory authority must make reasonable efforts to ensure that the lawyers and nonlawyers they supervise comply with the Rules. Where prosecutors have both managerial and direct supervisory authority, they may, depending on the circumstances, be required to fulfill both sets of obligations. The particular measures that managerial and supervisory prosecutors must implement to comply with these rules will depend on a variety of factors, including the size and structure of their offices.

A. Introduction

Prosecutors have special duties under the Model Rules of Professional Conduct. They have "the responsibility of a minister of justice and not simply that of an advocate."[1] They must "refrain from prosecuting a charge that [they know] is not supported by probable cause."[2] They must "make reasonable efforts to assure that the accused has been advised of the right to, and the procedure for obtaining, counsel and has been given reasonable opportunity to obtain counsel."[3] They must "make timely disclosure to the defense" of exculpatory and mitigating evidence.[4] In short, and in words long ago written by the Supreme Court in *Berger v. U.S.*,[5] a prosecutor's duties are "not of an ordinary party to a controversy, but of a sovereignty whose obligation

---

1. ABA Model Rules of Prof'l Conduct R. 3.8 cmt. [1].
2. ABA Model Rules of Prof'l Conduct R. 3.8(a).
3. ABA Model Rules of Prof'l Conduct R. 3.8(b).
4. ABA Model Rules of Prof'l Conduct R. 3.8(d). For additional special duties of prosecutors, see also ABA Model Rules of Prof'l Conduct R. 3.8(c)-(h) and cmts. [3]-[9].
5. Berger v. United States, 295 U.S. 78 (1935).

to govern impartially is as compelling as its obligation to govern at all; and whose interest, therefore, in a criminal prosecution is not that it shall win a case, but that justice shall be done."[6]

We believe that most prosecutors know and follow the rules of professional conduct. Indeed, the laudable efforts of such prosecutors have provided good examples, cited throughout this opinion. But there are prosecutors who do violate the rules, and for all prosecutors there are special challenges and obligations. This opinion provides guidance on the special challenges and obligations of prosecutors with managerial and supervisory responsibility.[7]

B. ABA Model Rules of Professional Conduct 5.1 and 5.3 Apply to Prosecutors

Rules 5.1 and 5.3 address obligations of lawyers with managerial authority (hereinafter sometimes referred to as "managers") and supervisory lawyers within a "firm" or a "law firm." Rule 1.0(c) defines "firm" or "law firm" to include "lawyers employed in a legal services organization or the legal department of a corporation or other organization." Comment [3] makes clear that government organizations are included.[8] The comments to Rule 5.1 also specifically reference government agencies.[9] Prosecutors' offices are *government* organizations.

Rule 3.8, which specifies the "Special Responsibilities of Prosecutors," also makes clear that prosecutors have supervisory obligations under Rules 5.1 and 5.3. Comment [6] to Rule 3.8 reads, "Like other lawyers, prosecutors

---

6. *Id.* at 88. *See also* ABA Comm. on Ethics & Prof'l Responsibility, Formal Op. 09-454 at fn. 9 ("References in U.S. judicial decisions to the prosecutor's obligation to seek justice date back more than 150 years.") (citations omitted). A "prosecutor" for purposes of this opinion is a lawyer employed by a government agency whose primary responsibility involves the investigation and prosecution of criminal cases and related matters. Where a prosecutor's duties also embrace civil authority, this opinion also applies to that sphere of their work. Federal prosecutors are covered by state ethics rules under the McDade Amendment, 28 U.S.C. §530B.

7. Of course all lawyers--e.g., lawyers in private practice, in public defender offices, and in other state and federal agencies--have supervisory obligations under Rules 5.1 and 5.3. We leave for another day a specific discussion of how Rules 5.1 and 5.3 must be implemented by them. The general obligations described in this opinion with respect to prosecutors, however, apply to lawyers in those offices as well.

8. ABA Model Rules of Prof'l Conduct R. 1.0 cmt. [3] ("[w]ith respect to the law department of an organization, *including the government,* there is ordinarily no question that the members of the department constitute a firm within the meaning of the Rules") (emphasis added).

9. ABA Model Rules of Prof'l Conduct R. 5.1 cmt. [1] ("[p]aragraph (a) [of Rule 5.1] applies to lawyers who have managerial authority over the professional work of a firm. . . . This includes . . . . lawyers having comparable managerial authority in a . . . government agency. . . ").

are subject to Rules 5.1 and 5.3, which relate to responsibilities regarding lawyers and nonlawyers who work for or are associated with the lawyer's office."[10] Finally, ABA Formal Opinion 09-454 emphasizes that these obligations apply to prosecutors: "Any supervisory lawyer in the prosecutor's office and those lawyers with managerial responsibility are obligated to ensure that subordinate lawyers comply with all their legal and ethical obligations."[11]

Formal Opinion 09-454 adds, "[S]upervisors who directly oversee trial prosecutors must make reasonable efforts to ensure that those under their direct supervision meet their ethical obligations of disclosure, and are subject to discipline for ordering, ratifying or knowingly failing to correct discovery violations."[12]

C. Who Has Responsibility Under ABA Model Rules 5.1 and 5.3 in a Prosecutor's Office?

Rules 5.1 and 5.3 set forth three types of responsibility for the conduct of lawyers and nonlawyers "employed or retained by or associated with a lawyer."[13] Paragraph (a) addresses lawyers "with managerial authority."[14] Paragraph (b) pertains to lawyers "having direct supervisory authority over another lawyer" or "having direct supervisory authority over the nonlawyer."[15] Paragraph (c) applies to lawyers who either (i) order or ratify the conduct of another, or (ii) have managerial authority or direct supervisory authority, know of the conduct at a time when its consequences can be mitigated, and fail to take reasonable remedial action.[16] We address each below.

1. Managerial Responsibility

Under paragraph (a), "managerial" lawyers "shall make reasonable efforts to ensure that [their organization] has in effect measures giving reason-

---

10. Comment [6] to Rule 3.8 gives examples: "Paragraph (f) [of 3.8] reminds the prosecutor of the importance of these [supervisory] obligations in connection with the unique dangers of improper extrajudicial statements in a criminal case." Paragraph 3.8(f) also "requires a prosecutor to exercise reasonable care to prevent persons assisting or associated with the prosecutor from making improper extrajudicial statements, even when such persons are not under the direct supervision of the prosecutor."

11. Formal Op. 09-454, *supra* note 6, at 8 (citing Rules 5.1(a) and (b)). See also the opening summary of Formal Op. 09-454: "Supervisory personnel in a prosecutor's office must take reasonable steps under Rule 5.1 to ensure that all lawyers in the office comply with their disclosure obligation."

12. Formal Op. 09-454, *supra* note 6, at 8 (citing Rules 5.1(b) and (c)).

13. ABA MODEL RULES OF PROF'L CONDUCT R. 5.1(a) (over lawyers) & R. 5.3(a) (over nonlawyers). With respect to nonlawyers, the obligation is to make sure that the nonlawyer's "conduct is compatible with the professional obligations of the lawyer."

14. ABA MODEL RULES OF PROF'L CONDUCT R. 5.1(a) & 5.3(a).

15. ABA MODEL RULES OF PROF'L CONDUCT R. 5.1(b) & 5.3(b).

16. ABA MODEL RULES OF PROF'L CONDUCT R. 5.1(c) & 5.3(c).

able assurance that all lawyers in the [organization] conform to the Rules of Professional Conduct." Managerial lawyers include "members of a partnership, the shareholders in a law firm organized as a professional corporation and [other lawyers] having comparable managerial authority."[17] This group also includes "lawyers who have intermediate managerial responsibilities."[18] Rule 5.3(a) imposes a corresponding obligation with respect to nonlawyers "employed or retained or associated" with the office.

In a prosecutor's office, managerial lawyers are the top prosecutors and all other prosecutors with managerial or executive functions in the office. This group would include, for example, the District or County or U.S. Attorney him or herself, as well as executive staff, bureau or unit heads, and similarly positioned others who, among other duties, make policies and set procedures for the office as a whole or for individual units. As part of their functions, these individuals may also be direct supervisors under 5.1(b) and 5.3(b) discussed below—depending on the facts and circumstances—but they have overarching special duties under Rules 5.1(a) and 5.3(a).[19]

Managers must make "reasonable efforts" to ensure compliance with the Model Rules of Professional Conduct by all lawyers in the office, including other lawyers with comparable managerial authority. As discussed further in this opinion, "these efforts can take many forms, so long as they are reasonably calculated to eliminate or inhibit violations [of the Rules]."[20]

2. Supervisory Responsibility

Under Rule 5.1(b) "[a] lawyer having direct supervisory authority over another lawyer shall make reasonable efforts to ensure that the other lawyer conforms to the Rules of Professional Conduct." Under Rule 5.3(b) "[a] lawyer having direct supervisory authority over [a] nonlawyer shall make reasonable efforts to ensure that the person's conduct is compatible with the professional obligations of the lawyer." This category "applies to lawyers who have supervisory authority over the work of other lawyers [and nonlawyers] in the [office]" regardless of their status in the organization.

In a prosecutor's office, a "supervisor" is a lawyer who—regardless of his or her position or title in the office hierarchy—directly supervises the

---

17. ABA MODEL RULES OF PROF'L CONDUCT R. 5.1 cmt. [1].

18. *Id.*

19. *See* GEOFFREY C. HAZARD, W. WILLIAM HODES & PETER R. JARVIS, THE LAW OF LAWYERING §42.4 (3rd Ed., Supp. 2010) [hereinafter HAZARD & HODES] (partners and other managers are "'supervisory' lawyers *per se*"); RESTATEMENT OF THE LAW GOVERNING LAWYERS (3rd Ed.) §11, at 112 (managerial lawyers have "general supervisory" duties over lawyers and nonlawyers).

20. HAZARD & HODES, *supra* note 19, §42.4.

work of another prosecutor in a particular matter, proceeding, inquiry or other event or series of events involving a case. "Even if a lawyer is not a partner or other general manager, he or she may have direct supervisory authority over another lawyer."[21]

Further, a manager within the meaning of paragraph (a) can also be a supervisor within the meaning of paragraph (b). For example, a unit or bureau chief whose job description consists mainly or principally of executive or managerial functions may also directly supervise individual prosecutors in any proceeding, application, inquiry, investigation, trial, appeal, or other matter. When managers function as direct supervisors, they have obligations under paragraph (b) as well.

The key to responsibility under paragraph (b) is the relationship between the two lawyers in the matter. The supervisory authority "need not be over the entirety of the second lawyer's practice. . . [5.1(b)] would apply to direct supervision in a particular case, to a senior or mid-level [lawyer] with supervisory authority over a junior [lawyer's] work in that or a series of cases, or to one partner [or manager] who has been given supervisory authority over another partner [or manager's] work in a case or practice area."[22]

Finally paragraphs (a) and (b) impose some overlapping duties. For, example, a direct supervisor "has the same responsibility as a partner or manager to assure compliance with the ethical rules by those lawyers under her direct supervisory authority."[23] In fact, as noted in G. Hazard, W. Hodes & P. Jarvis, *The Law of Lawyering* (3rd Ed., 2010 Supplement), Rule 5.1(b) "*is essentially identical to Rule 5.1(a)*, except that it applies to all lawyers who have 'direct supervisory authority over another lawyer,' whether or not they are partners or managers or other partner- equivalents" and whatever their practice setting.[24] And, "Rule 5.1(b), like Rule 5.1(a), can require proactive, as distinct from merely reactive or passive, measures."[25]

---

21. Ronald D. Rotunda & John S. Dzienkowski, Legal Ethics: The Lawyer's Deskbook on Professional Responsibility § 5.1-2(b), at 1009 (2014) [hereinafter Rotunda & Dzienkowski] (citing Rule 5.1(b)).

22. Hazard & Hodes, *supra* note 19, §42.5. *See also* ABA Model Rules of Prof'l Conduct R. 5.1 cmt. [5] ("Whether a lawyer has supervisory authority in particular circumstances is a question of fact. Partners and lawyers with comparable authority have at least indirect responsibility for all work being done by the firm, while a partner or manager in charge of a particular matter ordinarily also has supervisory responsibility for the work of other firm lawyers engaged in the matter.").

23. Rotunda & Dzienkowski, *supra* note 21, §5.1-2(b), at 1009.

24. Hazard & Hodes, *supra* note 19, §42.5 (emphasis added).

25. *Id.*

3. Responsibility for Another's Conduct Under ABA Model Rules 5.1(c) and 5.3(c)

Rules 5.1(c) and 5.3(c) make a lawyer responsible for another lawyer's or a nonlawyer's conduct if the lawyer "orders or, with knowledge of the specific conduct, ratifies the conduct involved" or if "the lawyer is a partner or has comparable managerial authority in the [office] where the other lawyer practices [or the nonlawyer is employed], or has direct supervisory authority of the other lawyer [or nonlawyer], and knows of the conduct at a time when its consequences can be avoided or mitigated but fails to take reasonable remedial action."[26]

These obligations supplement the obligations of managers and supervisors under paragraphs (a) and (b), even though they are not directed at supervisors and managers alone. Indeed, the obligations set forth in Rules 5.1(c)(1) and 5.3(c)(1) apply regardless of whether the ordering or ratifying lawyer is a manager or a direct supervisor. But it is important to make clear—as we do here—that a lawyer who is a manager or supervisor may be responsible under Rules 5.1(c) and 5.3(c) even though he or she has no formal or structural relationship to the misbehaving lawyer or nonlawyer.[27]

Rules 5.1(c)(2) and 5.3(c)(2) also impose a duty to avoid or mitigate the consequences of improper conduct if there is an opportunity to do so.[28] A lawyer who is "a partner or has comparable managerial authority . . . or has direct supervisory authority over the other lawyer [or non-lawyer] and knows of [misconduct] at a time when its consequences can be avoided or mitigated" must take "reasonable remedial action."[29]

What constitutes "reasonable remedial action" will depend on the circumstances, but in any event requires "prevention of avoidable consequences" of the misconduct if the manager or supervisor learns of the mis-

---

26. ABA MODEL RULES OF PROF'L CONDUCT R. 5.1(c) & R. 5.3(c).

27. RESTATEMENT OF THE LAW GOVERNING LAWYERS, *supra* note 19, §11, at 110 (the obligation of a partner or managerial lawyer to take remedial action as described in 5.1(c) "attaches even if [the partner or managerial lawyer] has no direct supervisory authority over the other lawyer"). *See also* HAZARD & HODES *supra* note 19 §42.6 ("[P]artners and those with comparable managerial authority cannot rely upon the fact that they have, or had, no direct responsibility for or supervisory authority over the lawyer engaged in wrongdoing. Partner status, equivalent managerial status, and direct supervisory authority all equally trigger a responsibility to take remedial action under Rule 5.1(c)(2)"). Further, "most violations of [(c)(1) will] also constitute violations of Rule 8.4(a)"). HAZARD & HODES, *supra* note 19, §42.6. Model Rule 8.4(a) provides that it is "professional misconduct for a lawyer to violate or attempt to violate the Rules of Professional Conduct, knowingly assist or induce another to do so, or do so through the acts of another."

28. *See* ABA MODEL RULES OF PROF'L CONDUCT R. 5.1(c)(1)-(2) & 5.3(c)(1)-(2). *See also* HAZARD & HODES, *supra* note 19, §42.6.

29. *Id.*

conduct when that can be achieved.[30] Steps to avoid future similar acts may be important for other reasons, but Rules 5.1(c)(2) and 5.3(c)(2) require steps that look back — that will "remedy or mitigate the consequences of [a] violation" that has already occurred. In the case of prosecutors, the immediate turnover of material to the defense might be required.[31] In other instances, reporting the conduct to disciplinary authorities might be required.[32] But the obligation to take reasonable remedial steps "extends to all known violations"—not only those covered by an applicable reporting obligation[33]—and should, in some recognizable measure, remedy or mitigate the consequences of misconduct that has occurred.

D. Background: The Need for Guidance

In recent years, reports, court opinions, and other authorities have drawn attention to prosecutorial misconduct—notwithstanding the many excellent prosecutors who scrupulously follow or exceed the mandates of the Rules of Professional Conduct. These reports, opinions and authorities suggest a need for more guidance.[34] For example, in *Connick v. Thompson*,[35] the Supreme Court reversed a $14 million judgment awarded against the New Orleans Parish District Attorney's Office in favor of John Thompson, an innocent man who spent 18 years in prison—14 of them on death row—because pros-

---

30. *See, e.g.*, ABA MODEL RULES OF PROF'L CONDUCT R. 5.1 cmt. [5] ("[a]ppropriate remedial action by a partner or managing lawyer would depend on the immediacy of that lawyer's involvement and the seriousness of the misconduct. A supervisor is required to intervene to prevent avoidable consequences of misconduct if the supervisor knows that the misconduct occurred. Thus if a supervising lawyer knows that a subordinate misrepresented a matter to an opposing party in negotiation, the supervisor as well as the subordinate has a duty to correct the resulting misapprehension"). *See also*, HAZARD & HODES, *supra* note 19, §42.6.

31. *In re* Myers, 584 S.E.2d 357, 362 (S.C. 2003) (Solicitor (a supervising or managerial prosecutor) violated Rule 5.1(c)'s obligation to remediate when he failed to notify the defense lawyer about improper eavesdropping by his subordinates immediately upon learning of the misconduct).

32. RESTATEMENT OF THE LAW GOVERNING LAWYERS, *supra* note 19, §11 cmt. e.

33. *Id.*

34. *See, e.g.*, Brad Heath & Kevin McCoy, *Prosecutors' Conduct Can Tip Justice Scales*, USA TODAY (September 23, 2010), http://usatoday30.usatoday.com/news/washington/judicial/2010-09-22-federal-prosecutors-reform_N.htm; Joaquin Sapien, *Out of Order: When Prosecutors Cross The Line*, PROPUBLICA, http://www.propublica.org/series/out-of-order (last visited July 6, 2014); KATHLEEN M. RIDOLFI & MAURICE POSSLEY, PREVENTABLE ERROR: A REPORT ON PROSECUTORIAL MISCONDUCT IN CALIFORNIA 1997-2009 (2010), *available at* http://www.veritasinitiative.org/downloads/ProsecutorialMisconduct_Exec_Sum.pdf. *See also* United States v. Olsen, 737 F.3d 625 (9th Cir. 2013) (denying petition for rehearing en banc, Kozinski, Pregerson, Reinhardt, Thomas, and Watford dissenting, writing, "There is an epidemic of *Brady* violations abroad in the land.").

35. Connick v. Thompson, 131 S.Ct. 1350 (2011).

ecutors withheld exculpatory evidence. The majority opinion rejected Mr. Thompson's theory of liability based on 42 U.S.C. §1983,[36] and did not address the Rules. But the opinions in *Connick*—both majority and dissenting—document events that demonstrate the need for guidance on the managerial and supervisory obligations of prosecutors under the Rules of Professional Conduct. And, only one year later in *Smith v. Cain*,[37] the Supreme Court reversed a conviction for *Brady* violations by the same office.[38]

In 2013 the Supreme Court of Oklahoma disciplined a former Assistant District Attorney for the Oklahoma County District Attorney's Office and criticized the District Attorney's office for a lack of managerial and supervisory effectiveness.[39] The Court said:

> We must recognize that the [Assistant District Attorney] was acting under the direction, supervision, and policies of the then elected District Attorney. Responsibility for the respondent's conduct and trial tactics falls partially to the District Attorney as the chief administrator of the office.[40]

The New Orleans and Oklahoma examples alone would justify examination of the obligations of managerial and supervising prosecutors under Rules 5.1 and 5.3. But the frequency of prosecutorial misconduct nationwide documented by, *inter alia*, opinions in criminal cases and disciplinary proceedings reported in the last fifteen years, also underscores this need. These

---

36. "Thompson alleged that Connick had failed to train his prosecutors adequately about their duty to produce exculpatory evidence and that the lack of training had caused [the District Attorney's Office to fail to disclose certain evidence to Thompson]." *Id.* at 1355. *See* 42 U.S.C. §1983 (1996) provides in relevant part: "Every person who, under color of any statute, ordinance, regulation, custom, or usage, of any State . . . subjects, or causes to be subjected, any citizen of the United States or other person within the jurisdiction thereof to the deprivation of any rights, privileges, or immunities secured by the Constitution and laws, shall be liable to the party injured in an action at law, suit in equity, or other proper proceeding for redress. . . ."

37. Smith v. Cain, 132 S.Ct. 627 (2012) (reversing a murder conviction for *Brady* violation by the New Orleans Parish District Attorney's Office).

38. Brady v. Maryland, 373 U.S. 83 (1963).

39. State ex rel. Oklahoma Bar Ass'n v. Miller, 309 P.3d 108 (Okla. 2013) (assistant prosecutor suspended for 180 days for violations of, *inter alia*, Rules 8.4, 3.8 & 3.4). The Tenth Circuit has also expressed concern about prosecutorial misconduct in the Oklahoma County District Attorney's office. *See* Le v. Mullin, 311 F.3d 1002, 1029 (2002) ("While it is true that any prosecutor will have his share of trial-outcome challenges, over the last fifteen years, the Oklahoma County District Attorney's office has been cited for actions deemed improper, 'egregiously improper,' deceitful and impermissible in striking foul blows, deplorable, 'perhaps inappropriate,' worthy of condemnation, and, in this very case, 'condemned' and 'certainly error.'"; "The prosecution's actions in this case suggest defiance of Oklahoma courts and disregard for Oklahoma law.") (footnotes omitted).

40. State ex rel. Oklahoma Bar Ass'n v. Miller, 309 P.3d at 119.

decisions reveal numerous violations of *Brady* in criminal cases[41] (which are also violations of Rule 3.8), and show other examples of misconduct, e.g., prosecutors using false evidence or failing to correct false statements to the court;[42] prosecutors engaging in other improper courtroom conduct;[43] and

---

41. *See, e.g.,* Monroe v. Angelone, 323 F.3d 286, 314 (4th Cir. 2003) (failure to reveal leniency agreements with key witness and then stressing absence of such deals in closing statement[s]); Tassin v. Cain, 517 F.3d 770, 781 (5th Cir. 2008) (failure to disclose a "beneficial sentencing agreement that hinged directly on [a government witness's] testimony"; failure to correct misleading statements by the witness regarding the agreement; and, arguing to the jury, on the basis of the misleading testimony, that the witness had no reason to lie) (footnote omitted); Silva v. Brown, 416 F.3d 980, 986 (9th Cir. 2005) (failure to disclose an arrangement where the prosecutor agreed to drop murder charges against the chief prosecution witness in exchange for the witness's agreement to refrain from undergoing a psychiatric evaluation before testifying; "The existence of this deal evidencing the prosecution's concern as to the mental state of [the witness] was obviously impeachment evidence favorable to the defense."); Douglas v. Workman, 560 F.3d 1156, 1174-76 (10th Cir. 2009) (failure to disclose plea deal with witness linking defendant to murder; the witness was "indispensible" to the state's case). *See also* Brad Heath & Kevin McCoy, *supra* note 34 (finding *Brady* violations in many federal cases). Indeed, the failure to turn over exculpatory evidence has been described as the "most common form of [prosecutorial] misconduct cited by courts in overturning convictions." *See* Radley Balko, *The Untouchables: America's Misbehaving Prosecutors, And The System That Protects Them*, Huffington Post, http://www.huffingtonpost.com/2013/08/01/prosecutorial-misconduct-new-orleans-louisiana_n_3529891.html (last visited July 7, 2014). *See also Rampant Prosecutorial Misconduct*, NY Times (Jan. 4, 2014), http://www.nytimes.com/2014/01/05/opinion/sunday/rampant-prosecutorial-misconduct.html?_r=0; Comm. on Prof'l Ethics & Conduct of the Iowa State Bar Ass'n v. Ramey, 512 N.W.2d 569 (Iowa 1994) (indefinitely suspending an experienced prosecutor for making false statements regarding a chain of custody and for failing to disclose exculpatory evidence); Office of Disciplinary Counsel v. Wrenn, 790 N.E.2d 1195 (Ohio 2003) (six month stayed suspension for failing to disclose DNA test results in a child sex abuse case); In re Jordan, 913 So. 2d 775, 784 (La. 2005) (deferred three month suspension for failing to disclose *Brady* material in violation of 3.8(d) and 8.4(a); deferral "subject to the condition that any misconduct . . . during a one-year period following [the date of the suspension] may be grounds for making the deferred suspension executory, or imposing additional discipline. . . .") (rehearing denied).

42. *See, e.g.,* Napue v. Illinois, 360 U.S. 264, 265, 269-270 (1959) (failure to correct witness testimony the prosecutor knew to be false); Drake v. Portuondo, 553 F.3d 230, 233, 241-243 (2d Cir. 2009) (knowingly presenting false expert-witness testimony); Hobbs v. Cappelluti, 899 F. Supp. 2d 738 (N.D. Ill. 2012) (helping detective coerce a false video confession and pursuing conviction with the false confession); Dow v. Virga, 729 F.3d 1041 (9th Cir. 2013) (knowingly eliciting and failing to correct a detective's false testimony; "textbook prosecutorial misconduct"); In re Jordan, 91 P.3d 1168, 1173-1175 (Kan. 2004) (public censure for prosecutor's, *inter alia*, false statements to the court and failure to disclose evidence in violation of Rules 3.3, 3.4, 3.8, and 8.4).

43. *See, e.g.,* United States v. Perlaza, 439 F.3d 1149, 1172-1173 (9th Cir. 2006) (improper comment that presumption of innocence disappears when jury starts to deliberate); Marshall v. Hendricks, 307 F.3d 36, 65 (3d Cir. 2002), *cert. den.*, 538 U.S. 911 (2003) (improper mischaracterization of defense witness's testimony); State v. Rogan, 984 P.2d 1231, 1249-1250 (Haw. 1999) (forbidding re-prosecution on double jeopardy grounds after mistrial based on prosecutor's impermissible appeals to racial prejudice during summation; discussing Rule 3.8 and ABA Prosecution Function Standards 3-5.8 (3d ed. 1993)).

prosecutors engaging in conduct that would violate, *inter alia*, Rule 4.2,[44] Rule 3.6,[45] Rule 8.4(a), and Rule 8.3(a).[46]

E. Basic Requirements
1. Establishing Office-Wide Policies

To accomplish the goals set forth in Rules 5.1 and 5.3, managers must "establish internal policies and procedures."[47] Generally, these policies and procedures should address confidentiality obligations, how to detect and resolve conflicts of interest,[48] "dates by which actions must be taken in pending matters,"[49] and ways to "ensure that inexperienced lawyers are properly supervised."[50] In the prosecutorial context, these policies and procedures should specifically facilitate compliance with ABA Model Rule 3.8. As we wrote in ABA Formal Opinion 09-454, "Supervisors who directly oversee trial prosecutors must make reasonable efforts to ensure that those under their direct supervision meet their ethical obligations of disclosure and are subject to discipline for ordering, ratifying or knowingly failing to correct discov-

---

44. *See, e.g.*, United States v. Koerber, 966 F. Supp. 2d 1207 (D. Utah 2013), *app. dismissed*, (10th Cir. 2014) (granting defendant's motion to suppress evidence gained by the prosecutor during interviews that violated Rule 4.2).

45. *See, e.g.*, United States v. Bowen, 269 F.Supp. 2d 546, 568, 574 (E.D. La. 2013) (granting defendants' motion for a new trial based on anonymous comments by prosecutors on a website that was viewed by jurors; noting, *inter alia*, the special duties of prosecutors under Rule 3.8; "[T]he government's actions, and initial lack of candor and credibility thereafter, is like scar tissue that will long evidence infidelity to the principles of ethics, professionalism, and basic fairness and common sense necessary to every criminal prosecution, wherever it should occur in this country."); Lawyer Disciplinary Bd. v. Sims, 574 S.E.2d 795 (W. Va. 2002) (public reprimand for violating Rules 3.6, 3.8, and 8.4(a) by, *inter alia*, making improper statements to the press); Att'y Grievance Comm'n. of Md. v. Gansler, 835 A.2d 548 (Md. 2003) (public reprimand for violating Rules 3.6 and 8.4(a) by making improper extrajudicial statements).

46. *See, e.g.*, *In re* Riehlmann, 891 So. 2d 1239, 1247-1249 (La. 2005) (public reprimand for violating Rule 8.3(a) by failing to report a colleague's suppression of exculpatory evidence).

47. ABA MODEL RULES OF PROF'L CONDUCT R. 5.1 cmt. [2].

48. *Id.* Situations that may give rise to conflicts for prosecutors include, for example, (i) former-client and revolving-door issues under Rule 1.11, (ii) negotiations for private employment, and (iii) relationships with defense counsel and other lawyers. *See also In re* McKinney, 948 N.E.2d 1154 (Ind. 2011) (prosecutor suspended for 120 days because he prosecuted criminal matters as a part-time prosecutor while, at the same time, pursuing related civil forfeiture cases as a private attorney, where he would earn 25% of the amounts collected in the civil forfeiture cases).

49. R. 5.1 cmt. [2], *supra* note 46. For example, prosecutors should know the timing requirements applicable to investigations and prosecutions so as not to prejudice a matter.

50. *Id.*

ery violations. To promote compliance with Rule 3.8(d) in particular, supervisory lawyers must ensure that subordinate prosecutors are adequately trained regarding this obligation. *Internal office procedures must facilitate such compliance.*[51] Further, in light of the "intensely difficult ethics issues" that arise for prosecutors, more elaborate procedures may be necessary to ensure compliance.[52]

With respect to nonlawyers, managers must establish policies and procedures that provide for "appropriate instruction and supervision concerning the ethical aspects of their employment . . . [that] . . . take account of the fact that [nonlawyers] do not have legal training and are not subject to professional discipline."[53] These policies and procedures for nonlawyers must, among other things, specifically facilitate compliance with Rule 3.8.

For lawyers and nonlawyers the policies and procedures set by managers should include substantive provisions that reasonably ensure compliance, as mandated by paragraph (a), and procedural provisions identifying specific measures that direct supervisors and other responsible individuals should implement to ensure that the policies and procedures established by the managers will be effectively executed. What those specific measures are will vary, depending on the size and structure of the office; no one size fits all. But some measures must be adopted and implemented. Recommendations for such measures are set forth below.

2. Guidance on Specific Measures

The ABA Standards for Criminal Justice Prosecution Function and Defense Function Standards (the "ABA Standards"), the National District Attorneys Association, National Prosecution Standards published by the National District Attorneys Association (the "District Attorneys Standards"), substantial literature on prosecutorial conduct,[54] and compliance programs implemented by law firms and corporate legal departments in response to the

---

51. Formal Op. 09-454, *supra* note 6, at 8 (emphasis added) (footnotes omitted).

52. *See, e.g., In re* Myers, 584 S.E.2d 357, 360-361 (S.C. 2003) (public reprimand of the Solicitor for the Eleventh Judicial District for violation of Rule 5.1(b) by failing to ensure that a deputy prosecutor disclosed, *inter alia*, eavesdropping by investigators on a confidential conversation between the defendant and his lawyer; "We hold that . . . the Solicitor's Office is a law office where complex ethical questions arise, which necessitate a more elaborate system to ensure that the attorneys in the Solicitor's Office comply with the Rules [of Professional Conduct]").

53. ABA MODEL RULES OF PROF'L CONDUCT R. 5.3 cmt. [2].

54. *See, e.g.,* Rachel E. Barkow, *Organizational Guidelines for the Prosecutor's Office*, 31 CARDOZO L. REV. 2089 (2010) (advocating an entity-based compliance approach in prosecutor's offices).

requirements of the Sarbanes-Oxley Act[55] all provide examples of the types of measures that might be adopted. We set forth our recommendations below, based on these and other sources.

a. Training

The ABA Standards recommend that supervising prosecutors train incoming lawyers regardless of their previous experience.[56] We recommend that the training cover the ethical and legal obligations imposed by the Rules of Professional Conduct, including what disclosures and other obligations Rule 3.8 imposes, what public statements may be made under Rules 3.6 and 3.8 (including statements on social media, websites, and blogs), what must be revealed to a tribunal under Rule 3.3, what contacts may be made with represented and unrepresented persons under Rules 4.2 and 4.3, what statements may be made in closing argument, and what conduct by other prosecutors must be reported under Rule 8.3(a). We also recommend that training cover what constitutes *Brady* material. Others have suggested that the initial train-

---

55. Responding to the regulations promulgated by the Securities and Exchange Commission (the "SEC") under Section 307 of the Sarbanes-Oxley Act—which sets forth minimum standards of professional conduct for attorneys—law firms and corporate legal departments adopted internal policies which include but are not limited to distributing written policies describing the up-the-ladder reporting requirements, creating compliance committees and setting up training programs. *See* James L. Sonne, *Sarbanes-Oxley Section 307: A Progress Report on How Law Firms and Corporate Legal Departments Are Implementing SEC Attorney Conduct Rules*, 23 GEO. J. LEGAL ETHICS 859, 864-65, 868-69 (2010).

56. *See* ABA STANDARDS FOR CRIMINAL JUSTICE, PROSECUTION FUNCTION AND DEFENSE FUNCTION STANDARDS § 3-2.6 & Commentary (3d ed. 1993) (the "ABA Standards") ("[t]raining programs should be established within the prosecutor's office for new personnel and for continuing education of the staff"; "[e]ven lawyers with extensive experience in the trial of civil cases must undergo new training ... before they can function effectively in the trial of a criminal case"). *See also* National District Attorneys Association, NATIONAL PROSECUTION STANDARDS §§ 1-5.3, 1-5.4 (2009) (the "District Attorneys Standards") ("At the time they commence their duties and at regular intervals thereafter, prosecutors should participate in formal training and education programs. Prosecutors should seek out continuing legal education opportunities that focus specifically on the prosecution function . . . . Each prosecutor's office should develop written and/or electronically retrievable statements of policies and procedures that guide the exercise of prosecutorial discretion and that assist in the performance of those who work in the prosecutor's office."). Both the ABA Standards and the District Attorneys Standards state that they are intended only as guides to professional conduct, but the ABA Standards constitute ABA policy. The District Attorneys Standards do not constitute ABA policy. For additional guidance *see, e.g.,* Barry Scheck, *Professional and Conviction Integrity Programs: Why We Need Them, Why They Will Work, and Models for Creating Them*, 31 CARDOZO L. REV. 2215, 2244-46 (describing benefits of "Clear Office-Wide Definitions of What Is or Is Not Brady Material").

ing also address office policies and procedures, technical skills, other relevant substantive law, and court rules.[57] In addition, making office policies and procedures available to all lawyers in hard copy or electronically retrievable format may help ensure compliance. Updating those policies and procedures regularly is advisable.

Supervising lawyers should also provide initial training for nonlawyers who are "employed, retained or associated with" the office. This group would ordinarily include detectives and investigators, forensic experts in the office, paralegals and clerical staff. The training should include education on the ethical and legal obligations of prosecutors and related office procedures, e.g., proper handling, filing, and retention of forms and documents, and the preservation of evidence.[58] The training should be adequate to insure that the conduct of nonlawyers is compatible with the professional obligations of prosecutors.

Training sessions should be offered as frequently as needed to update lawyers and nonlawyers on relevant subjects, for example, when an important decision is rendered that directly bears on a prosecutor's professional obligations. Policies, procedures, and training manuals should also be updated regularly, as events require, and key court decisions on prosecutorial conduct should be circulated with explanatory memos.[59] When a court criticizes the conduct of a lawyer or nonlawyer in the office, supervising prosecutors should consider holding special training or educational sessions as appropriate to avoid any repetition.

---

57. *See* NATIONAL PROSECUTION STANDARDS § 5, Commentary (2009) ("A basic orientation package for assistants could include familiarization with office structure, procedures, and polices; the local court system; the operation of local police agencies; and training in ethics, professional conduct, courtroom decorum, and relations with the court and the defense bar."); CTR ON THE ADMINISTRATION OF CRIMINAL LAW, ESTABLISHING CONVICTION INTEGRITY PROGRAMS IN PROSECUTORS' OFFICES: A REPORT OF THE CENTER ON THE ADMINISTRATION OF CRIMINAL LAW'S CONVICTION INTEGRITY PROJECT, at 17 (2012), available at http://www.law.nyu.edu/sites/default/files/upload_documents/Establishing_Conviction_Integrity_Programs_FinalRepo rt_ecm_pro_073583.pdf [hereinafter CONVICTION INTEGRITY PROJECT REPORT] ("Both new and experienced prosecutors must be trained and educated about their ethical and professional obligations. Ongoing training programs are not an admission that an office has a problem with attorney misconduct; they are a necessary component of reminding prosecutors about their unique job responsibilities.").

58. *See* NATIONAL PROSECUTION STANDARDS § 5, Commentary.

59. For a sample manual, *see, e.g.,* DIST. ATT'YS ASS'N OF THE STATE OF N.Y., "THE RIGHT THING:" ETHICAL GUIDELINES FOR PROSECUTORS, *available at* http://www.daasny.org/Ethics%20Handbook%209.28.2012%20FINAL.pdf (last visited July 3, 2014).

b. Supervision

Effective supervision would require that supervisors keep themselves informed of the status of and developments in pending cases by, for example, requiring periodic written or oral reports on pending cases.[60] Other examples of appropriate measures include: (i) requiring that supervising prosecutors participate in major decisions, e.g., granting immunity, deciding charges, identifying *Brady* material, and, where feasible, documenting the basis for these decisions in writing;[61] (ii) establishing a system of individual oversight of line prosecutors, including during the preparation for and the conduct of trials; (iii) pairing untrained or newly-trained prosecutors with more experienced prosecutors; (iv) holding prosecutors with Rule 5.1(b) and 5.3(b) obligations accountable for the conduct of their subordinates; and (v) designating a specific attorney to oversee the review of files for *Brady* material.

F. Other Recommendations
1. Creating a Culture of Compliance

"[T]he ethical atmosphere of [an organization] can influence the conduct of all its members . . . ."[62] Managers and supervisors in prosecutors' offices should create a "culture of compliance."[63] This can be done by, e.g., (i) emphasizing ethical values and imperatives during the hiring process;[64] (ii) providing incentives for ethical behavior, such as positive reviews, promotions,

---

60. ABA Model Rules of Prof'l Conduct R. 5.1 cmt. [3] notes managerial lawyers "may not assume that all lawyers associated with the firm will inevitably conform to the Rules." Keeping abreast of the developments in the matters under supervision and requiring such periodic reports are reasonable measures to check any such assumptions. *See In re* Anonymous Member of S. Carolina Bar, 552 S.E.2d 10, 14-15 (S.C. 2001) ("[u]ndoubtably, the supervision of attorneys by other attorneys in their firm is one of the most effective methods of preventing attorney misconduct"; "[w]hen an attorney has allegedly violated Rule 5.1, it is not a complete defense to prove that the attorney did not know about the underlying misconduct. . . . In fact, a complete lack of knowledge can lead to a finding of poor supervision if the subordinate's violation is such that reasonable supervision would have discovered it.").

61. *See generally* Stephanos Bibas, *Prosecutorial Regulation Versus Prosecutorial Accountability*, 157 U. Pa. L. Rev. 959, 1005-06 (2009).

62. ABA Model Rules of Prof'l Conduct R. 5.1 cmt. [3].

63. *See* Barkow, *supra* note 53, at 2116 ("Whether or not an office is responding to a history of misconduct, creating a culture of compliance and ethical behavior is in the interests of prosecutors who head the office.").

64. *See* Conviction Integrity Project Report, *supra* note 56, at 16 (recommending posing ethical hypotheticals and asking "potential hires to discuss key ethical rules or obligations").

and raises; (iii) protecting and rewarding lawyers who fulfill their up-the-ladder duties;[65] (iv) promoting initiatives that make compliance with ethical obligations less demanding for line prosecutors[66] such as "open-file" discovery policies;[67] (v) publicizing ethical compliance reforms and internal policies both within the office and to the public;[68] and (vi) internally disciplining lawyers and reporting lawyers who violate the Rules of Professional Conduct.[69]

2. Enforcing "Up-the-Ladder" Obligations

Prosecutors, like lawyers in other government offices, have obligations under Rule 1.13 to report conduct by an employee or other constituent that is a violation of law that might be imputed to the office.[70] This raises especially

---

65. See discussion of a prosecutor's up-the-ladder duties, *infra* at Part F2.

66. *See, e.g.*, Formal Op. 09-454, *supra* note 6, at 4 (Rule 3.8 "requires the disclosure of evidence or information favorable to the defense without regard to the anticipated impact of the evidence or information on a trial's outcome. The rule thereby requires prosecutors to steer clear of the constitutional line, erring on the side of caution.") (footnotes omitted).

67. An "open-file" discovery policy includes, for example, the office disclosing all exculpatory evidence of which they are aware, without evaluating materiality, in an effort to avoid both intentional and unintentional withholding of *Brady* evidence. *See* Barkow, *supra* note 53, at 2111 ("Another way of improving transparency and monitoring without imposing substantial costs would be for prosecutors' offices to adopt an 'open-file' discovery process. Many offices already follow open-file policies, and several scholars have touted these policies as a protection against Brady violations.") (footnote omitted); *See also* CONVICTION INTEGRITY PROJECT REPORT, *supra* note 56.

68. This provides interested "stakeholders" the opportunity to comment on these policies. *See* Barkow, *supra* note 53, at 2111; CONVICTION INTEGRITY PROJECT REPORT, *supra* note 56, at 33-34 (discussing the benefits to prosecutors of publicizing their efforts to curb prosecutorial misconduct).

69. ABA MODEL RULES OF PROF'L CONDUCT R. 8.3(a) provides: "A lawyer who knows that another lawyer has committed a violation of the Rules of Professional Conduct that raises a substantial question as to that lawyer's honesty, trustworthiness or fitness as a lawyer in other respects, shall inform the appropriate professional authority."

70. *See* ABA MODEL RULES OF PROF'L CONDUCT R. 1.13(b). R. 1.13 cmt. [9] reads, "The duty defined in the Rule [1.13] applies to governmental organizations." "Up the ladder" obligations are also imposed by the Sarbanes- Oxley rule for lawyers appearing and practicing before the SEC. *See* 17 C.F.R. §§ 205.3(b), 205.4 & 205.5 (2013) (establishing responsibilities for supervisory and subordinate lawyers to report material violations of the Sarbanes-Oxley Act). For a model up-the-ladder policy, see ASSOC. OF THE BAR OF THE CITY OF NEW YORK, REPORT OF THE TASK FORCE ON THE LAWYER'S ROLE IN CORPORATE GOVERNANCE, App. F (2006), which establishes specific procedures, provides for an appropriate level of confidentiality, prohibits retaliation, requires training on reporting requirements, and provides for annual written certification by all lawyers that they are aware of their obligations and will comply.

complex issues for prosecutors and other lawyers who work in government offices about the identity of their clients and the nature of their obligations.[71] We do not address these Rule 1.13 issues in this opinion. We focus here on how prosecutors might implement their supervisory and managerial obligations under Rules 5.1 and 5.3 by developing an internal system for "up-the-ladder" reporting of violations of the Rules of Professional Conduct whether or not such violations would also trigger the up-the-ladder reporting obligations of Rule 1.13.

Though not addressing Rule 1.13, we recommend that managerial and supervising prosecutors establish a similar system for up-the-ladder reporting concerning possible violations of the Rules of Professional Conduct by lawyers in the office. Such internal reporting procedures would enable managers and supervisors to correct, remedy, and sometimes avoid such violations. A system for this up-the-ladder reporting could include (i) designating a specific attorney or committee to receive reports and address and resolve the issues; [72] (ii) permitting confidential review, as appropriate, to promote increased reporting of potential ethical issues;[73] and (iii) requiring the reporting of any reprimand or other criticism by a judge, as well as written complaints or allegations of ethical misconduct by any person, to a supervising prosecutor or to a prosecutor designated for this purpose.[74] In addition, supervising prosecutors should make clear that any lawyer who knows of a violation of the rules of professional conduct may be required to report that information to a supervising prosecutor, or pursuant to an established up-the-ladder regime instituted to comply with Rules 5.1 and 5.3.

3. Discipline

The training and supervision described in this opinion can be enhanced with appropriate remediation and discipline. For example: (i) imposing sanctions within the office; (ii) requiring remedial education targeted at particular types of misconduct;[75] (iii) intensifying, in appropriate cases, the scrutiny of

---

71. For example, actions by constituents in a prosecutor's office could lead to liability under 42 U.S.C. §1983, as alleged in Connick v. Thompson, 131 S.Ct. 1350 (2011), and might require up-the-ladder reporting under Rule 1.13. So too might the apparent failure to supervise and train in the Oklahoma County District Attorney's office noted by the Tenth Circuit in Le v. Mullin, 311 F.3d 1002 (2002), where the Court said that the prosecutor's actions "suggest defiance of Oklahoma courts and disregard for Oklahoma law." In such instances there could be violations of Rule 1.13 separate from any violations of Rules 5.1 and 5.3.

72. *See* ABA MODEL RULES OF PROF'L CONDUCT R. 5.1 cmt. [3] ("Some firms, for example, have a procedure whereby junior lawyers can make confidential referral of ethical problems directly to a designated senior partner or special committee.").

73. *Id.*

74. *See* Barkow, *supra* note 53, at 2110.

75. For example, if the office is criticized for a *Brady* violation, appropriate remedial education is imperative.

prosecutors who have engaged in improper conduct or whose conduct has been criticized by a court; (iv) demotion or dismissal; and (v) where appropriate, referring the matter to an outside authority under Rule 8.3(a).[76] It may be effective to have responsibility for in-house review placed with a specific supervisory lawyer or a group of lawyers within the office.[77]

G. Organizational and Structural Variables

Organizational and structural differences, such as the size of an office, the personnel turnover rate, the manner in which cases are prosecuted, the size of caseloads,[78] and the hierarchical structure may have an impact on which of the measures we recommend should be used to ensure compliance. Large offices with several layers of hierarchy may need to establish a formal committee to coordinate and direct the internal reporting of misconduct and the monitoring for ethics violations. Such formalized assignments, on the other hand, are unlikely to be required for small prosecutor's offices that employ 10 to 15 prosecutors, or even fewer. Supervising prosecutors in these smaller offices may make "reasonable efforts" by simply, for example, adopting an open-door policy for reporting misconduct or assigning a specific person in the office to hear such reports.

Direct supervision and monitoring also may vary with organizational and structural differences. For example, some offices assign multiple prosecutors to handle a case and each prosecutor is responsible for only one stage

---

76. *See, e.g., In re* Brizzi, 962 N.E.2d 1240 (Ind. 2102) (public reprimand for improper public statements); *In re* McKinney, 948 N.E.2d 1154 (Ind. 2011) (120 day suspension for conflict of interest); *In re* Miller, 677 N.E.2d 505 (Ind. 1997) (reprimand for advancing the cause of a civil litigant while serving as a prosecutor). *But see,* Joel B. Rudin, *The Supreme Court Assumes Errant Prosecutors Will Be Disciplined by Their Offices or the Bar: Three Case Studies That Prove That Assumption Wrong,* 80 FORDHAM L. REV. 537, 541-42 (2011); ABA Comm. on Ethics & Prof'l Responsibility, Formal Op. 09-454, at 2 ("[D]isciplinary authorities rarely proceed against prosecutors in cases that raise interpretive questions under Rule 3.8(d)"); United States v. Olsen, 737 F.3d 625, 630 (9th Cir. 2013) (Kozinski, Pregerson, Reinhardt, Thomas & Watford dissenting) (denying petition for rehearing en banc) ("[p]rofessional discipline [for Brady violations] is rare").

77. *See* CONVICTION INTEGRITY PROJECT REPORT, *supra* note 56, at 16 (discussing creation of "Best Practices Committees"). For an analogous discussion of the benefits of having a general counsel in private firms, *see* ROTUNDA & DZIENKOWSKI, *supra* note 21, § 5.1-1.

78. High caseloads are a particular risk factor. Whether a caseload is manageable may depend on, *inter alia,* the type and complexity of cases being handled by each lawyer, the experience and ability of each lawyer, and the resources available to support the lawyers. *See also* Va. Standing Comm. on Legal Ethics, Advisory Op. 1798 (2004) (addressing whether a chief prosecutor violates Rule 5.1 when he assigns too high a caseload; "[w]here a supervising attorney assigns a caseload so large as to preclude any hope of the supervised attorney's ethically representing the client (or clients), that supervisor would be in violation of Rule 5.1").

of the process.[79] In these offices, a monitoring scheme is unlikely to be reasonable if no special attention is paid to ensure that important information, such as *Brady* material, is not lost in the transition from prosecutor to prosecutor. The handling of this transition is especially delicate in offices with high turnover rates—much can be lost with frequent transitions. By contrast, where only one prosecutor handles a case from start to finish and through all stages in the process, a different monitoring regime will be appropriate.[80]

H. Conclusion

Prosecutors with managerial authority and supervisory lawyers must make "reasonable efforts to ensure" that all lawyers and nonlawyers in their offices conform to the Rules of Professional Conduct. Prosecutors with managerial authority must adopt reasonable policies and procedures to achieve these goals. Prosecutors with direct supervisory authority must make reasonable efforts to insure that the lawyers and nonlawyers they supervise comply with the Rules. Where prosecutors have both managerial and direct supervisory authority, they may, depending on the circumstances, be required to fulfill both sets of obligations. The particular measures that managerial and supervisory prosecutors must implement to comply with these rules will depend on a variety of factors, including the size and structure of their offices, as set forth in this opinion.

---

79. Don Stemen & Bruce Frederick, *Rules, Resources, and Relationships, Contextual Constrains on Prosecutorial Decision Making*, 31 QUINNIPIAC L. REV. 1, 13 (2013) ("horizontal prosecution" refers to matters handled by "multiple prosecutors, each handling the case at one stage of the process").

80. *Id.* at 12 ("vertical prosecution" refers to matters handled by one prosecutor at all stages). *See also* Formal Op. 09-454, *supra* note 6, at 8 ("[W]hen responsibility for a single criminal case is distributed among a number of different lawyers with different lawyers having responsibility for investigating the matter, presenting the indictment, and trying the case, supervisory lawyers must establish procedures to ensure that the prosecutor responsible for making disclosure obtains evidence and information that must be disclosed. . . . Similarly, procedures must ensure that if a prosecutor obtains evidence in one case that would negate the defendant's guilt in another case, that prosecutor provides it to the colleague responsible for the other case.").

AMERICAN BAR ASSOCIATION
STANDING COMMITTEE ON ETHICS AND PROFESSIONAL RESPONSIBILITY
321 N. Clark Street, Chicago, Illinois 60654-4714 Telephone (312) 988-5310
CHAIR: Paula J. Frederick, Atlanta, GA ■ T. Maxfield Bahner, Chattanooga, TN
Barbara S. Gillers, New York, NY ■ Amanda Jones, Chicago, IL
Donald R. Lundberg, Indianapolis, IN ■ Myles V. Lynk, Tempe, AZ
J. Charles Mokriski, Boston, MA ■ Ellen A. Pansky, South Pasadena, CA
Jennifer A. Paradise, New York, NY ■ Richard H. Underwood, Lexington, KY

CENTER FOR PROFESSIONAL RESPONSIBILITY:
Dennis A. Rendleman, Ethics Counsel ■ Mary McDermott, Associate Ethics Counsel

Formal Opinion 468   **October 8, 2014**

Facilitating the Sale of a Law Practice

When a lawyer or law firm sells a law practice or an area of law practice under Rule 1.17, the seller must cease to engage in the private practice of law, or in the area of practice that has been sold, in the relevant jurisdiction or geographic area. But the selling lawyer or law firm may assist the buyer or buyers in the orderly transition of active client matters for a reasonable period after the closing of the sale. Neither the selling lawyer or law firm nor the purchasing lawyer or law firm may bill clients for time spent only on the transition of matters.

Until 1990, lawyers were unable to sell any part of a law practice except for the physical assets such as furniture, office equipment, and books. Rule 1.17, first adopted in 1990, rejected the traditional prohibition on the sale of a law practice and permitted such transactions under certain conditions, including the condition that the selling lawyer or law firm "ceases to engage in the private practice of law, or in the area of practice" that was sold, in the relevant jurisdiction or geographic area. A question has arisen as to whether a selling lawyer or law firm may nevertheless continue to "practice" to assist the buyer or buyers in the orderly transition of active client matters.

Traditional Prohibition on Sale of a Law Practice

Various reasons were typically given for the traditional prohibition on the sale of a law practice. First, the uniform position of the courts and bar associations was that there was no legally or ethically recognized "good will" in a law practice that a lawyer might sell, pledge, assign, or even give away.[1] This position was reflected in ABA Formal Opinion 266 (June 2, 1945), which stated that the "good will," or intangible going-concern value, of a lawyer's practice was not an asset that either the lawyer or the lawyer's estate could sell because ". . . clients are not merchandise. Lawyers are not tradesmen. They have nothing to sell but personal service. An attempt, therefore, to bar-

---

1. *See* CHARLES W. WOLFRAM, MODERN LEGAL ETHICS § 16.2, at 879 (1986).

ter in clients, would appear to be inconsistent with the best concepts of our professional status."

A second reason was concern that the sale of a law practice, whether by the estate or the survivor of a deceased sole practitioner to a lawyer or by a lawyer or law firm to another lawyer or law firm, would constitute an impermissible sharing or division of legal fees. With regard to a sale of a practice by the estate or survivor of a deceased sole practitioner, the pre-1990 provisions of Rule 5.4(a), as well as DR 3-102(A) of the 1969 Model Code of Professional Responsibility, generally prohibited lawyers or law firms from sharing legal fees with nonlawyers, with certain limited exceptions including payments made to the survivors or estates of deceased law firm partners and law firm compensation and retirement plans. Thus, compensation for the "good will" of a sole practitioner's law practice, paid by the purchasing lawyer or law firm to the estate or survivor of the sole practitioner and derived from fees paid by the clients of that practice, was considered an improper sharing of a legal fee with a nonlawyer.[2] With regard to a sale of a practice by a lawyer or law firm to another lawyer or firm, both Rule 1.5(e) and DR 2-107(A) of the Code prohibited the division of legal fees between lawyers who are not in the same firm, with limited exceptions not applicable to the sale of the "good will" of a law practice.

A third reason was the long-established ban on payments by a lawyer to anyone for recommending the lawyer's services, as expressed in DR 2-103(B) of the Code and Rule 7.2(b). When a lawyer sells a practice, the lawyer presumably recommends the buyer to the clients of the practice, and thereby receives payment for those recommendations.

A fourth reason was concern that confidential client information might be disclosed as the result of the sale of a law practice. The 1983 version of the Model Rules did not address this issue. However, EC 4-6 of the Code explained: "The obligation of a lawyer to preserve the confidences and secrets of his client continues after the termination of his employment. Thus a lawyer should not attempt to sell a law practice as a going business because, among other reasons, to do so would involve the disclosure of confidences and secrets."

Whatever the reason or reasons given in any particular situation, it was generally held prior to 1990 that a law practice could not be sold, either by a sole practitioner or a law firm or by the survivor or the estate of a deceased sole practitioner.

---

2. *See, e.g.,* O'Hara v. Ahlgren, Blumenfield & Kempster, 537 N.E.2d 730 (Ill. 1989) (contract with widow to sell practice of deceased sole practitioner violated public policy against fee sharing and would not be enforced).

New Model Rule 1.17

In 1990, the ABA House of Delegates adopted new Model Rule 1.17 that permits the sale of a law practice, including the "good will" of the practice, if the detailed requirements of the rule are followed. According to its sponsors, the new rule was designed to accomplish two goals. The first was to address the disparity of treatment of clients of sole practitioners and clients of law firms when a lawyer responsible for a client matter leaves the practice, by ensuring that client matters handled by sole practitioners are attended to when the sole practitioner leaves practice. Formerly, clients of sole practitioners were left to fend for themselves after their lawyer left the practice because the lawyer had no legal way to sell the practice. Second, the new rule put sole practitioners in a financial position equal to partners of law firms regarding the value of the "good will" of their practice because most jurisdictions had limited a sole practitioner's ability to value his or her practice upon retirement or other cessation of practice to physical assets.[3]

Comment [1] to Rule 1.17 reaffirms the traditional notion that the "... practice of law is a profession, not merely a business. Clients are not commodities that can be purchased and sold at will." However, the black letter of the rule and the remaining comments outline and explain the conditions for the sale of a practice or area of practice, including requirements that the entire practice or an entire area of practice must be sold;[4] that the seller give written notice of the proposed sale to each client;[5] and that the fees charged to the client shall not be increased by reason of the sale.[6]

Another key requirement of Rule 1.17, expressed in paragraph (a) of the black letter and Comments [2] and [3], is that the seller must cease to engage in the private practice of law, or in the area of practice that has been sold, in the relevant geographic area or jurisdiction. Comment [5] explains that if an area of practice is sold and the lawyer otherwise remains in the active practice of law, then "the lawyer must cease accepting any matters in the area of practice that has been sold, either as counsel or co- counsel or by assuming joint responsibility for a matter in connection with the division of a fee with another lawyer as would otherwise be permitted by Rule 1.5(e)."

Comment [11] notes that lawyers participating in the sale of a practice or practice area remain subject to the ethical standards applicable to the involvement of another lawyer in the representation of a client, including,

---

3. *See* A LEGISLATIVE HISTORY: THE DEVELOPMENT OF THE ABA MODEL RULES OF PROFESSIONAL CONDUCT, 1982-2013, at 383 (Art Garwin ed., 2013).

4. ABA MODEL R. 1.17(b) & cmt. [6] (2014).

5. ABA MODEL R. 1.17(c) & cmt. [7] (2014).

6. ABA MODEL R. 1.17(d) & cmt. [10] (2014).

for example, the seller's obligation to exercise competence in identifying a purchaser qualified to assume the practice and the purchaser's obligation to undertake the representation competently;[7] the obligation to avoid disqualifying conflicts of interest and to secure informed consent where appropriate;[8] and the obligation to protect information relating to the representation.[9]

Comment [12] also explains if approval of the substitution of the purchasing lawyer for the selling lawyer is required by the rules of a tribunal, that approval must be obtained before the matter can be included in the sale.

Other provisions of the Model Rules have been amended to reflect the changes made by Rule 1.17. For example, with respect to the prohibition of the sharing of legal fees with a nonlawyer, Rule 5.4(a)(2) now permits a lawyer who purchases the practice of a deceased, disabled, or disappeared lawyer to pay, pursuant to the provisions of Rule 1.17, the agreed-upon purchase price to the estate or other representative of that lawyer. An exception to the general ban expressed in Rule 7.2(b) on payments for recommending a lawyer to clients was adopted that permits a lawyer to "pay for a law practice in accordance with Rule 1.17." Comment [13] to Rule 1.6 now recognizes that lawyers may need to disclose limited information to each other to detect and resolve conflicts of interest in various situations, including when considering the purchase of a law practice. And Comment [3] to Rule 5.6, which generally prohibits agreements that restrict the right of a lawyer to practice, explains that the rule does not apply to "restrictions that may be included in the terms of the sale of a law practice pursuant to Rule 1.17."

Transition of Client Matters

Neither the black letter nor the comments to Rule 1.17 address the timing of when a seller "ceases to engage" in the private practice of law for purposes of the rule. In particular, there is no discussion of whether a selling lawyer may continue to be involved in the practice to assist in the orderly transition of active client matters. It is clear from Comment [5] that the selling lawyer may no longer accept new matters in the relevant practice or area of practice, and that prohibition should logically take effect immediately upon the closing of the sale. However, given the history and purpose of the rule, as well as the black letter provisions and comments to the rule, it seems reasonable to conclude that the transition of pending or active client matters from a selling lawyer or firm to a purchasing lawyer or firm need not be immediate or abrupt.

For example, one of the purposes stated by the sponsors of new Rule 1.17 was to address the disparity of treatment of clients of sole practitioners and

---

7. ABA MODEL R. 1.1 (2014).
8. ABA MODEL R. 1.7 & 1.0(e) (2014).
9. ABA MODEL R. 1.6 & 1.9 (2014).

law firms. Lawyers retiring or withdrawing from law firms are not precluded from assisting their former colleagues in the transition of responsibility for pending matters from the retiring or withdrawing lawyer to another firm lawyer. Where appropriate, a selling lawyer or firm should be given a similar opportunity, for a reasonable period of time after the closing of the sale, to assist in the transition of active client matters.

This conclusion is consistent with Comment [12] to Rule 1.17, which notes that if "… approval of the substitution of the purchasing lawyer for the selling lawyer is required by the rules of any tribunal in which a matter is pending, such approval must be obtained before the matter can be included in the sale…." The drafters of this comment anticipated situations where the selling lawyer or firm would need to stay involved to accomplish the transition of a pending matter.

This conclusion is also consistent with Rule 1.16(d), which provides that upon termination of representation, a lawyer "shall take steps to the extent reasonably practicable to protect a client's interests…." The duty to protect the client's interests appears to apply regardless of the reason for the termination of the representation, and should therefore include any steps reasonably necessary to protect the interests of the client, even if those steps must be taken after the sale of a lawyer's practice or area of practice has closed.[10]

The period of time required for the selling lawyer to comply with Comment [12] to Rule 1.17 or Rule 1.16(d) in any particular client representation will necessarily depend on the circumstances, including the rules and rulings of courts or other tribunals in pending matters. It is therefore impractical to propose any prescriptive time limitation for when the selling lawyer "ceases to engage" in the private practice of law in the relevant practice area or jurisdiction following the sale of a law practice or area of law practice, as long as the selling lawyer stops accepting new matters in the practice or area of practice that has been sold and also limits his or her activities to acts reasonably necessary to accomplish the orderly transition of active client matters.

Charging Clients for Time Spent on Transitioning Matters

Finally, neither the selling lawyer or law firm nor the purchasing lawyer or law firm may bill clients for time spent on transition activity that does not advance the representation or directly benefit the client. The clear intent of the black letter and the comment of Rule 1.17 is that clients should not experience any adverse economic impact from the sale of a practice or area of practice. As noted above, Rule 1.17(d) unequivocally states: "The fees charged clients shall not be increased by reason of the sale." And Comment [10] fur-

---

10. *See also* AMERICAN LAW INSTITUTE, RESTATEMENT (THIRD) OF THE LAW GOVERNING LAWYERS (2000) § 33(1) (in terminating representation, lawyer must take steps to extent reasonably practicable to protect client's interests).

ther explains: "The sale may not be financed by increases in fees charged clients of the practice. Existing arrangements between the seller and the client as to fees and the scope of the work must be honored by the purchaser."

The need to spend time on transition activity arises only because of the sale of a practice or area of practice. Charging clients for time spent implementing the sale, activity that would not have been undertaken but for the sale, constitutes an "increase" in the original fee arrangement between the seller and the client "by reason of the sale." Even if the hourly rate is unchanged, billing for the additional time spent on transitioning matters will necessarily increase the fee otherwise due for the representation.[11] Thus, time spent implementing the sale may not be billed to clients.

The compensation, if any, to the selling lawyer or law firm for time spent on transitioning matters should be a matter of negotiation between the seller and the buyer in determining the consideration for the sale.

Conclusion

The requirement of Rule 1.17(a) that the seller of a law practice or area of practice must cease to engage in the private practice of law, or in the area of practice that has been sold, does not preclude the seller from assisting the buyer or buyers in the orderly transition of active client matters for a reasonable period of time after the closing of the sale. However, neither the selling lawyer or law firm nor the purchasing lawyer or law firm may bill clients for time spent only on the transition of matters.

---

11. *See also* ABA Comm. on Ethics & Prof'l Responsibility, Formal Op. 93-379 (1993) (client should only be charged for legal services performed).

AMERICAN BAR ASSOCIATION
STANDING COMMITTEE ON ETHICS AND PROFESSIONAL RESPONSIBILITY
321 N. Clark Street, Chicago, Illinois 60654-4714 Telephone (312) 988-5310
CHAIR: Paula J. Frederick, Atlanta, GA ■ T. Maxfield Bahner, Chattanooga, TN
Barbara S. Gillers, New York, NY ■ Amanda Jones, Chicago, IL
Donald R. Lundberg, Indianapolis, IN ■ Myles V. Lynk, Tempe, AZ
J. Charles Mokriski, Boston, MA ■ Ellen A. Pansky, South Pasadena, CA
Jennifer A. Paradise, New York, NY ■ Richard H. Underwood, Lexington, KY
CENTER FOR PROFESSIONAL RESPONSIBILITY:
Dennis A. Rendleman, Ethics Counsel ■ Mary McDermott, Associate Ethics Counsel

AMERICAN BAR ASSOCIATION
STANDING COMMITTEE ON ETHICS AND PROFESSIONAL RESPONSIBILITY

Formal Opinion 469   **November 12, 2014**

Prosecutors and Debt Collection Companies

A prosecutor who provides official letterhead of the prosecutor's office to a debt collection company for use by that company to create a letter purporting to come from the prosecutor's office that implicitly or explicitly threatens prosecution, when no lawyer from the prosecutor's office reviews the case file to determine whether a crime has been committed and prosecution is warranted or reviews the letter to ensure it complies with the Rules of Professional Conduct, violates Model Rules 8.4(c) and 5.5(a).

Introduction

Debt collection companies are contracting with local prosecutors' offices to use prosecutor letterhead to create and mail collection demand letters. These demand letters typically cite the criminal law allegedly violated (such as making or delivering a check with insufficient funds) and advise the debtor that she/he could avoid the possibility of further action from the prosecutor's office by paying the amount of the debt, and in a significant number of cases, a substantial additional fee to attend a mandatory debtor education course. Typically, no lawyer in the prosecutor's office reviews the case file to determine whether a crime has been committed and prosecution is warranted or reviews the letter to ensure it complies with the Rules of Professional Conduct prior to the mailing.[1]

---

1. For a full discussion of this country-wide practice, see Jessica Silver-Greenberg, *In Prosecutors, Debt Collectors Find a Partner*, NY TIMES (Sept. 15, 2012), http://www.ny times.com/2012/09/16/business/in-prosecutors-debt-collectors-find-a-partner.html ?pagewanted=all&_r=0; Joel Cohen, *When District Attorneys Become Bill Collectors*, AMERICAN LAWYER (Nov. 19, 2012), http://www.americanlawyer.com/id=1202578727214/When-Dis trict-Attorneys-Become-Bill-Collectors?slreturn=20140311111758; Mosi Secret, *Bounced Checks: How Local District Attorneys Get a Cut of the Debt Collection Business*, PROPUBLICA (Mar. 2, 2009), http://www.propublica.org/article/bounced-checks-how-local-das-get-a-cut-of-the-debt -collection-business. While programs vary depending on the terms of the contract between the prosecutor's office and the collection company, one thing does not: prosecutors allow debt collection companies to misrepresent the author and sender of this threatening letter. To review a copy of a debt collection letter issued by collection companies on prosecutor letterhead see *Letter from Bad Check Restitution Program*, NY TIMES (Sept. 16, 2012), http://www.nytimes.com/

The Committee concludes that prosecutors involved in this late Model Rules of Professional Conduct 8.4(c) and 5.5(a).

Application of the Rules of Professional Conduct to Prosecu
Jurisdictional Statement

There is no question that prosecutors are subject to the rules of professional conduct. As ABA Formal Opinion 97-405, Conflicts in Representing Government Entities (1997), explained, "While lawyers who serve as public officers or employees are singled out for special treatment under a few rules, e.g., Rule 1.11 ('Successive Government and Private Employment') and 3.8 ('Special Responsibilities of a Prosecutor'), it has generally been assumed—correctly in our view—that such lawyers are in most other respects subject to the same obligations in representing their client that apply to lawyers representing private clients."

Prosecutors acknowledge their ethical obligations as lawyers. Most prosecutors fulfill those obligations conscientiously and live up to the even higher responsibility of a minister of justice, as prescribed by Comment [1] to Rule 3.8. However, occasionally practices have taken hold in prosecutors' offices that, while driven by budgetary exigencies, fall short of their higher calling. It is such practices that have created the need for this opinion.

Model Rule 8.4, *Misconduct*

A prosecutor who enters into the type of agreement described in this opinion violates Model Rule 8.4(c), which provides that: "It is professional misconduct for a lawyer to engage in conduct involving dishonesty, fraud, deceit or misrepresentation."

In 1943, the ABA issued Formal Opinion 253, which determined that it would be unethical for a lawyer to allow a client to use the lawyer's stationery to deceive a debtor into believing that the debt had been referred to the lawyer and that the lawyer had written the collection letter. Specifically, the Committee noted that the practice violated Canon 15, which read in part: "The office of attorney does not permit, much less does it demand of him for any client, violation of law or any manner of fraud or chicane. He must obey his own conscience and not that of his client."[2] The Committee explained that a lawyer who allowed a client to send a collection letter on the lawyer's stationery was a party to deception and violated Canon 15. Today, Model Rule 8.4(c) addresses this same conduct.

---

interactive/2012/09/16/business/20120916_DEBT_LETTER.html?ref=business. In 2013, the Oregon legislature passed a state bill prohibiting prosecutors from allowing collection companies to use their letterhead. OR. REV. STAT. §646.639 (2013), *available at* http://www.oregonlegislature.gov/bills_laws/lawsstatutes/2013orLaw0551.pdf.

2. ABA Canons of Prof'l Ethics, Canon 15 (1908).

To the same effect is a joint opinion of the New Jersey Committee on the Unauthorized Practice of Law and Advisory Committee on Professional Ethics, which determined that a lawyer who sold his "name and letterhead to a collection agency in exchange for a monthly fee" violated Rule 8.4(c).[3] The conduct enabled the debt collection agency to deceive the debtor into believing that the lawyer was about to institute proceedings to collect the alleged debt by sending a collection letter on firm stationery, giving the debtor reason to believe that "there has been an evaluation by an attorney of the claim asserted with a determination by the attorney that proceedings to ensure collections are warranted."

Such letters written on prosecutors' letterhead are even more deceptive than the letters dealt with in ABA Formal Opinion 253 and in the New Jersey Joint Opinions 48 and 725. This is because they misuse the criminal justice system by deploying the apparent authority of a prosecutor to intimidate an individual. They carry with them the implication that the prosecutor or associates in the prosecutor's office have reviewed the facts and found that a crime has been committed and criminal prosecution is warranted. To create such a false impression violates Rule 8.4(c).[4]

Model Rule 5.5, *Unauthorized Practice of Law; Multijurisdictional Practice of Law*

Since at least 1932, the ABA Standing Committee on Ethics and Professional Responsibility has written about lawyers working for and with creditors to collect allegedly delinquent debts.[5] Many of these opinions have focused on what is the proper allocation of duties between lawyers and laymen in collection matters to ensure that the lawyer is not aiding in the unauthorized practice of law.

---

3. N.J. Comm. on the Unauthorized Practice of Law & Advisory Comm. on Prof'l Ethics, Joint Ops. 48 & 725 (2012).

4. Believing that ABA Model Rule 8.4(b) addressed the crimes of extortion and compounding a crime, when the ABA adopted the Model Rules in 1983, it deliberately omitted former Disciplinary Rule 7-105(A), which prohibited a lawyer from threatening criminal changes to gain an advantage in a civil matter. *See* ABA Comm. on Ethics & Prof'l Responsibility, Formal Op. 94-383 (1994) (threatening a disciplinary complaint against opposing counsel to gain an advantage in a civil matter may violate Rule 8.4(b) if the conduct is extortion under jurisdiction's law). Therefore, depending on the jurisdiction in which the prosecutor practices, if the threat to file a criminal action meets the jurisdiction's elements of extortion, the prosecutor could also be in violation of Rule 8.4(b). Prosecutors have not been excluded from the application of Rule 8.4(b). In *In re* Gobel, the Supreme Court of Nebraska suspended a lawyer for three months because, while county attorney, he threatened the debtor of a private client that unless a debt was immediately paid, the lawyer would file criminal charges against the debtor. *In re* Gobel, 271 N.W.2d 41(1978).

5. *See* ABA Comm. on Ethics & Prof'l Responsibility, Formal Op. 68 (1932), Formal Op. 253 (1943) & Informal Op. 1368 (1976).

Only a licensed lawyer may practice law, and states prohil censed practice to protect consumers. Limiting the practice of la\ bers of the bar "protects the public against rendition of legal se unqualified persons"[6] and serves to protect the public from unscr ..ous persons' engaging in abusive conduct and misuse of the law. Model Rule 5.5(a) prohibits a lawyer from "assisting another" in practicing law in violation of that jurisdiction's regulations.[7]

The practice of law is defined by state statute and case law.[8] In the collection area, generally, a nonlawyer may negotiate, adjust, and settle a debt on behalf of a creditor, but a nonlawyer cannot give legal advice, institute litigation, or threaten to sue on behalf of another.[9]

The participation by a prosecutor in the conduct described in this opinion, wherein the prosecutor supplies official letterhead to a debt collection company and allows the debt collection company to use it to send threatening letters to alleged debtors without any review by the prosecutor or staff lawyers to determine whether a crime was committed and prosecution is warranted, violates Rule 5.5(a) by aiding and abetting the unauthorized practice of law.[10]

In ABA Formal Opinion 68 (1932), the Committee determined that a lawyer who provided a client corporation with signed letterhead so that the client could write to persons who owed the client money "over the attorney's supposed signature" violated Canon 35 of the ABA Canons of Professional Ethics (1928). The Committee explained that by giving the client signed letterhead, the lawyer delegated his professional functions - which were strictly personal to the lawyer - to a nonlawyer. This conclusion is consistent with state Supreme Court decisions and bar association ethics opinions.[11]

The conduct at issue in this opinion is even more abusive than that in Formal Opinion 68 because it gives the impression that the machinery of the

---

6. ABA MODEL R. 5.5, cmt. [2] (2014).

7. *See* ABA MODEL R. 5.5(a) (2014).

8. ABA MODEL R. 5.5, cmt. [2] (2014).

9. ABA/BNA Laws. Man. on Prof. Conduct § 21:8011 (ABA/BNA 2011).

10. The Committee has become aware of a similar practice that involves a state overpayment of a benefit to a recipient. In that situation, a prosecutor lends office stationery to a state agency so that the agency's employees can use prosecutor letterhead to threaten criminal prosecution for failure to remit the overpayment. This practice, structured similarly to the one presented, would also violate the Rules of Professional Conduct.

11. *See* Yount v. Zarbell, 135 P.2d 309 (Wash. 1943) (lawyer who lends her signature to collection agent aids in the unauthorized practice of law); *In re* DeVinny, 255 N.W.2d 832 (Minn. 1977) (lawyer who allows collection agency to draft letters to debtors under his signature and who does not review and approve said letters aids unauthorized practice of law); Adams v. Kentucky Bar Ass'n, 843 S.W.2d 898 (Ky. 1991) (Assistant County Attorney aided the unauthorized practice of law when he "delegated authority and responsibility for deciding which parents of students in the Christian County School System would receive"

criminal justice system has been mobilized against the debtor, and that unless the debtor pays the debt, the debtor faces criminal prosecution and possible incarceration.

Conclusion

A prosecutor who provides official letterhead of the prosecutor's office to a debt collection company for use by that company to create a letter purporting to come from the prosecutor's office that implicitly or explicitly threatens prosecution, when no lawyer from the prosecutor's office reviews the case file to determine whether a crime has been committed and prosecution is warranted or reviews the letter to ensure that it complies with the Rules of Professional Conduct, violates Model Rules 8.4(c) and 5.5(a).

---

letter threatening jail for nonpayment of school fees.); *In re* Scheck, 574 N.Y.S.2d 372 (N.Y. 1991) (lawyer who allowed collection company to use his name, letterhead and signature to send letters to debtors without actually reviewing letters sent out under his name aids in unauthorized practice of law); *In re* Hear, 755 N.E.2d 579 (Ind. 2001) (lawyer, who contracted with debt collector to perform services, and failed to make reasonable efforts to ensure that collector's conduct complied with rules of professional conduct, violated Rule 5.3). *See also* Ill. State Bar Ass'n, Op. 85-7 (1985) ("A lawyer may not allow unsupervised lay persons to prepare letters on the lawyer's stationery, with or without the lawyer's signature, if the letter states or implies legal conclusions- i.e., that the addressee is liable for the amount claimed- or threatens litigation if the purported debt is not paid. Such activities would constitute unauthorized practice of law by lay persons . . ."); State Bar of Georgia, Formal Op. 00-2 (2000) ("[A] lawyer is aiding a nonlawyer in the unauthorized practice of law when the lawyer allows a nonlawyer member of his or her staff to prepare and sign correspondence which threatens legal action or provides legal advice or both. Generally, a lawyer is aiding a nonlawyer in the unauthorized practice of law whenever the lawyer effectively substitutes the legal knowledge and judgment of the nonlawyer for his or her own."); L.A. County Bar Ass'n Prof'l Responsibility & Ethics Comm., Op. 522 (2009) ("[A]n attorney may not lend his or her name to be used by an unlicensed person. . . . The power and privileges attendant to the right to practice law may not be delegated to a nonlicensed person . . . To facilitate or assist an unlicensed person such as a legal assistant to engage in the practice of law would constitute aiding and abetting UPL." (internal citations omitted)).

AMERICAN BAR ASSOCIATION
STANDING COMMITTEE ON ETHICS AND PROFESSIONAL RESPONSIBILITY
321 N. Clark Street, Chicago, Illinois 60654-4714 Telephone (312) 988-5310
CHAIR: Paula J. Frederick, Atlanta, GA ■ T. Maxfield Bahner, Chattanooga, TN
Barbara S. Gillers, New York, NY ■ Amanda Jones, Chicago, IL
Donald R. Lundberg, Indianapolis, IN ■ Myles V. Lynk, Tempe, AZ
J. Charles Mokriski, Boston, MA ■ Ellen A. Pansky, South Pasadena, CA
Jennifer A. Paradise, New York, NY ■ Richard H. Underwood, Lexington, KY
CENTER FOR PROFESSIONAL RESPONSIBILITY:
Dennis A. Rendleman, Ethics Counsel ■ Mary McDermott, Associate Ethics Counsel
©2014 by the American Bar Association. All rights reserved.